DEATH ROW WELCOMES YOU

MELVILLE HOUSE
BROOKLYN · LONDON

DEATH ROW WELCOMES YOU

Visiting Hours in the Shadow of the Execution Chamber

STEVEN HALE

Death Row Welcomes You

First published in 2024 by Melville House
Copyright © 2023 by Steven Hale
All rights reserved
First Melville House Printing: January 2024

Melville House Publishing
46 John Street
Brooklyn, NY 11201
and
Melville House UK
Suite 2000
16/18 Woodford Road
London E7 0HA

mhpbooks.com
@melvillehouse

ISBN: 978-1-61219-928-3
ISBN: 978-1-61219-923-8 (eBook)

Library of Congress Control Number: 2023949076

Designed by Patrice Sheridan

Printed in the United States of America
10 9 8 7 6 5 4 3 2 1
A catalog record for this book is available from the Library of Congress

To Mallory, with love and gratitude:
This would not exist without you.

And to Leighton and Holland:
You make everything worth it.
If you read this one day, I hope it makes you proud.

"But if people are shown the machine, made to touch the wood and steel and to hear the sound of a head falling, then public imagination, suddenly awakened, will repudiate both the vocabulary and the penalty."

– ALBERT CAMUS, "REFLECTIONS ON THE GUILLOTINE"

"Prisons do not disappear problems, they disappear human beings."

– ANGELA DAVIS, "MASKED RACISM: REFLECTIONS ON THE PRISON INDUSTRIAL COMPLEX"

Introduction

The first execution I remember being aware of is the lethal injection of Timothy McVeigh. I was thirteen when the Oklahoma City Bomber was put to death at the United States Penitentiary in Terre Haute, Indiana, on June 11, 2001. I cannot claim to have had any precocious thoughts about his crime—blowing up a federal building, killing 168 people including 19 children—or his punishment. I remember the pictures of him that appeared on the television and in the newspaper—his gaunt face and sunken eyes topped with a military-style crew cut, an orange prison uniform hanging on his lean frame. I remember the way his surname's second syllable sounded menacing to my young ears and that the words "lethal injection" conjured for me the image of a hooded man approaching him with a cartoonishly large needle. I never imagined then that I would witness the strange horror of executions myself or that I would come to know some of the men condemned to them.

I grew up in a conservative Christian home, on the east coast of Florida, a state with a long history of grisly executions of which it is not particularly ashamed. But if the death penalty ever came up in our house, I don't remember it. I believe my parents would have told a pollster at the time that they supported capital punishment in certain cases; it was not an animating political or religious issue for them, and so it was not a subject on which I felt I inherited a position.

They did, however, raise my sister and me in the church, and into a sincere Christian faith. Despite growing up in a community whose politics tended toward the law-and-order Right, I heard far more about the grace of Jesus Christ growing up than I did the state's duty to repay killing with killing. I suppose this is why, at some point in my teenage years, I came to the belief that an earth as it was in heaven would not include the execution of prisoners if it had any prisoners at all.

Still, the death penalty remained largely abstract to me, the subject of the occasional adolescent philosophical debate. Nearly 500 executions were carried out in the United States between McVeigh's in 2001 and the day I graduated college—485 men and 4 women strapped to a gurney or an electric chair—and I don't recall being aware of a single one.

That changed in the late summer of 2011. My wife and I were fresh out of college, newly married, and living in a small condo on the west side of Nashville, Tennessee. She was working nights as a nurse, I was working at a sandwich shop and writing as a freelancer for two local publications—the since-shuttered *City Paper* and the alt-weekly *Nashville Scene*. On the evening of September 21, I was scrolling through Twitter when I started seeing reports from the preposterously named Georgia Diagnostic and Classification State Prison, where a Black man named Troy Davis was set to be executed for the 1989 murder of a police officer in Savannah, Georgia. He'd also been convicted of shooting a man and assaulting another. But for more than twenty years, he'd maintained his innocence.

I pulled up a livestream of Democracy Now! and watched rapt as host Amy Goodman reported from outside the prison where crowds were gathered waiting to find out if Davis had been put to death or granted an eleventh-hour reprieve. In the end, it would be both. After the appointed hour came and went, word came that Davis was still alive, and that the execution had been delayed pending a review of his petition for a stay by the Supreme Court of the United States. Several hours later, though, the court denied his request. In a final statement, he expressed condolences to the victim's family, declared his innocence one last time, and asked God to have mercy on those about to execute him. Davis was declared dead shortly after midnight in the central time zone where I was still following on my laptop.

The experience lingered with me like a stubborn cold. I was troubled by the possibility that Georgia had executed a man for a crime he didn't commit, but I had not followed the case closely up to that point, and I felt ill-equipped to take a firm stance on his guilt or innocence. I was compelled, though, by the activists and journalists who had insisted that the nation—and the world, even—knew what the state of Georgia was doing, that it was killing a man behind closed doors.

Three years later, Tennessee was planning to do the same, and I was preparing to go behind those doors. The state was set to execute a man named Billy Ray Irick, and I—then a staff writer at the *Scene*—had been selected as one of seven members of the media who would witness it. I'd volunteered without much hesitation, but the truth is I had done very little research on the case or the man at the center of it. I hadn't the slightest idea how Billy Ray Irick became the sort of man capable of the unfathomable crime that sent him to death row, nor the faintest sense of who he'd become in the decades since. I did know that he was one of ten men on Tennessee's death row who were suing the state over the constitutionality of its then newly adopted and heavily shrouded lethal injection protocol. That was the basis for an order from the Supreme Court of Tennessee on September 25, 2014, calling off the execution which was then less than two weeks away. I was relieved. But the state's invitation to the execution chamber would come again soon.

In January 2018, the state Supreme Court set a new execution date for Irick later that year—a date the executioners would keep.

Over the next two years, Tennessee would execute seven men, and on three occasions I went to the execution chamber to watch them do it. It was an execution spree unseen in Tennessee since the 1940s.

As that streak of state killings was just beginning, though, I also received another invitation, this one to the death row visitation gallery. It turns out that for many years, a quiet community has existed in the shadow of Tennessee's execution chamber, one made up of death row prisoners and the men and women who visit them regularly. As I would learn, these gatherings are so ordinary as to be extraordinary and so life-giving as to feel defiant. They prove, I would come to see, that the very premise of death row is false.

This book is, in large part, the story of evenings spent in those two places—the execution chamber and the visitation gallery—and the lives of the people I have encountered in each of them. It is an attempt to show what our death penalty system has been built to obscure—the true horror of executions and the full, beautiful, and painful humanity of the condemned. And it is an account of how I went from writing about the men on death row to becoming friends with one of them.

The people, experiences and research that make up this book have changed my life. I hope that by preserving them here I can contribute in some small way to the idea that we are, all of us, capable of terrible and beautiful things, that people are so often harmed before they harm others, and that, as the lawyer and activist Bryan Stevenson says, each of us is more than the worst thing we've ever done.

This is the story of how I went to death row and found I was welcome.

1

Tennessee houses and kills its condemned men at Riverbend Maximum Security Institution, a prison that disturbs an otherwise peaceful field around ten miles from downtown Nashville. The collection of beige buildings sits in a bend of the Cumberland River, a bit of geography that gives the *institution* the only part of its name that isn't draped in euphemism. In the evenings, turkeys and deer meander in and out of the glare of floodlights on the perimeter of the grounds, unbothered by the razor wire fencing that surrounds the prison and seemingly oblivious to what it implies.

I went to Riverbend for the first time on August 9, 2018, to witness the revival of Tennessee's death penalty, the lethal injection of a man named Billy Ray Irick. When the state kills someone, the law requires them to let a small group of people watch them do it.[1] Prison officials solicit applications for media witnesses, which, as if to signal the archaic nature of the whole exercise, must be submitted by fax. There is a drawing to select seven reporters to be admitted to the execution.[2] I was one of the winners, chosen to witness the execution for the *Scene*.

It had been nearly ten years since the state had executed one of its prisoners.[3] So-called capital punishment had been steadily declining in the United States since the late 1990s,[4] with a number of states abolishing the practice and others allowing their death chambers to go dormant. In 2017, only eight states carried out executions for a total of twenty-three, the second fewest in the United States in twenty-five years.[5] But Tennessee was now going the other way. Its hiatus had not been the result of a merciful impulse, but a mere delay caused by a series of legal and logistical dams which had now burst, allowing the river of retribution to flow.

It was still light out, just before 5 p.m., when I turned onto a long, winding driveway that led to the prison. An official checked my ID while a German shepherd sniffed around the outside of my car for signs of contraband. Armed officers waved me on. In the prison's parking lot, a large, white canopy tent and a wooden lectern marked the spot where we would hold a press conference to describe the execution after it was finished. To the hundreds of men inside, looking out through thin, vertical windows, we must have looked like vultures descending on a carcass.

I parked in between two satellite trucks and sat in my car for fifteen or twenty minutes. I felt weighed down in my seat by the crime and the punishment that had brought us there. Nearly thirty-three years earlier, Irick had raped and murdered a little girl named Paula Dyer, a seven-year-old he'd been left to babysit. Paula's mother and other members of her family were at the prison now too, waiting for the state to deliver what it had promised, an act it claimed would bring justice. The details of the crime and the image of a girl too young to know what human beings could do to one another had been on an endless scroll in my mind for months as I reported on the upcoming execution. Alongside those facts were others—details of Irick's lifelong severe mental illness and the brutal abuse he'd endured as a child. There was also the near certainty among medical experts that we were about to watch him be tortured to death.

Soon, the Tennessee Department of Correction's communications director—our chaperone for a night at the death house—gathered us in the parking lot and led us inside the prison. The entryway smelled of fresh paint. Still-visible brush strokes on the walls betrayed a hasty whitewash in preparation for the arrival of what some men on the inside call "free-world" people. Prison officers directed us through a security checkpoint, sending our shoes and jackets through an X-ray machine and us through a metal detector and full-body scanner. We were there to see a homicide, but first they had to make sure we didn't have anything in our pockets. On the walls, framed placards declared the department of correction's "guiding principles" and offered information about the exciting opportunities available to staff.

From security we were led into the first of two holding rooms we'd spend time in on the way to the execution chamber—a small conference room with light-blue cinder-block walls and a long wooden table. Prison staff brought us our notepads and pencils as we'd been prohibited from bringing any reporting materials inside. They also offered us bottled water and coffee—a kind and unsettling gesture. Should one accept a cup of coffee at the gallows? In any case, I did.

Three men joined us in the conference room: Irick's longtime attorney, Gene Shiles, Deputy Attorney General Scott Sutherland and Sheriff Jimmy "J. J." Jones, who was there to represent Knox County, where Irick had been convicted. Jones, who wore his uniform with his gray hair parted in the middle, framing a round face, was new to me. But I was familiar with Sutherland.

Weeks earlier, the state's execution method had gone on trial. After difficulty obtaining its preferred lethal injection drug, pentobarbital, Tennessee had adopted a new protocol that called for the use of a three-drug cocktail—midazolam, to sedate the prisoner; vecuronium bromide, to paralyze them; and potassium chloride, to stop their heart. In a lawsuit citing warnings from the state's own associates and the results of executions using similar protocols in other states, attorneys representing thirty-three condemned men argued that Tennessee's new protocol would amount to cruel and unusual punishment. One leading anesthesiologist testified that there was "no debate" about the fact that midazolam was not sufficient to prevent a person from experiencing the torturous effects of the next two drugs, which he likened to being buried alive and then being burned alive, all while paralyzed.[6]

Sutherland had argued the state's case, dismissing the horrifying testimony of medical experts as hyperbole and emphasizing that the Constitution does not require executions to be painless. Crucially, he argued that the death row plaintiffs had not met the legal burden established by the U.S. Supreme Court in *Glossip v. Gross*, which held that death row prisoners challenging an execution method must provide a feasible and available alternative.[7] A sort of "bring your own execution method" rule. In many ways, the trial was not so different from the lethal injection we were about to witness: Barbarism dressed as bureaucracy and armed with legal jargon. I'd sat in the court gallery, listening as the state's lawyers split legal hairs over when a certain amount of pain becomes cruel or unusual, making arguments whose logic could only work in a cruel and unusual society.

The judge hearing the case upheld the protocol as constitutional.[8] Irick's attorneys asked the U.S. Supreme Court to stay his execution so they could have more time to appeal the decision. But the court denied that request over the objection of Justice Sonia Sotomayor.

"In refusing to grant Irick a stay, the Court today turns a blind eye to a proven likelihood that the State of Tennessee is on the verge of inflicting several minutes of torturous pain on an inmate in its custody, while shrouding his suffering behind a veneer of paralysis," Sotomayor wrote. "If the law permits this execution to go forward in spite of the horrific final minutes that Irick may well experience, then we have stopped being a civilized nation and accepted barbarism. I dissent."[9]

The sheriff and the deputy attorney general weren't interested in talking while we waited to be led to the execution chamber, but Shiles, a gentle man with a warm Southern accent who'd represented Irick for more than twenty years, was more than willing. What else was left for him to do? Neither the courts nor then Governor Bill Haslam was stepping in to stop the execution. The attorney's face showed the strain of the years he'd spent fighting on behalf of someone society had cast off as a monster. He mourned Paula Dyer and he mourned Billy Ray Irick and it was clear that for him these were not at all contradictory feelings. It was all tragedy, all loss. Irick had now spent more years on death row than he had in the outside world, and his life before death row had been consumed by darkness.

"I don't know if there's been one day in his whole life when his life was celebrated," Shiles said. "Even the day he was born, I don't think, was a happy day."

His sadness was mixed with shock. Holding a folder stuffed with papers, he referred to Irick's long history of severe mental illness, a history that had prompted calls for mercy from state and national mental health advocacy organizations. Shiles said he didn't truly believe the execution would happen until the Supreme Court had denied Irick's request for a stay earlier that afternoon, forcing Shiles to go to his client and tell him no one was going to spare his life.

"I thought someone would look at the facts," he told me.

At some point—time, I found, was hard to track inside the prison—we were told it was time to move on. Our chaperones led us out of the entry building and down a narrow sidewalk toward a large chain-link gate topped with razor wire. We waited as the gate opened in front of us, allowing us to crowd into a small piece of sidewalk between the first gate and a second identical one which would not open until the first one had closed. Stretching out to our left was a long gravel path in between the two fences that formed a waterless moat between the prison units and the outer rim of the facility.

Once the gate opened in front of us, we were led into another building, down a hallway and into another conference room. The sounds of heavy doors slamming shut and walkie-talkies crackling echoed outside the room. We waited. Eventually, the officer who'd been leading us through the prison looked up from where she was standing at the door and asked, "You guys ready?" She didn't wait for an answer.

We walked out of the room and into a large visitation gallery used by the prison's general population. Small clusters of chairs filled the room where incarcerated men and their loved ones gather for visits, sharing snacks from the vending machines that line one of the gallery's walls. The death chamber is on the other side.

Again, we walked through one door and huddled in a small closet-sized space, waiting for the door behind us to close before the door in front of us could open. And then we were there.

In the small witness room, there were about a dozen chairs arranged in front of a large four-paneled window with a curtain drawn across it. A small digital clock on a phone that hung on the wall revealed the time: 6:43 p.m. We took our seats, and the lights were shut off.

We sat in the dark, waiting for the killing to begin.

▦ ▦ ▦

I knew Billy Ray Irick as he was rendered in years of court filings,[10] a catalog of the worst things he had ever done and the worst things that had ever been done to him. Those pages contained a roster of his demons and a record of their manifestations.

Billy was the second of four children, born in Knoxville, Tennessee, in 1958, to a harsh, violent father and an unstable mother. He was rarely at peace with society, and society was rarely at peace with him.

The first time someone raised questions about his mental health was when he was just six years old, nearly the same age Paula Dyer would be when he raped and strangled her to death. His school's principal referred him to the Knoxville Mental Health Center for an evaluation, hoping to determine whether his behavioral issues stemmed from emotional problems or some kind of "organic brain damage."[11]

A clinical social worker at the Knoxville Mental Health Center who performed an initial assessment described six-year-old Billy as "overly aggressive." She noted that he "apparently mistreats animals," adding, "this is something that is particularly evident with his cat."

"He prowls and meddles a great deal at home and at school," she wrote. "He has for a couple of years been telling people outside the home that his mother mistreats him, that she ties him up with a rope and beats him."

A psychologist who interviewed Billy around the same time wrote that the boy felt "intense hostility" toward his family and that Billy "tends to fear his own impulses."

If his parents, Nancy Stevens and Clifford Irick, were willing and able to care for their son, it is not evident from the records of his childhood. The same social worker who first assessed Billy would later testify that his mother "had psychiatric problems of her own and was just not able to function in the role of a parent for Billy."

The staff at the Knoxville Mental Health Center became so convinced that the Irick home was degrading the boy's mental health that they had him hospitalized and later placed him in a residential school called the Church of God Home for Children, a former orphanage that provided care for abused and emotionally disturbed children. His parents rarely, if ever, visited him between the ages of eight and thirteen.

When they were reunited, it did not go well. Court documents bluntly summarize what took place during a home visit when Billy was thirteen: "During the visit, Billy used an axe to destroy the family television set, clubbed flowers in the flower bed, and, in a very disturbing incident, used a razor to cut up the pajamas that his younger sister was wearing as she slept. The razor was later found in his sister's bed."

Later, back at the Home for Children, he broke into the girls' dormitory and was discovered hovering over a sleeping girl. A knife was found in her bed.

Billy was briefly hospitalized again, and after his discharge the Home for Children would not take him back. Just entering his teenage years, he was like a transplanted organ repeatedly rejected by unsuitable bodies.

Back at what was supposed to be home, he found no peace or love. His father, a Korean War veteran, beat him often. Years after Billy was sent to death row, a neighbor named Inez Prigmore told an investigator working on his case that she regularly heard Clifford Irick's verbal and physical abuse from her home two doors down. On one occasion, she said, she saw Billy's father hit him across the head with a two-by-four.

By the time he was sixteen, Billy had been expelled from school. At the urging of his father, he joined the Army but was discharged after only a few weeks.[12]

For years after he was kicked out of the military, Billy lived as a drifter, hitchhiking around the country and traveling as far as Alaska and Hawaii. It was during these years, he would later say, that he took a serious interest in Lakota Native American spiritual traditions. He worked as a short-order cook and a maintenance worker and did a stint on a fishing boat in the Gulf of Mexico. He would later describe those years, on the road with no permanent mooring, as the best years of his life.

In 1983, after leaving the Gulf, Billy returned to the Knoxville area and found work washing dishes. While he was working eighty-hour weeks in the kitchen at a truck stop, he crossed paths with Kenny Jeffers, a man he'd known as a child. Billy later lost his job when the truck stop closed down, and he set off with his backpack toward the highway again. He was making his way down the road when Kenny drove up alongside him and offered him a place to stay. Billy moved in with Kenny, his wife, Kathy, and their five children, including a little girl named Paula. Decades later, in an interview with a Knoxville TV station, WBIR, Kathy Jeffers would describe her daughter as an outgoing girl who loved to pick flowers and bring them to new neighbors.[13]

Billy's time living with the family was short and turbulent, but as Kathy would tell a local reporter decades later, he became part of the family. When Kathy and Kenny worked, Billy would watch the kids. For a brief time, he appeared to have a home and family relationships that were not deformed by illness, hostility, and violence. He was said to love the children as if they were his own, and they called him "Uncle Bill." One night when the family's home caught fire, Uncle Bill saved two of the children's lives.[14]

When Kenny and Kathy divorced, Billy and Kenny moved in with Kenny's parents, Ramsey and Linda Jeffers.[15] It was there that Billy's mental health quickly deteriorated. In affidavits more than a decade later, the elder Jeffers and one of their daughters, Cathy, described a man coming unhinged. Billy's personal hygiene was "atrocious," and he rarely took a bath or washed his clothes. He repeatedly told the Jeffers that he talked to the devil every day and that "voices" told him what to do.[16]

Late one night, Ramsey Jeffers stopped Billy walking down a hallway in the apartment, mumbling to himself and holding a machete. When Ramsey asked Billy what he was doing, Billy said "I'm gonna kill Kenny." Ramsey took the machete away.

But soon after that incident, he saw Billy with the machete again. This time, Billy was chasing a young girl down the street. He followed her into an apartment nearby and screamed that he wanted to kill her. According to Ramsey, when he asked Billy why he had chased after the girl, Billy told him he wanted to kill her because "I don't like her looks."

Billy's preoccupation with violence seems to have been a near constant, but it was not always directed at others. He also became increasingly paranoid. Ramsey and Linda's daughter, Cathy, was awoken one night by Billy, who warned her that the police were at the apartment and were going to kill the family with chainsaws.[17]

It wasn't long before Billy's increasingly disturbing behavior led to an intense argument between Billy and Linda, which ended with Linda kicking Billy out and literally chasing him from the house with a broom.[18] More than thirty years later, in a letter to then Governor Bill Haslam's general counsel, in which he pleaded for the governor to spare Billy's life, Gene Shiles would point to this moment as a reenactment of "a recurrent theme in in Billy's life of being removed and exiled from family."[19]

Later that same day, on April 15, 1985, Kenny Jeffers showed up at his ex-wife's home with Billy, who later told police he'd been drinking and smoking marijuana. Kathy Jeffers had to work a night shift at a nearby truck stop. She told detectives that she'd expected Kenny to watch the kids that night, but he took off to pick up his sister. Kathy headed off to work a little before 10 p.m., leaving Billy alone with the sleeping children, including seven-year-old Paula.[20]

She didn't feel good about it, though. She told detectives the following day that Billy wasn't "drunk-drunk, but he was well on his way" and that he'd been "talking crazy." Not long after Kathy had arrived at the truck stop, Kenny walked in with a box of donuts. Kathy asked him to go home and stay with the kids because she was uneasy about Billy's behavior, but Kenny brushed it aside, saying, "Aw, kids'll be alright." He left to do some work of his own.[21]

Kathy's elderly neighbor would later report that, around midnight, she heard a knock on her door. She refused to open it, but Billy called to her from outside, telling her that it was an emergency.

"Paula is bleeding," he said. "I can't get her to wake up and breathe, and I want to use your phone."

The neighbor placed the phone on the porch and Billy called Kenny.

"It's Paula," he told his friend. "I can't wake her up."

Billy walked back to Kathy's house, the neighbor recalled. He kicked a bucket and a dog that was sitting on the porch, before kicking a post and cursing. She asked him why he hadn't called 911, and he replied, "I think it's too late for that."[22]

Kenny arrived at the home to find Billy standing on the porch. Inside, Paula was lying motionless and half-naked with blood pooling between her legs. Kenny wrapped her in a blanket and rushed her to the hospital where doctors tried in vain to resuscitate her. Paula was later pronounced dead from asphyxiation.[23, 24]

In her interview with WBIR, Kathy Jeffers described arriving at the hospital where she'd rushed to be with her daughter.

"I kind of went nuts. They finally let me go back [where Paula's body was] and I kept trying to wake her up. I kept telling her, 'Mommy is here. Mommy is here.' That is when the chaplain came in and took me into the room to talk about what happened to her."

The station reported that Paula's first-grade classmates at Beaumont Elementary School collected donations to help pay for her funeral, and that she was eventually buried with a Cabbage Patch doll she'd been wanting.[25]

Police arrested Billy the day after the murder when he was spotted under a bridge near the interstate, where he said he'd been hiding all day.

His guilt was never really in question. But his culpability—whether he could truly be held responsible for his heinous acts—was a different matter. At least, it might have been if the jury heard the whole story.

The Jeffers family—Ramsey and Linda, as well as their daughter Cathy, with whom Billy had been living in the weeks prior to Paula's murder—was not interviewed by Billy's defense team before trial. Despite the fact that the Jeffers resided in downtown Knoxville, no one spoke to them about the case for fourteen years. It wasn't until 1999 that an investigator working with the legal team representing Billy, as his case wound through the federal appeals system, interviewed the Jeffers on his very first day in town.[26]

As a result, the jury at Billy's trial never knew about his psychotic behavior leading up to the night of April 15, 1985. They didn't hear the testimony of the victim's family members about his violent outbursts and paranoid delusions. They heard only that as a troubled young child he had received some outpatient treatment.

It's impossible to know for sure how the full story would have affected the jurors who decided Billy's fate. But it was persuasive to experts. After reviewing the Jeffers' affidavits, Dr. Clifton Tennison Jr., the psychologist who performed an initial assessment of Billy to deem him competent to stand trial, said he no longer had confidence in his original conclusion.[27] Dr. Peter Brown, who performed a psychiatric evaluation on Billy in 2010, wrote of the earlier evaluations: "This was not a situation in which examiners 'failed to connect the dots.' Rather they were faced with a puzzle in which several critical pieces were missing."[28]

■ ■ ■

Billy's parents, and his mother in particular, remained a toxic presence in his life even after he was sent to death row. Nancy Irick refused to provide any assistance for his defense. In 1990, she declined to be interviewed by a neuropsychologist who was evaluating Billy, saying, "I don't care if my son's helped or not." She accused Billy's defense team of trying to control her by sending messages through her television set, disrupting her favorite shows.[29] Later, she claimed to have placed a "curse" on Billy's attorney, Gene Shiles, telling Shiles that she hoped his own two children met the same fate as Paula.[30]

During a psychiatric evaluation in 2010, Billy said that his mother was a practicing witch who "regularly used spells and witchcraft directed against others." Although he denied that she had special powers, the evaluation says, he also said, "Things do happen that you cannot explain."[31]

He told the doctor performing the evaluation that his mother had fully disowned him after his father's death in 2002 and that he no longer had any contact with any members of his family.

"He spends most of his time alone whether working or engaged in solitary recreational activities such as painting and drawing," the evaluation reads. "He listens to music and watches television. He reads very little. His interactions with others are limited to structured fantasy games or activities such as watching television."

Billy's relationship with the actions that sent him to death row remained largely incoherent. He denied having raped and murdered Paula Dyer, saying, "If I thought I had done this I would kill myself." However, he could not offer any account of what had happened, and he also consistently denied having any kind of mental illness.

In a separate evaluation that same year, a psychologist described Billy's views of the death penalty. Billy was "aghast" at how inconsistently it was applied, the psychologist wrote, and felt that executions had become a "circus." He said he believed that the media should not be allowed to attend them.[32]

Less than a week before his execution, I sent word to Billy through an attorney, offering him the chance to answer questions or make a statement. I was told that Billy "politely" declined.

■ ■ ■

It was past 7 p.m., the appointed hour. The execution seemed to be running behind schedule. We'd been sitting in the dark viewing room for more than half an hour, occasionally straining our eyes to check the time. No one spoke, really. But what was there to say?

It had been almost ten years since the last time the viewing room had hosted witnesses for an execution. But that didn't mean the executioners were out of practice. The state's execution protocol calls for monthly mock executions, rehearsals known to some inside the prison as "band practice." The simulation, according to the state's

Lethal Injection Execution Manual, "includes all steps of the execution process with the following exceptions: A. Volunteers play the roles of the condemned inmate and physician; B. Saline solution is substituted for the lethal chemicals; C. A body is not placed in the body bag."[33]

Now the real thing was here, and we were the audience.

At around 7:12 p.m., the deputy attorney general and Shiles were taken out of the room so that they could observe the IVs being placed in Billy's arm. As we sat in the darkness, we could hear what sounded like the rattling and squeaking of a gurney being wheeled into the execution chamber. Sutherland and Shiles returned around 7:25, and Shiles told us that he'd touched Billy's arm and kissed him on the forehead.

Around a minute later, the curtain jerked open, and we peered into hell—the brightly lit execution chamber where Billy was lying on his deathbed. Above him, a large clock hung on the wall to help us take accurate notes on his execution. A heavy-set man with shoulder-length hair and an unkempt beard, he wore an off-white Tennessee Department of Correction jumpsuit. There were heavy straps across his chest, arms, and legs. His hands were taped down and his belly protruded from between the straps, contracting with each of his labored breaths. His eyes were open.

Two men stood in the chamber with him, a few steps from the gurney. It was Riverbend warden Tony Mays, a short Black man with a bald head, and a towering Black deputy who looked chiseled out of stone. Both wore black suits and straight faces, with their hands folded in front of them. The rest of the execution team was hidden behind a wall, but the presence of Mays and his deputy clarified an easily obscured truth. The State does not execute prisoners. People do.

"Billy, do you have any last words?" Mays asked, his voice carried into the witness room through a microphone hanging in the middle of the execution chamber.

Billy sighed. "No."

Mays wiped his hand over his own face, signaling the executioners—who were behind a wall—to start administering the drugs. But it was at that point that Irick spoke, offering what seemed like a spontaneous apology.

"I just wanna say I'm really sorry, and that—that's it."

I knew Paula Dyer's mother and other members of her family were watching too, seated in a witness room adjacent to ours. While we had a side-view of the gurney, they were positioned at the foot of it, looking at their daughter's killer in the face. I remembered that same interview with the Knoxville TV station weeks before the execution in which Kathy Jeffers said her daughter's story had too often been displaced by coverage of Irick's abusive parents and mental illness.

"All you ever hear about is him. Nothing about her," she told the station. "What he did to her is the reason he's where he is. I am sick of hearing about his pain and his suffering. What about her pain and her suffering? She was seven years old, raped, sodomized, and strangled to death. I'm sorry, I feel nothing for his pain. Nothing at all. God, forgive me, but I don't."[34]

In the run-up to the execution, as I wrote thousands of words about Billy's mental illness, his traumatic childhood, and the possibility that his lethal injection would amount to a slow, torturesome death, angry readers had emailed me. Repeating the horrific details of little Paula's rape and murder, they would ask: What if that had been your daughter? It wasn't as hard a question as they seemed to imagine. I was as certain about the injustice of the death penalty as I was about what I would want to do if it had been one of my daughters, who were sleeping in their beds at home as I sat there looking into the execution chamber: I would want to light the man on fire myself.

After his hurried final words, Billy faded quickly. His eyes soon closed, and he began to snore loudly. Around seven minutes passed before Mays stepped forward to perform a consciousness check. The protocol called for the warden to reach down and pinch the muscle between Billy's shoulder and his neck, which he appeared to do although our vantage point made it tough to see clearly. Then the warden shouted.

"Billy!" he yelled, his voice carried into the witness room through a microphone hanging in the middle of the execution chamber.

"Billy!"

His executioners knew him on a first name basis.

But there was no response.

Around two minutes later, though, Billy's body appeared to react to the second drug. He jolted and made what sounded like a cough or a choking noise. He moved his head slightly and appeared to briefly strain his forearms against the restraints. We scribbled furiously on our legal pads, a task that momentarily kept the horror at bay.

A few minutes later, his face turned almost purple. We sat in the dark, watching for nearly ten minutes as he lay there. He did not appear to be breathing. At 7:46 p.m., Mays shut the blinds and our room went dark again. Soon his voice came through the speakers.

"That concludes the execution of Billy Ray Irick. Time of death, 7:48 p.m. Please exit now."

■ ■ ■

Not long before the execution, a note had been passed to me from death row, written in blue ink on a cheap prison napkin. This is what it said:

"Am a friend of Billy, I was asked how he is feeling, my opinion is, okay. He spends his days painting what he feels, which is some of the most beautiful paintings I've ever seen. He doesn't complain, he just rolls with it. How do I feel about him having a date. It's not easy because I care, he's a human being like we all are."

Standing in the prison as we waited for Billy's execution to begin, his attorney, Gene Shiles, had lamented his client's mostly loveless life. "I don't know if there's been one day in his whole life when his life was celebrated," he told me. But it turned out that wasn't entirely true. I was beginning to learn that there was a community transcending the boundaries of death row and the "free world," a fellowship of the living and the condemned. There were men and women who regularly came to the prison to visit the condemned men in Riverbend's Unit 2. They had come to know Billy as something more than the horrible act that put him on death row. They had celebrated him, and they would mourn him.

2

In July 2018, while I was attending the trial over Tennessee's lethal injection drugs, I ran into Demetria Kalodimos. A short woman with short hair and the charisma for television, Demetria was an icon of Nashville media. For more than thirty years, starting when she was just twenty-five, she was a lead anchor for WSMV, Nashville's NBC affiliate. To more than one generation of Nashvillians, Demetria *was* The News, having anchored the station's most prominent broadcasts and memorable investigations. She was so beloved that even the local store that was named in every broadcast's credits for providing her wardrobe, The French Shoppe, became famous. But her decorated tenure at the station had ended earlier in the year, when the station announced on New Year's Day that her contract had expired and was not being renewed.[1] Demetria would later sue the station, citing age discrimination—she was not the only longtime reporter who appeared to have been forced out of the station—and the two sides eventually settled out of court.[2]

I was not surprised to see a veteran newshound like Demetria at the courthouse, but her interest in the case went beyond a reporter's curiosity.[3] Years earlier, alongside her broadcast journalism, she had started producing independent documentaries, and in 2014 she'd gone to the Tennessee Department of Correction with a pitch. Prison officials had granted her access to several men on death row, allowing her to talk to them informally, but she wanted to interview them on camera and follow their daily routines to explore how a man copes and grows under the specter of execution. Eventually, the prison said yes. They didn't allow her and her camera to spend a day with the men, but they selected two—Charles Wright and Bill Stevens—and allowed her to interview them for one hour, on camera, for two days in a row. By 2018, that kind of official access to death row was unimaginable, but she'd gotten in under the wire. Bill died in 2016, but Demetria had kept in touch with Charles and started to visit him regularly at the prison. He'd recently been diagnosed with advanced prostate cancer that had spread to his bones. Demetria had been diligently visiting him and started working on a campaign aimed at securing his compassionate release, so that, at least, he could die with his family outside of the prison.

But I didn't know all that yet when one day as we left the courthouse, she casually said, "I have visiting privileges on death row," and talked about recent conversations with "the guys." I wasn't entirely sure what this even meant. The only people I had ever spoken to who visited death row were officers of the court or people of the cloth. As executions loomed, state officials had not seemed at all interested in facilitating media coverage of the condemned that went beyond a crime and a mugshot. And yet here was someone talking about "the guys." She knew them, and she wasn't the only one.

Demetria put me in touch with another regular death row visitor, a man who would later invite me into a community I never thought was possible.

■ ■ ■

One weekday evening, I walked into Gold Rush, a dimly lit and since-shuttered midtown bar that had been a popular local haunt since it opened in 1974. The execution of Billy Ray Irick was around a week away. Seated at a table near the back was David Bass. A convivial middle-aged man, he greeted me warmly, his conservative appearance befitting his Alabama accent. But he admitted he felt a bit uneasy about speaking to a reporter.

"I'm not an activist," he said.

It was not a derogatory statement about activists or their work but an acknowledgment of his shock that he'd ended up being the sort of person who meets a reporter in a bar to talk about death row. I could tell he wouldn't be here but for the fact that, as he would tell me later while the state kept adding execution dates to the calendar, "they're trying to kill my friends."

We were both able to relax a little bit when we realized we shared an alma mater, Auburn University, which meant we also shared a familiarity with the state of Alabama and probably a less-than-healthy relationship with college football. Soon I could see how David's personality must have made him a natural fit for his job as a university fundraiser. He began to speak as if we'd known each other for years, and I became convinced that if he'd wanted to, he could have gotten everyone in the bar to go in together on appetizers. He seemed like a man driven by an innate urge to make sure everyone he knew met everyone else that he knew. Now, some of those people were on death row, and so, here we were. Over the next few months, in this awful context, we got to know each other.

For most of his life, David did not fret over the fates of death row prisoners. In fact, born and raised in Alabama—and brought up in the Southern Baptist church—he'd been far from indifferent on the topic.[4] From a state with one of the nation's largest death row populations[5]—and an electric chair named Yellow Mama, because it was covered in a coat of yellow highway-line paint from the Alabama State Highway Department[6]—he'd inherited an enthusiasm for executions. His time in church did not temper that verve for retributory violence. The Southern Baptist Convention is one of the few prominent Christian denominations that still supports the death penalty.[7, 8]

As a younger man, David had adopted the words of former Alabama attorney general Charlie Graddick, who reportedly pledged while campaigning for the job in 1978 that when it came to convicted murderers in the state, he'd "fry 'em until their eyes pop out."[9] Now David seemed almost to choke on the words, repeating them only as a confession.

There came a point in his life that he became disillusioned with the Southern Baptist church and felt increasingly alienated from its more legalistic teachings. He began to wander spiritually, reading the work of the Catholic monk Thomas Keating and even going on a silent retreat. Around 2013, he found his way to a regular gathering at Christ Church Cathedral, an Episcopal church in downtown Nashville. It was a meeting devoted to Centering Prayer, a form of Christian meditation that originated with Trappist monks, including Keating, in the 1970s. There, he encountered a man named Joe Ingle.

David found himself intrigued by Joe, a blunt older reverend who often spoke about prisons at the meeting. He looked him up online and discovered that Joe had been an advocate and spiritual adviser for death row inmates across the southeast since 1974. He'd also written two books about his experiences.

"I would read the synopsis of his books, and I would go, 'Now that makes a lot of sense and I agree with that,'" David told me. "Then I would read his detractors that were coming at him, and I would go, 'That makes a lot of sense and I agree with that.' Right there started the turmoil."

David sees most interactions as the potential starting point of a relationship, but in Joe he also saw a possible spiritual guide. So, he asked him to lunch. They met and Joe just listened.

"He didn't quite know what to do with me," David recalled.

But after about six weekly lunches, Joe had an idea about what to do.

"You need to go to death row," he told David.

That was how David became friends with the men now facing execution. Over the course of five years he had been making almost weekly Monday night visits with a condemned man named Terry King. During that time, the state tried to start up the death penalty machine, at one point scheduling ten executions across 2014 and 2015.[10] But those dates were all canceled due to pending legal challenges around the state's execution methods.[11] And so, David had been able to operate with a sort of denial about what the prison really was and what the state really meant to do with the men on Unit 2. The reality of executions was, for him, like a far-off storm whose thunder was not close enough to wake one from a dream. But now the storm was overhead.

David, like many others close to death row, strongly suspected that Billy had been chosen as the first man to be executed because his crime had been so heinous. In Tennessee, the state Supreme Court sets execution dates, and since they refuse to comment on how they make these grim scheduling decisions, the theory was all but impossible to confirm. But it was easy to see the logic in it. The state and the governor seemed far less likely to face significant resistance to resuming executions after nearly a decade if they did so by first executing a man convicted of raping and killing a little girl. The fact that Billy was a white man—as were most of the men who would be scheduled after him—also obscured the fact that Tennessee's death row, like death rows around the country, is disproportionately Black and diverted attention from the racism of the death penalty.[12]

The truth, as we would all learn in the months to come, was that officials in this state were unlikely to face significant resistance to executions, no matter the circumstances of the crime or the particular history of the condemned.

In his years visiting the prison, David had seen and spoken to Billy once or twice. Billy was a fairly quiet guy. But he knew one of

Billy's visitors and offered to connect us, as came naturally to him. It was a young attorney named Alvaro Manrique Barrenechea, one of Billy's last and only close friends on earth.

■ ■ ■

As he grew up in Lima, Peru, in the 1990s and early 2000s, Alvaro Manrique Barrenechea had little reason to think about state executions, or the men condemned to them. The last time a death sentence had been handed down in Peru was in 1979, when an Air Force officer was charged with spying. Since then, the penalty had been eliminated, except for the crimes of treason during times of war and terrorism.[13] So, Alvaro was only familiar with the death penalty through American entertainment. He read John Grisham novels and saw the film adaptation of Stephen King's *The Green Mile*, which was filmed in part at the old Tennessee State Prison in Nashville.[14]

While his father worked as the loss prevention chief for a Peruvian supermarket chain and his mother served as the general manager of a large nonprofit organization, Alvaro busied himself with school and soccer. He never visited a prison, even later when he was in law school, although his Criminal Procedure professor did take his class to the morgue. The professor reasoned that, if ever in their legal career they needed to identify a dead client, it would be better if it wasn't their first time seeing a dead body.

"It was hard," Alvaro told me. "I will never forget the smell."

But it was an experience he had while he was an undergraduate that would set him on a path to America and to Tennessee's death row. During a semester abroad in Munich, Germany, he met Megan, an American student from Nashville. At first their relationship was casual, a friendship. But after they each went back home and found themselves talking by Skype nearly every day for nearly a year, they decided, as Alvaro put it, to give it a go. It wasn't easy.

Over the next several years, Alvaro would do a stint as a student in Milledgeville, Georgia, through an exchange program, commuting to Nashville by bus or plane for weekend visits. Later, Megan moved to Peru for two years before returning to the United States to attend Vanderbilt Divinity School. International borders and oceans do not make good conduits for a long-term romantic relationship. They briefly separated but soon reconnected. Eventually the two got married, and Alvaro immigrated to the United States in 2015.

In Nashville, they started attending Christ Church Cathedral, the same church where David had stumbled into the meeting for Centering Prayer. And it was there that Alvaro also found himself drawn to Joe Ingle and the death row visitation program he spoke about. When Alvaro approached him about participating, Joe quickly paired him up with an inmate who was interested in having a visitor, told him to write the man a letter, and sent him off without much fuss.

Alvaro did not research the man Joe had asked him to write. He did not scour the internet for details of his crimes. He knew that men on death row had been convicted of violent acts, and that was enough for him. He wanted to meet the man as he was, not as he had been, and he would remain dedicated to that idea for the entirety of their relationship, never diving into his past.

"If I meet someone in the street, I don't Google him," he told me. "I don't do a background check."

He sat down to write a letter to the man Joe had pointed him to—Billy Ray Irick.

Billy's response came from the prison, a handwritten, one-page letter.

"Hey fella," Billy wrote. "Really nice to hear from you. I am glade [*sic*] that Joe told you about me. He has told me nothing about you. :)"[15]

In his letter, Alvaro had mentioned that he liked to cook, and Billy told him he used to love cooking too.

"Not anything fancy," he wrote. "I worked at different restaurants. I was a short order (no jokes) and a grill cook. Not what you would call real cooking. I also do bead work and painting. I am hoping to get started doing leather paintings real soon."

He signed off: "Later, Bill."

In a letter soon after that, Billy informed Alvaro that he'd been approved to start coming to the prison as a visitor.

"For me Mondays are best, but whenever you want to is fine," Billy wrote. "The only time I don't visit is on the holidays. I would rather you spend those with your family."[16]

At the bottom of the short note, he added one more question: "P.S. Is it OK if I call you 'Al'?"

Alvaro made his first visit to the prison on a Monday night in the spring of 2017. He was in his mid-twenties at the time, a young man with a buoyant personality and welcoming demeanor walking largely unprepared into a prison staffed by people who may possess those qualities but are not always compelled to display them.

On that first night, as he made his way back to Unit 2, he was unnerved by the way that he could only ever move forward after the door behind him had shut.

"It's part of a thing of keeping things away," he told me. "Not only inside but also keeping things outside. You're breaking through. You have to go through all these hurdles to get to the inside."

Because he had not looked Billy up, he had never seen his mugshot. He did not know what the man he was going to meet looked like, setting up the death row version of an awkward first coffee meeting arranged only by email. He'd spent a lot of time gaming out how the conversation might go. How does one make small talk with a man on death row, he wondered, and what if you run out of things to talk about?

As he approached the unit, he saw somebody on the other side of the door looking through the window, a bearded man with

shoulder-length hair waiting for someone to arrive. He knew it
was Billy.

The fifty-eight-year-old man Alvaro met on that first Monday
night was a man with boyish enthusiasm for his few interests: football,
painting, and the fantasy trading card game Magic: The Gathering.

They talked about Billy's travels and the various jobs he'd had
along the way. At a later visit, Billy said he wanted to paint something
for Alvaro, and he asked his visitor for any requests. Alvaro asked him
to paint a time in his life when he had been truly happy. Billy settled
on a shrimping boat he had worked on in the Gulf of Mexico, and
Alvaro hung the painting in his office.

Among the other memories of true happiness Billy recalled to
Alvaro was that of the best hamburger he ever had, one he got from
a place in Santa Fe, New Mexico. Once Alvaro figured out the somewhat complicated system for putting money on a special card that
prison visitors must use to purchase food at the vending machines
inside, he started bringing a hamburger (such as it was) and a soda to
Billy on Monday nights.

The two were also able to bond over a shared love of sports. Billy
didn't share Alvaro's interest in soccer, but they both loved American
football.

When it came to Magic: The Gathering, though, Alvaro had
some catching up to do. He remembered other kids playing the game
when he was growing up, but he'd never played himself. He bought
a starter deck as a way to connect with Billy and began helping Billy
acquire various cards that were missing from his collection. The game
came up often in their letters, with Billy listing the specific cards
he was looking for: Evasive Maneuvers—Green, White, and Black;
Eternal Bargain—White, Blue, and Black; Nature of the Beast—Red,
Green, and White.

At one point, Billy mentioned that he and the few other men he
often played with were regularly frustrated by one thing—they didn't

have a rule book. This small detail led to the occasional disagreement or unanswerable question. So, Alvaro tracked one down online, printed it out and sorted through the various procedures in order to mail it to the prison. Billy was thrilled.

Despite his surroundings and a pending execution, Billy had a certain sense of humor. He would crack jokes during Alvaro's Monday night visits and become very expressive and animated while telling stories, a part of his personality that had rarely been seen for many years. In his letters to Alvaro, he would make dry remarks followed by little smiley faces—analog emojis.

"Sorry for not writing," he wrote in a letter in early 2018. "Things have been really messed up. This cold got the state off guard. That was real hard to do . . . not."

On what turned out to be his last visit with Billy, Alvaro stopped at the vending machines and got the usual—a hamburger and a Mountain Dew. When he got back to the visitation gallery, though, he saw that another one of Billy's regular visitors was there, and had brought him the same combo.

Billy ate the burger, but told Alvaro to keep the Mountain Dew, joking that he should wait for the right moment to drink it. Alvaro took it home and put it in his refrigerator. He saved it until the following spring and drank it in his full graduation regalia on the day he graduated from Vanderbilt University Law School.

He would not see Billy or the prison again before the execution. Billy had asked him not to come for the vigil that regular visitors and death penalty opponents were planning to hold outside the prison.

"If you want to think about me," Billy told him, "have a burger."

The day before his execution, Billy ordered his last meal—a Super Deluxe Combo, including a super deluxe burger, onion rings, and a Pepsi.

■ ■ ■

On the day Billy died, Alvaro was on Anna Maria Island, off the west coast of Florida with his wife, Megan. He honored Billy's wish for him to stay away from the prison on the night of the execution, and he continued to preserve his image of the man he knew. Megan followed the news for updates, sparing Alvaro from headlines that reduced a man he called a friend to the author of a heinous crime. He would not find out more details about Billy's case until weeks later.

But there were people gathered at Riverbend that night. In a field adjacent to the prison, two patches of grass had been fenced off, one for opponents of the death penalty and one for its supporters. David was there, huddling with other death row visitors and activists, many of whom were taking part for the first time in what would become a painful ritual. It was not a protest, exactly, although they did object to what was being done in their name inside the prison. It was more like a vigil and a way to show publicly that there were people who would mourn the man on the gurney inside. Standing there with David was a man named Al Andrews. He was David's former therapist, one of many people David had brought and would bring to the prison, to this place that had turned his life upside down. Now Al was a regular visitor himself.

In the weeks before the execution, the mood among the group of visitors was a mix of defiant hope and denial. Billy had been scheduled for death before, and many in the group had seen him outlive execution dates. As this new one approached, David had gone to Joe, casting about for guidance.

"Joe, what are we going to do if this comes about?" he'd asked.

"We're going to do everything we can to make sure it doesn't come about," Joe told him.

But Al, a gentle man with thinning gray hair and a calming voice, was struck by the seeming inevitability of the execution. Weeks before he would drive out to the vigil at the prison, he felt its crushing weight.

"All of a sudden there was someone I'd seen in that room, who was just kind of a gentle, quiet soul [who] was gonna be dead and be executed," he told me.[17]

At one point, Al had called the prison chaplain to see if Billy would have anyone there when the curtains were opened, anyone he could look to in his final moments—someone beyond his attorney, who didn't want him to die. The answer was no.

Al couldn't shake the thought. So just days before Billy was put to death, he called the prison chaplain again and asked if he could attend the execution himself. The answer was no, again. Al sobbed on the phone and asked the chaplain to tell Billy that someone had tried to be there for him.

David had been at the prison just a few days earlier for a Monday night visit. He had seen Billy there and seen his visit cut short so that prison guards could take him to death watch, to a cell outside the execution chamber where he would wait for death for the next seventy-two hours. Before Billy left, David had walked over to him and put his hand on his shoulder.

"I said, 'Billy, I love you and I'll be praying for you,'" David told me later. "I don't even know that he responded."

Billy slowly made for the door, a dead man walking, as calls came from the room behind him—"hang in there man, we love you."

On the afternoon of the execution, David had gone to a small chapel to pray for Paula Dyer, the girl Billy had raped and murdered.

Now, as the group stood in the field waiting for word that the execution was done, a lone man in the area reserved for death penalty supporters hurled taunts at them. At first, he played AC/DC's "Hell's Bells," which brought some smiles to the vigil on an otherwise distressing night. The man couldn't know that he was paying an unintentional tribute to Billy, who regularly listened to AC/DC on his headphones as he painted.

But what the man shouted next startled some of the group. After the executioners were done, he shouted that they should throw Billy's body in the dump.

The truth, as David and Al had learned days earlier, was not so different from the cruel and unusual wish of the man who had cheered on Billy's execution. If no one came forward to claim him, Billy's body would be buried in an unmarked grave outside the city.

Al knew that to many people this would seem appropriate. In Billy, he told me later, the state had picked the perfect person to execute first as it revived the death penalty. Who is going to stand up for a man who raped and murdered a seven-year-old girl? And yet.

"If you're against the death penalty, you're against the death penalty," he said. "And that means you have to say of Billy Ray, he did a horrific thing *and* given what we know about his childhood, I know that he was mentally ill."[18]

To him, erasing Billy, even in death, felt like the final step of a violent and dehumanizing process.

"I don't know, there was just something about that that got all over me," Al told me. "I just think the idea of somebody being put in the ground without a name, they just disappear—it just bothered me."

It bothered him so much that on the morning of Billy's execution he had emailed the prison chaplain and asked him if a group of death row visitors could claim the body after the execution. He wasn't even entirely sure what he was asking.

3

Billy's body had been a legally contested object since before the first lethal drug entered his veins. After the legal fight over the chemicals that would be used to kill him, there was the matter of whether his body would be pried open and picked over just as his life had been, by lawyers and people like me. On the day of his execution, Billy's attorneys had filed suit on his behalf to block an autopsy, citing his Native American religious beliefs. A judge granted his wish, signing an order that prevented the medical examiner in Nashville from cutting into his body.[1] Billy had also made it known before his death that he wished to be cremated.

In his final months, he had worked with several other condemned men on a large painting of the Stations of the Cross, a depiction of Jesus' path to his own state execution. Now, Al and David were stepping into the role of Joseph of Arimathea, the man who is said in the New Testament to have claimed Christ's body and buried it in a tomb he owned. The men didn't really think of it this way, though. They were acting on what to them seemed like a moral impulse, but the truth was they hadn't really even thought through the logistics of their plan.

Soon, though, a prison official told Al that if a family member did not claim Billy after a certain number of days, the visitors could take him. Al already knew there would be no family coming for Billy. The only family he had left was this peculiar community—the other men on death row and the people who spent Monday evenings with them. Al contacted the person who managed the small graveyard at his church and got a recommendation for a local funeral home. A professional there would take care of the rest—picking up Billy's body and transporting it to be cremated—for $900.

David started fundraising, albeit with a pitch quite different from the ones he was used to making in his day job. He was already in for $100. So was Al. The Catholic priest of a local parish quietly sent them a $100 check. After that, the rest came in quickly. Not a single person David called said no.

They were also planning a memorial service. The group wanted to mourn Billy's death, yes, but also to make right the tragedy that Billy's lawyer had lamented before his execution—they wanted to celebrate Billy's life.

Having read my coverage of the execution, Al reached out to me by email. He told me about the memorial and invited me to attend.

"So many people just labeled him as a monster, and I guess it's easier to murder a monster than a human," he wrote. "I visit a man who is on death row. He is becoming a friend. I hope your article will help in the fight to end this barbaric practice. I hope that it will help to save the life of the next person in line. I hope it helps to save the life of my friend."

In another email days later, he wrote, "I fear that Billy's execution is opening the door for more."

■ ■ ■

On September 30, a little more than seven weeks after many of them had gathered in a field outside the prison, a small group of death row visitors came together at St. Augustine's Episcopal Chapel on the campus of Vanderbilt University. Near the altar at the front of the A-frame sanctuary, two of Billy's paintings were on display. One showed what looked like a fairy surrounded by the branches of a rose bush. In the other, a person on horseback was riding through snow-covered mountains, a large moon hovering in the night sky above them.

A painting could not mitigate the rape and murder of Paula Dyer any more than Billy's tortured childhood and mental illness could exonerate him of the crime. But they complicated the picture. Days before the execution, I had spoken to Alvaro. He didn't know all the details of Billy's crime then, but he had been scrolling online one day and seen an old mugshot of Billy's.

"It just looks so different from the person that I know," he said. "It's completely different from the person that I've known for the past year and a half."

Can a man who raped and murdered a seven-year-old girl ever be anything else? Does it matter if he can? The state of Tennessee had given its answer, at least to the latter question. An execution insists that there is nothing worth preserving that will be lost by killing the condemned, and only justice to be gained. Many times since the execution I had thought of Paula's family. I hoped they'd arrived at something like peace, although I didn't know if that was possible. Still, I felt certain that the world was no safer now that Billy Ray Irick was gone. And the men and women gathered in the chapel were there to insist that something had been lost.

Among those who spoke at the service was Joe Ingle, the reverend who first brought David and Alvaro and many others into this community. He had been here many times before, marking the death of a man whose life he'd fought to save, and it showed on his face. Billy had always thought God abandoned him as a child, Joe said. But God had never abandoned him. The state of Tennessee had, he said, watching a troubled young boy bounce from institution to institution, in and out of a violent and unstable home, until he grew into a disturbed man. In the end, Joe said he felt he'd let Billy down too.

Another eulogy came from Alvaro, who began by following through on the request that Billy had used as a sign-off on every one of his letters—"Tell all, 'hey.'"

"On those Monday nights, you could locate Billy and I by the up-roarious laughter coming from our chairs," he said, reading what he'd written as he stood toward the front of the chapel. "We spent those hours telling stories of our lives and cracking jokes. Billy's elaborate stories were punctuated by exaggerated facial expressions that never failed to make me laugh. This laughter was contagious and caused us to be somewhat loud. It wasn't until much later that I learned Billy mostly kept to himself, he didn't talk much and very rarely shared his emotions. Our friendship, however, made room for laughter, and it was through laughter that I came to know my friend Billy."

Russell Mills, another death row visitor who goes by Hank, shared with the group a plan in progress, another longshot idea to give Billy the dignity they believed he deserved. Because of Billy's long-held belief in Lakota Native American spiritual traditions, Hank had reached out to the organization overseeing the Crazy Horse Memorial, a massive mountain carving of the Lakota warrior that is still in progress. He hoped that after hearing Billy's story, they'd allow Hank and his wife to travel to their native South Dakota and spread Billy's ashes in the Black Hills.

There were also words from Billy's fellow death row prisoners. Don Johnson, who'd known Billy since they both arrived on death row in 1985, wrote a short note to be read in Billy's memory.

"He was the same every day and I never knew him to strike out at anyone," Don wrote. "He was straightforward and honest."

Some men on the unit had written notes to Billy ahead of his execution, meant to comfort him before his death and honor him after it.

"Billy," wrote a man named David Duncan, in red ink and beauti-ful cursive handwriting, "the eyes of heaven have looked down upon

you and saw the love and joy you've brought to this family. You have
left friends, but your friends have not left you. You still rest in our
hearts and will always have a place there. Save us a place on the bench
in the wonderful sunshine. We'll bring the food, and the smiles."

Terry King had also written Billy a short note.

"Billy, I want you to know I think you are a great guy. I am so
sorry you are having to go through all this. Please ask God for forgiveness. God will hear you. My heart hurts for you."

In a letter to some death row visitors, he'd offered some context
for his words.

"The reason I wrote 'ask God for forgiveness' is because Billy has
always said he didn't believe in God," Terry wrote. "Billy always wondered where God was when he was a boy being mistreated. If you
had asked me 8 years ago, would I have sent such a note to Billy I
would have said NO WAY. See, I used to think I was better than him
because I hadn't done what he had done. I thank God I no longer
think like that."

Later, Alvaro attended a small service for Billy on Unit 2. He
shared with me a handwritten note signed by eleven men from death
row and addressed to him and one of Billy's other visitors.

"Thank you for being friends with Billy," it read. "Those of us who
were his real friends know how much like a damaged child he was in
a grown-up's body. We never forget the victims harmed in the cases,
but we know the stories of those here, like Billy, whose childhoods
were so tormented."

■ ■ ■

The death penalty was alive in Tennessee again. The next execution
was less than two weeks away and another was scheduled around
two months after that. As the visitors walked out of the chapel that
Sunday, they were only at the beginning of a historic streak of state

killings, an execution spree unlike any seen in Tennessee since the 1940s. Though they had been able to push it off for a time, the visitors had always been aware of a fact their friends on the row lived with every day—that the condemned are standing always in a line that leads to the execution chamber.

Now the line was moving.

4

In the summer of 1971, almost forty-seven years before he stood in a small Nashville chapel eulogizing Billy Ray Irick, Joe Ingle was living in east Harlem.[1] It was a stricken corner of New York City where Black, white, Puerto Rican, Italian and Chinese residents lived in close quarters, bound by poverty. Joe was in his mid-twenties then, outside of the south for the first time in his life.

He'd grown up in the various small North Carolina towns where his parents worked as teachers. Sorrow found him early in life. He was seven when his father, who'd just taken a job as a principal in Jonesville, died at the age of forty-two. Joe and his mother moved back to Greenville, where they spent the miserable year following his father's death living with Joe's grandparents. The fog lifted eventually, though. They spent what Joe would recall as five wonderful years in Asheville, where his mother was the head librarian of the city's public school system before another job brought them to Raleigh. Joe spent his high school years there before heading off to St. Andrews Presbyterian College.

It was the 1960s, a decade that seemed to affirm Jesus' notion that prophets are never welcome in their own country. Joe learned this truth in his own way. After graduating from St. Andrews, he spent a short time as a student at what is now Union Presbyterian Seminary in Richmond, Virginia, where he marched against the Vietnam War and helped start an alternative newspaper on campus. As he writes in his 2008 memoir, *Last Rights*: "The erstwhile fair-haired boy had begun to be seen as a radical peacenik by a seminary establishment that considered itself liberal by denominational—Southern Presbyterian—standards. I was part of a group of Union students who sought to learn more about the Christian faith without committing ourselves to serving the institutional church."[2]

He'd come to New York to study at New York Theological Seminary and to be a part of their East Harlem Urban Year program, which embedded students in area public housing projects. It gave Joe just what he was looking for: the chance, he writes, "to integrate the study of the Christian faith with the living of it."[3]

The program required seminary students to put twenty hours a week into some form of community service, and after spending his first year there working with the youth at an area church, Joe was certain he didn't want to be that sort of clergyman. He was searching for the focus of his second year, when images and reports of an uprising at Attica Correctional Facility in upstate New York started appearing on his black-and-white television.

Attica was a cauldron that had been threatening to boil over for some time, with more than 2,200 people imprisoned there in a facility built for around 1,600. White guards wielded their power over the disproportionately Black prisoners. The incarcerated men had already been pushed to their limit by abuse and appalling living conditions when news came from the opposite coast that the Black revolutionary George Jackson had been killed by guards at San Quentin State Prison in California on August 21. Two weeks later, Attica erupted. Nearly 1,300 men rebelled after a confrontation between a small group of prisoners and guards escalated into a riot. The incarcerated men took control of the prison, holding dozens of guards hostage and releasing a list of demands. The standoff lasted four days, until negotiations between the men inside and the authorities outside broke down. On September 13, New York State Police troopers stormed the prison, dropping tear gas and opening fire. It was a massacre. When the shooting stopped, twenty-nine incarcerated men were dead, along with seven guards and three civilian prison employees—all killed by state police bullets. The death toll also included three incarcerated men who had been killed by other prisoners during the rebellion and one guard who was beaten by prisoners during the initial riot. A state commission that investigated the rebellion and the retaking of the prison concluded that, excluding the Indian massacres of the late 1800s, the Attica uprising was the bloodiest single encounter between Americans since the Civil War.[4]

From his apartment in east Harlem, Joe was riveted. The prisoners' rebellion looked to him like a response to blatant and persistent injustice. He was as compelled by their demands as he was heartsick over the slaughter that put down the uprising. For him, Attica had exposed the carceral state as a violent place that dehumanizes and disregards those exiled to it. He didn't know then that he would spend the next fifty years resisting it in one way or another. But he wanted to know more about the people locked inside these places, the prisons and jails that dotted the country and kept a lid on the sort of truths that had exploded out of Attica.

He wasn't completely naive to the realities of the criminal legal system, though. It was a beast he'd seen snatch up his neighbors, those who were regularly hassled by the police, arrested, and thrown in jail. That's where he decided to go. He arranged to spend the next nine months visiting people detained at the Bronx House of Detention.

Soon he was walking up to the tall, Art Deco–detailed jail building that sat just blocks away from Yankee Stadium. He walked through the front doors and took an elevator to the sixth floor where a guard led him toward the visitation area designated for clergy and attorneys. They walked around the perimeter of a giant cage that surrounded the cell block where men were held in individual cells. When they reached the visitation room in the corner, Joe looked at the men inside the cage and asked if he could be let in there instead. The guard looked at him, as if to make sure his guest understood what he was asking. Then he shrugged and let Joe into the cage.

Joe stepped inside. But at the sound of door slamming behind him, his nerve and his righteous drive to know the people behind the bars was overtaken by an ugly thought he would come to regard as evidence of the cultural and societal ideas he had internalized: *Oh my God, I'm locked in here with these animals.*

He was shaken out of the thought, and somewhat relieved, when a man in a cell called out to him.

"Man, what are you doing here?"

Soon, the man was taking Joe from cell to cell, introducing him to around two-dozen men, most of whom were Black or Puerto Rican. Some had been convicted of crimes, while others were simply locked up because they could not afford bail. Confronting the humanity of these caged men and the depravity of his initial reaction to them shook him.

"Gradually," he writes in *Last Rights*, "I began to understand why the prisoners at Attica had rebelled. I was stunned."[5]

For the next nine months, Joe visited them. He got to know them, and he let them get to know him. He helped where he could, buying them postage stamps or helping them stay in touch with their attorneys. Mostly, he came to see them as friends and brothers in his evolving Christian faith. And this new knowledge that the people inside America's jails and prisons could come to feel like brothers and sisters to him sunk deep within him.

In 1973, after he graduated and was ordained as a minister in the United Church of Christ, he decided to head back south and make the prisons there his parish.

■　■　■

Joe made his way to Tennessee the following year. He'd fallen in love with the woman who would later become his wife, and she lived in Nashville. He arrived in the city still intent on working with people in prisons, but he needed a way in.

He found one in an issue of the quarterly journal *Katallagete* that was entirely devoted to prisons.[6] The journal, which took its name from the Greek word for the Biblical exhortation to "be reconciled," was published by the Committee of Southern Churchmen, led by the renegade Reverend Will Campbell.

A self-described "bootleg preacher," Campbell was known to say that he preferred to preach anywhere but under a steeple. He was just the sort of minister Joe hoped to become. Campbell had been raised on a Mississippi cotton farm during the Great Depression and baptized in a river. He was ordained as a Baptist minister while he was still a teenager, but soon became the sort of preacher who wasn't necessarily welcome in many Southern Baptist churches. He sermonized about the evils of racism and segregation, made moonshine, counseled Freedom Riders, and ministered to Klansmen. When the Southern Christian Leadership Conference, led by Martin Luther King Jr., was founded, Campbell was reportedly the only white person in the room. In the 1960s, Campbell faced down fire hoses alongside those civil rights activists and he rushed to the Lorraine Motel in Memphis to grieve with Black leaders when King was assassinated. Later, though, he would visit King's assassin, James Earl Ray, in prison. To him, these were not contradictions. He fought racism, stood with the poor, and believed that "Mr. Jesus died for the bigots as well."[7, 8]

In 1974, when Joe got to Nashville, Campbell was living just outside the city, on a family farm where he regularly led house church services. Joe had been to the farm before as he crisscrossed the region. So, after reading *Katallagete*, Joe called him up and asked for advice on getting into prison ministry. It turned out that the journal's prison issue had brought in several thousand dollars in donations, enough to start the Southern Prison Ministry. Campbell had hired a man named Tony Dunbar to lead it, and he sent Joe to go meet with him.

As tends to happen with such ragtag outfits, anyone expressing interest in the mission was put to work. Dunbar—who would later resettle in New Orleans, working as an attorney and writing crime fiction—quickly made Joe the director of the ministry's operation in Tennessee. He would make fifty dollars a week to do the same kind of work he'd done at the Bronx House of Detention, visiting incarcerated people and helping them however he could. It wasn't long before the Southern Prison Ministry spawned the Southern Coalition on Jails and Prisons, an avowedly abolitionist organization that connected grassroots groups across the southeast.

With little direction beyond the Biblical mandate to "remember those in prison, as though in prison with them," Joe started making visits to prisons around Tennessee and became a regular presence at the Tennessee State Prison in Nashville.

The fortress-like penitentiary known as the Walls had been in operation since 1898 and held more than 2,000 prisoners. It also housed Tennessee's death row. A Gothic-style administration building stood like a castle at the front of the prison, which was rimmed by a twenty-foot-high rock perimeter. The prison's imposing appearance was matched by a dungeon-like atmosphere inside. Guards and incarcerated men were rivaled in number by the rats and roaches that infested the facility. It sweltered in the summer and froze in the winter. A man could spread his arms wide and touch both walls of his cell. Cells were stacked one on top of another to form walls of prisoners.

Inside the Walls there were echoes of Attica. Built to hold 800 men, the prison was filled with more than 1,400 on its first day in operation and, for the most part, remained severely overcrowded from then on. By 1975, more than 1,800 men were imprisoned there.[9] Grievances over policy and practice were compounded by the unforgiving conditions. After beginning to meet with the men imprisoned there, Joe quickly became convinced that they needed to organize. He was especially drawn to the men serving longer sentences. They were the backbone of the prison, men who would not be leaving the Walls soon, if ever, and who had a deeply vested interest in how the place was run. It took a year or so and some changes in the leadership of the Tennessee Department of Correction—state officials weren't typically thrilled about collective action by prisoners—but Joe and a group of men on the inside eventually formed the Lifer's Club. Members had to be serving sentences of twenty years or longer. They met twice a month, elected officers, and even had an office inside the prison. Joe became more familiar with the Walls as an ecosystem, which meant becoming more familiar with the specter of violence that always hung over it. During a visit to the prison in the early summer of 1975, he was chatting with a captain he'd come to know and respect when the captain took a call. Joe watched as he responded to the person on the other end of the line, his voice growing increasingly agitated.

"No, no," he said, then yelling, "no!" before slamming down the phone.

The call had been from a guard in a tower, who had his rifle trained on a prisoner crossing the yard. He was calling for permission to shoot the man because he didn't have a required pass prominently displayed.

Tensions were high at the Walls that summer and not just because of tower guards with itchy trigger fingers. The prison had a new acting warden, Robert Morford, who saw himself as tough but fair and who instituted a series of new policies he saw the same way. The Lifers saw them differently, and Joe started to hear increasing frustration from the men. They saw Morford's new policies as overly punitive. In particular, they objected to his decision to strip them of the ability to spend visiting hours at an outside picnic area with their loved ones. As the list of grievances grew, the Lifers warned Joe that the situation was becoming untenable. Joe went to the warden to advocate for the men in the prison and to warn him that the rising pressure could lead

to violence. Then on September 11, 1975, almost four years to the
date after Attica, the dining room ran out of pork chops.

The quality of the chow on offer at the Walls was already among
the incarcerated men's long list of unaddressed grievances that night's
dinner service started. Meals were distributed one unit at a time, and
pork chops had been on the menu. When the men from Unit 2—
many of them members of the Lifer's Club—arrived for their por-
tions, they were told there was only bologna left. It wasn't the first
time something like this had happened, and the slight triggered what
was likely coming soon anyway. An argument ensued. Men started
throwing trays and overturning tables. It wasn't long before prisoners
had taken over large sections of the prison.

As the revolt was escalating, Joe got a call from an assistant warden asking him to come out to the prison. He'd established himself
as a liaison of sorts between the incarcerated men and the administration, and the assistant warden on the phone indicated that both
sides wanted him to come out to the Walls immediately. He arrived
to find reporters and TV news crews swarming outside and learned
he'd been invited to a riot. Soon, he was standing in the eye of the
storm with a group of the Lifers who were facing down the warden
and a group of armed guards Joe would remember as a "goon squad."
The two groups shouted at one another as chaos swirled all around
them. The Lifers refused to back down without a discussion of the
issues they'd been raising for months. Joe was trying to get the commissioner of the Department of Correction on the phone when a
shot rang out. Morford would later tell the press that he'd fired the
shotgun he was carrying in the air.[10] But if it was meant as a warning shot, it proved to be a catalyst. The Lifers, with Joe standing
among them, started shouting back at the goon squad, daring the
guards to shoot them where they stood. The warden and his men had
overplayed their hand. They backed down and the imprisoned took
control of the prison.

Joe stayed at the Walls through the night. At one point he walked from unit to unit using a bullhorn to try to restore calm as men set fires inside the prison. Later, they formed a committee of incarcerated men who would meet with the commissioner, and they sat in the prison basement until the morning hours hammering out the conditions of a truce. Joe made it back to his bed across town around 5 a.m., believing they'd managed to avoid a disaster. Several hours later, though, he was awakened by another phone call, this time from one of the incarcerated men he'd spent the night with. Joe drove back to the Walls and found a bloody mess, holes in the walls from shotgun pellets and men brutalized by police and their dogs. At some point, while the small committee was working on negotiations, prison guards and some 100 local police officers had come in force to put down the rebellion. Ten prisoners had been shot and two dozen more were injured, along with two guards. One incarcerated man had been stabbed to death during the unrest.

In the aftermath, the press referred to the revolt as the Pork Chop Riot, but Joe and the men inside knew better. The inciting incident was just the last of a long line of indignities that had set the stage for a rebellion. Lawyers working with the Southern Coalition on Jails and Prisons undertook a legal effort on behalf of the men who were wounded when the authorities retook the prison, ultimately winning financial compensation for some of them.

State prison officials threatened to pursue murder charges against Joe as a participant in the riot that led to the death of a prisoner. He and three other volunteers from the free world were also banned from visiting the prison, tarred as outside agitators who had disturbed the peace. Their real crime had been standing on the side of the condemned.

The murder charges never materialized, though. And with the help of Will Campbell, Joe had his visiting privileges restored in 1976 when a new governor came into office.

■ ■ ■

At the same time Joe was working with men sentenced to life, he'd also been getting to know another group of prisoners at the Walls—the men sentenced to death.

He'd started visiting the prison during a period of transition for state killings in America—the brief intermission before the death penalty's so-called modern era. In 1972, the U.S. Supreme Court's decision in *Furman v. Georgia* declared the current death penalty regimes unconstitutional, effectively putting in place a moratorium on executions as states worked to pass new laws that would survive the court's scrutiny.[11] Death rows across the country were emptied. In Tennessee, state lawmakers were eager to get capital punishment back on the books, and they would spend several years crafting new death penalty statutes only to see them struck down by the Tennessee Supreme Court. The state's death row was cleared more than once as condemned men saw their sentences commuted amid the legal battles. In 1976, though, the U.S. Supreme Court would clear the way for the return of the death penalty nationally, and the following year it would be enshrined again in Tennessee law.[12, 13]

Death row at the Walls was in a standalone unit, a dungeon-esque concrete building with low ceilings and low light that stood separate from the rest of the prison. When the men there saw sunlight, it was whatever could make it through the unit's thick glass block windows or during the time they were allowed to pace in a series of chain-link cages attached to the outside of the building. Inside, at the end of a hallway lined with narrow cells, the electric chair sat in a room under a large exhaust fan, waiting.

When Joe started visiting in 1974, there certainly wasn't much in the way of programming. Condemned men who arrived at the prison after being sentenced to death were given a Bible and sent to isolation. He started to meet with them, and he quite liked them. In *Last Rights*, he recalls finding that the men on death row were "no different from any other prisoners, except that they were generally better behaved and were more serious about their religious inclinations."[14]

But he was troubled to find that, although the death row prisoners were allowed to receive visitors from the free world, most didn't have any. He set out to recruit volunteers to visit them on a regular basis and soon—in between working with the Lifers and maintaining correspondence with a growing number of incarcerated people around the southeast—he was going to Nashville area churches to speak about the prison and pitch congregants on visiting the condemned men there.

In 1976, Joe became head of the Southern Coalition on Jails and Prisons, and in anticipation of the death penalty's return the organization decided to focus its efforts on the fight against executions. His new role meant he'd be on the road more, visiting with incarcerated men across the southeast. But by then he'd attracted some comrades to the cause in Nashville, fellow travelers who were helping to sustain and formalize the death row visitation program.

One of them was a man named Harmon Wray. He'd grown up in Memphis and marched with striking sanitation workers as a college student after Martin Luther King Jr.'s assassination. Like Joe, his theological studies had convinced him that he—and all Christians—belonged in the dark and broken places. After graduating with a Master of Divinity from Duke University, he'd come to Nashville and thrown himself into activism and advocacy on behalf of the poor and imprisoned. He spent more than fifteen years pursuing a doctorate at Vanderbilt Divinity School—a study of religious radicals in the south, like Will Campbell—but ultimately never finished. The business of being a religious radical in the south was too all-consuming. A bearded and busy man with a somewhat disheveled manner in some areas of his life, Harmon's seemingly harried days were balanced by an inner calm and a seemingly unending well of passion for the work, which for Harmon and Joe and the others was always personal. Early on in his time going to the Walls, Harmon started visiting a condemned man named Bill Groseclose, who'd been sentenced to death for hiring two men to kill his wife, and Harmon continued doing so regularly for nearly thirty years until his death in 2007. After hearing of his sudden death that year from a massive brain hemorrhage, Harmon's friends went to death row, to share the news and to mourn.[15]

Another person pulled into the Walls' orbit during those years was John Lozier, a Vanderbilt Divinity School student who'd met Joe and Harmon while working on a paper for one of his courses. Soon afterward, they offered him a job. John jumped at the chance to work in proximity to Will Campbell. After Joe took over as head of the Southern Coalition on Jails and Prisons, John spent a few years leading the Tennessee operation, carrying on the work of recruiting visitors and aggressively fighting the return of the death penalty in the state. At one point, John, Harmon, Joe, and a group of other men and women all lived together in a house on Nashville's Music Row, a commune of radicals in the middle of the city's country music establishment. The prison had opened its doors to a group of people that was dedicated to the elimination of the institution and didn't try to hide it. One day, John and a group of advocates went out to the prison and marched around the flagpole, banging pots and pans with wooden spoons and calling on the Walls to "fall down." They did not fall, but the group made their position clear.[16]

As they attracted more regular visitors to the prison, they developed an orientation of sorts to help free-world people know what to expect and how to navigate the prison system. The intersection of the free world and death row was complicated, of course. Some visitors— John's wife, among them—had bad experiences with the men they met inside. In other cases, yes, the visits led to somewhat problematic romantic relationships between visiting women and isolated men on death row. But many men and women developed friendships with condemned men that would last for decades. More than forty years later, John would still be in regular contact with the man he started visiting in those years.

Alongside their work getting new visitors to death row, John and his colleagues also worked to facilitate time for the condemned men to spend with their families. A December 19, 1976, article in *The Tennessean* describes a Christmas banquet John had arranged on death row.

"The visitors' gallery, filled with redwood picnic tables but no windows, was decorated with green and red crepe paper, a real tree and a banner proclaiming, 'Merry Christmas,'" the paper noted.[17]

Although the death penalty would soon become legal again in Tennessee, the death chamber would sit dormant for the rest of the century. From 1960 to 2000, there were no executions in the state, a forty-year reprieve that allowed the visitation program to grow and stabilize without the traumatic disturbance of periodic killings. But as soon as the U.S. Supreme Court reinstated the death penalty in July of 1976, other states quickly started working to start up the machinery of death again.

Joe responded to the court's ruling by fasting, going without food as he continued working to organize resistance to the coming executions.

"It's a customary form of penance," he told *The Tennessean* on September 11, 1976, sixty days into the fast. "This goes all the way back to the prophets. When the people of the community are committing a great wrong, or about to commit a great wrong, one person or a group of people would do penance."[18]

On October 10, *The New York Times* interviewed him on day ninety-five, as he sipped on tomato juice and decaf coffee, down forty-five pounds.

"The Lord led me into it," he said, "and he'll lead me out."[19]

He eventually ended his fast, after 134 days. And the executions came.

The first was that of Gary Gilmore, the man who demanded to be executed in Utah in 1977 (and would later be the subject of Norman Mailer's Pulitzer Prize–winning true crime novel *The Executioner's Song*). The next was John Spenkelink, a man on Florida's death row who had become "like a brother" to Joe. He traveled to Florida to plead for mercy and joined a delegation of religious leaders in beseeching then Florida Governor Bob Graham to stop the execution. They worked to show the governor the injustice not just in this specific case, but in the newly reinstated death penalty as a whole. John Lozier and Harmon Wray were among a group of eight anti–death penalty activists who chained themselves to a fence outside the governor's mansion. But in the end, Graham would not spare John Spenkelink's life. Joe was in a car with a colleague, driving down the highway from Tallahassee back to the Florida State Prison when they heard the news on the radio that a stay had been lifted and John would be executed the next day.

"I leaned out the car window and screamed into the rushing wind, 'Is there no justice? Is there no justice? My God, is there no justice?'" he writes in *Last Rights*.[20]

The following day, on May 25, 1979, Joe shepherded John's mother away from the prison and to a roadside motel where she wouldn't be bothered by the press as her son's execution neared. Eventually, finally giving way to exhaustion, she fell asleep. Joe learned that his friend had been executed in the electric chair when the news scrolled across a television screen during a rerun of *All in the Family*.

He told himself after that that he would keep a safer distance from executions and the men facing them after that. But he never could stay away. In *Last Rights*, he documents his relationship with twelve men, including Spenkelink, and one woman who went on to be executed. People whose stories and families he came to know, whose lives became inextricably tangled up with his. Each execution brought a unique pain that landed with the combined weight of all the ones preceding it.

"It's kind of like being in a vise, an emotional vise, and they're grinding it shut and you're trapped with the condemned person and there's really not a whole lot to stop it," he told the crowd at a reading in Nashville when *Last Rights* was released.[21]

He continued his work with the coalition on behalf of prisoners across the south and was nominated for the Nobel Peace Prize in 1988 and 1989. But the work for which he became so admired came at a cost that was paid by his body and spirit. In 1991, burned out and battling depression, he took a sabbatical, studying at Harvard.

There were victories too, though. Although the Walls never did come down, the prison was eventually condemned. In 1982, after a series of lawsuits brought by prisoners, U.S. District Judge L. Clure Morton declared the state's prisons system unconstitutional on account of appalling conditions in facilities that were "unfit for human habitation." At the Walls, he wrote that units were "unconscionably overcrowded" and that the men incarcerated there were "double celled in tiny cages like so many animals in a zoo."[22] By 1985, prison officials were making plans to abandon the Walls and seeking funding to build a new maximum security prison nearby that would house death row. Riverbend Maximum Security Institution opened in 1989, and the Tennessee State Prison was closed for good in 1992.

Joe had been to every death row in the southeast, and he was one of many people consulted about how Tennessee's should operate. As officials planned the new unit at Riverbend, he impressed upon them how appalling most death rows were. Many of them kept condemned prisoners in their cells for twenty-three hours of the day. He believed the visitation program at the Walls, which had been ongoing for more than a decade, showed that it didn't have to be that way. In the end, what resulted at Riverbend was a system that rewarded men on death row for good behavior, increasing their privileges as time went on. Yet there was no redeeming the place. In his first year, a man in Unit 2 would be in almost total isolation, and for some men, mental illness meant they would likely never know anything but a disturbed existence behind the door. But for others, after a few years without incident, the highest level of privileges allowed them to spend the whole day outside of their cells, working jobs or building arts and crafts. They could also have contact visits, free from shackles or a glass barrier between them and their guests.

The men on death row settled into the new prison and received visitors for a decade before the state started killing them again. From 2000 to 2009, six men were put to death at Riverbend before legal challenges stalled the executions again.

By the time I met Joe, he had all this behind him and within him. All the years and all the killings had left him hardened, but not unkind. He'd long ago lost any naive optimism about the courage or merciful inclinations of state officials, but that had not deterred him from hurling himself into the fray again and again. How could he not? The state sought to carry out a mass killing of his dear friends. To be with him was like gaining entry into a world—dark and painful but also beautiful and true—that was invisible to most.

Several times, as the new wave of executions began, I met him for lunch at Rotier's, the since-closed restaurant in midtown Nashville where he'd been a regular since the members of the Southern Prison Ministry used to gather there in the seventies. On one occasion, while we were eating, a man bussing tables stopped and struck up a conversation with Joe. It was clear they'd known each other for some time. His name was Eddie. Joe went to introduce me and added, "Eddie used to be on death row at the Walls." I don't remember what I said hearing this information, but Eddie just looked at me and smiled. He made a crack about how easy the men had it now at Riverbend and chuckled, then picked up his dishes and disappeared into the kitchen.

5

On a Monday night in early October, around two months after Billy's execution and a few days before another, I made my first visit to Unit 2 at Riverbend. I had seen the death, but not the row—the dying, but not the living.

Shortly before 5 p.m., I met David and Al in a parking lot on the west side of town and climbed into the back seat of David's car. They were buzzing with the energy of people going to see friends. The return of executions had brought a weight to their evenings on death row and forced the reality of the place into clear, distressing view. But to David and Al, these visits were still life-giving. And they seized opportunities to bring new visitors into their peculiar community.

The men on Tennessee's death row who have visiting privileges are allowed to designate eight people, in addition to their immediate family members, who can visit them once a week. But they can also invite others to come as guests for special visits, subject to the warden's approval. So, by meeting David or Al, a person was suddenly just one degree removed from the men on death row. With Terry's permission, they had invited a number of people out to the prison—friends, family, professional acquaintances, well-connected businessmen, and me.

But their drive to introduce people to Terry and the other men on death row wasn't just an outgrowth of their sociable personalities. It was a conscious and, to some, subversive act. David and Al, along with many of the other regular visitors, had come to believe that support for executions, or indifference to them, could not survive a Monday night with the men facing them; that the best way to expose the inhumanity of the death penalty was to expose people to the humanity of the men condemned to it.

We started driving out toward the prison, winding through industrial areas and working-class neighborhoods that were rapidly gentrifying. We passed the Walls, where many of the men we were going to see had started their time on death row.

It had been around four years since David drove out to Riverbend for the first time. After Joe's invitation, he'd eagerly told everyone in his life about his plans, which seemed to them to be a sign of an ongoing crack-up.

"We've got the kind of family with the picket fence," he said when he first told me the story. "And all of a sudden dad and husband comes home going, 'guys, I got this great idea, I'm gonna go to death row' and everybody looked at me like I was crazy. And some of 'em still feel that way. But most of the family has come around on it."[1]

Four years later, David's wife, Michelle, had still never met Terry and he didn't think she ever would. He attributed this, at least in part, to her past experiences with murder and the trauma that emanates from it. She'd worked for the Georgia Bureau of Investigation, and taken part in the autopsies of victims, including children. David was open about the fact that his relationship with Terry and the other men he'd come to know on death row had complicated his marriage. But he did not expect his wife, or anyone else in his life, to share the passion he'd fallen into. One of their two sons had visited Terry, though. And to their two daughters, Katie Ann and Caroline, he'd become like an uncle. They corresponded with Terry regularly and often visited him with David when they could.

But the man who later felt comfortable bringing his then teenage daughters along for visiting hours at the prison would be unrecognizable to the one who showed up to Riverbend on his first Monday night. Sitting in his car in the prison parking lot that evening, before leaving his phone and heading inside, David sent a final text to his family and loved ones, as if he might not make it out.

"I'm going in . . ."

His friends on death row would tease him about this for years.

But the man who went into Riverbend that night didn't really make it out after all. That first Monday night visit upended David's life. He met men he previously would have simply called murderers. And they were murderers, of course. But as he sat with them, he realized that was a lie by omission. These men had not been wheeled out on a dolly to speak to him from behind a leather muzzle. They were sitting unshackled before him, looking into his eyes. They even seemed to care about him. He felt destabilized in their presence, not because they were menacing but because they were not.

The first man David met that night was Abu-Ali Abdur'Rahman, a slight, Black man known among the community of people close to death row simply as Abu. He'd been sentenced to death for his role in the 1986 killing of a small-time drug dealer named Patrick Daniels and the stabbing of Daniels' girlfriend, Norma Jean Norman, in Nashville. His case had become well known for its myriad problems, not the least of which was an overwhelmed defense attorney who later admitted he'd hardly given Abu a defense.[2]

But it wasn't the injustices of Abu's case that left David feeling, as he put it to me, like his whole world was breaking down. It was the fact of the man himself, whose peaceful presence seemed to contradict the very premise of the place where he was confined. In more than thirty years on death row, Abu had maintained a deep interest in spirituality. He'd adopted his name after converting to Islam. Later, he converted again and was confirmed as an Episcopalian in a service on death row where he sang "Amazing Grace." Among the several degrees he'd earned during his incarceration was one as a mediator, and he was an active part of a conflict resolution program in the unit.

After Abu, David met Terry, who told him a story of murder, yes, but also a curious story of redemption, one deemed impossible by the sentence handed down before Terry turned twenty-three years old. David would recall how uniquely present Terry seemed, and how aware he was of the overwhelming effect that the setting could have on a first-time visitor from the free world. Occasionally during their conversation, he would reach over and gently touch David's shoulder, asking "Are you OK?"

Toward the end of their visit, Terry asked David a question that he regularly asks new visitors. For David, who had already lost his sense of equilibrium, it was the blow that knocked him over.

"How do you feel about the death penalty?"

David didn't really answer. He stammered through a response, finding that he was unable to look this man in the face and tell him, "As it happens, I think people like you should be exterminated." He left the prison in an existential fog. A couple years later, though, after spending many Monday nights at the prison, he went to death row and told Terry about that old line he used to repeat about the condemned, that "we need to fry 'em until their eyes pop out." That was how he felt, he said, and he asked for Terry's forgiveness.

■ ■ ■

We arrived at Riverbend around 5 p.m., about the same time I'd arrived for Billy's execution, only now it was quiet and still. There were no armed guards at the top of the driveway, no white tent prepared for a press conference. We got out of the car and walked toward the entrance, assured that everyone we saw in the prison that night would be alive when we left.

A small group of men and women sat on benches outside the prison's front doors. They greeted us like regulars at a neighborhood bar, and David introduced me around.

Like us, they were waiting for visiting hours to begin. Some were going to death row, others had family members in the prison's general population. One of the women was the mother of a man whose crime and trial had made national headlines. David had gotten to know her well and soon they were laughing, but she looked to me like a person smiling from behind a veil of grief.

Sitting there on the benches, as afternoon turned to evening, the group seemed a lonely few. But they are not, of course. Around two million people are incarcerated somewhere inside America's sprawling system of prisons and jails. On that day, more than 2,700 people were languishing on death rows around the country. For so many of those locked-away men and women there are people like these, people who have not forgotten them.

Soon, the small group started jokingly bickering about who would go first through the door, risking the ire of the corporal who was perched at a desk behind the security checkpoint. She was short in stature and in temperament and particularly intimidating to un-easy newcomers. This tension did at times give way to some levity, though. Alvaro had told me how his long last name used to peeve the corporal when he first started visiting Billy but eventually became a sort of running joke between the two of them. David, who seemed to view tough personalities as a kind of challenge, worked to win her over. Still, the visitors found her whims somewhat difficult to predict. Visitation began at 5:30 and the group was typically allowed to come inside around 5:15 to start going through security. But on the wrong day, for reasons that were not always obvious, they might be bluntly told to go back outside and wait longer.

An even bigger hassle, though, was the prison's dress code for visitors, the enforcement of which seemed to ebb and flow on an arbitrary basis. This trouble mostly affected the women, whose outfits were scrutinized according to the visitation handbook's various dictates. A visitor's attire could not be "provocative or offensive to others"; clothing was to "fit in an appropriate manner," neither too tight or too loose; underwear was required, but underwire bras and thongs were banned, as were pieces of clothing with rips in them, such as a pair of jeans with a hole in the knee.[3] After a while, most of the women who visited the prison regularly had cordoned off a collection of approved clothes in their closets. But they found that even an outfit they'd worn multiple times without incident could get them sent back to their cars or their homes for a wardrobe change. Looming executions also seemed to put the guards on edge. On the Monday night before Billy's execution, the visitors had seen an unusual number of people turned away for minor violations.

On this night, though, we made it through security without any problems. After passing through the metal detector and the body scanner and retrieving my belt and shoes on the other side, I approached the desk where the corporal oversaw the proceedings. With David's direction, and the corporal's prodding, I leaned over a large black binder and wrote Terry's name and the Department of Correction ID number assigned to him—103308—followed by my own name. We repeated the same process in another binder designated for Unit 2 visitors. Its pages were a picture of radical solidarity, a catalog of people associating themselves in ink with men the state was determined to kill.

We waited quietly for a moment before the corporal waved us out the door and down the same path I'd taken to the execution a couple months before. We walked through the first of the two tall barbed-wire gates, waiting for it to close behind us before the next one would open in front of us. From there, we entered the central building that houses a large visitation gallery for men from the general population. Some of the visitors left us there to find a seat with their loved ones. Soon, an officer arrived to escort the rest of us to death row.

As we made our way down a long sidewalk, I saw what looked like large rectangular cages with concrete floors outside the unit buildings. A tiger pacing back and forth in one of them would not have looked out of place. Several of the regular visitors had told me about how the men on death row often spoke about how long it had been since they'd stepped foot on grass. I later learned that these cages—surrounded by grass the men couldn't quite touch—were as close as they got. Small red signs beside the sidewalk urged us to stay off the grass; they felt almost like taunts.

When we arrived at Unit 2, we stood outside a heavy metal door, waiting for the guard seated at a desk inside to unlock it. We stepped inside, crowding into a small space between the first door and a second, waiting again for a door to close behind us before another could open in front of us. We each handed the guard a slip of paper we'd been given at the security checkpoint, to prove, I suppose, that we hadn't gotten to death row's door by some other means. With that, we were in.

■ ■ ■

The death row visitation gallery looked something like a small indoor bus station or the waiting room at a dystopian doctor's office. An arrangement of blue and red chairs connected in groups of two and three were surrounded by off-white concrete walls and overseen by a large convex mirror hanging near the ceiling. In a corner near the entrance, there was a microwave and a cooler of water with a stack of small cups. Nearby, a small shelf held items for children—puzzles, games, a Mr. Potato Head.

We'd just walked in when a man emerged from a door toward the back of the room wearing a white T-shirt and beige Tennessee Department of Correction–issued pants. It was Terry. He was fifty-six years old then, with a bald head, a gray goatee, and skin paled by more than thirty-five years without sunlight. He walked toward us and reached his hand into a manilla envelope he was carrying, revealing its contents with a smile.

"I brought popcorn."

Terry knew I was a reporter, but I'd agreed not to write about the visit for the paper. We all understood that, given the prison's aversion to granting media access, a story like that could get me banned from visiting, and possibly have repercussions for David and Terry as well. I knew of Terry what I'd heard from David and gleaned from a brief Google search. The latter informed me that in 1983, during a drunken and drug-fueled summer when he was twenty-one years old, Terry had participated in two Knoxville-area murders.

The first took place in early July, when Terry and a friend named Joe Sexton met Todd Millard, a twenty-year-old soldier on leave from Fort Knox. Terry and Joe spent most of the night drinking and playing pool with him. Later, they robbed Todd before Joe shot him to death.

It was several weeks later that Terry committed the murder for which he was sentenced to death. Drunk again and high on Quaaludes, Terry and his cousin were cruising around the Cherokee Reservoir east of Knoxville when they met a thirty-one-year-old housewife named Diana Smith. The chance meeting led to a night of partying, more drugs, sex, and cruising. At some point, Diana looked at Terry and said, "Why did you all rape me?" Panicking, he met up with his friend Joe, who gave him a rifle, and the two drove out to a wooded area with Diana in the trunk. Terry shot her, and later, he and Joe dumped her body in a quarry lake.

There was more to the stories, but those were the blunt facts, and Terry did not dispute them.

Now, thirty-five years later, he was greeting me on death row with a bag of popcorn. He handed the bag to David and reminded him of just how long to cook it, repeating the instructions facetiously in a loud East Tennessee twang. Apparently, during a previous visit, David had overdone it, ruining the snack and filling the small visitation gallery with an incriminating stench. On this night, he returned to the group with an unburnt bag, and we each shook a bit of popcorn out onto the napkins we'd laid on our laps. We sat close in the hard plastic chairs, our knees nearly touching. The room filled up with around fifteen or twenty people and we leaned in closer to hear each other as voices and laughter bounced off the concrete walls.

We talked without any particular aim, David and Al and Terry catching up a bit, me and Terry sharing bits and pieces about ourselves as we went. I mentioned that I'd grown up in Florida, not far from Daytona Beach, and Terry recalled how he'd driven down there on a few occasions. We laughed about how crazy it seemed that they used to let people drive their cars on the beach and Terry shook his head, remembering out loud how he'd spent much of his time there getting drunk and chasing women. Later, when I told him about my newborn daughter who was sweet and healthy but still crying all through the night, his face softened, and he told me how lucky I was. After more than three decades in prison, he said, he could not even summon the sound of a crying baby in his mind.

I didn't ask him about the murders that night, but his address was on death row and that fact hung in the air between us. He referenced the time he "got in trouble," and more than once he urged me to ask him "anything at all." It seemed to me he'd learned to account for the skepticism a new visitor might have about a condemned man claiming to have changed. I only really took him up on it once, though. I asked if there was anyone in the unit that he wouldn't be comfortable having out with us in the visitation gallery—anyone he wouldn't turn his back on. He looked at me as if I must've forgotten where I was and said, "Hell yes!"

It took him years, he said, to truly reckon with who he'd been and what he'd done. A breakthrough had come in 2011, almost thirty years after he went to prison, when he read William Paul Young's international bestselling novel *The Shack*, and became a professing Christian. Years later, the author had come to meet Terry at the prison, and they kept in touch by writing letters. Terry told me he hated who he'd been but that he loved who he'd become. As he told me these things, it did not seem like he was trying to convince me of his redemption so much as he was claiming it for himself. The state, he said, wanted to strap him to his past.

"They want to kill the man who did those things," he said, "but they killed him a long time ago when they sent me here."

I looked around at the old men eating vending machine snacks and chatting with their free-world guests and understood the disorientation David had described to me. Walking into the prison, through its heavy metal doors and menacing razor wire, it was easy to feel what Joe felt stepping into the cell block at the Bronx House of Detention, to think, *I don't belong here.* But after only a short time in the visitation gallery, where around half of the people in the room had been convicted of murder, another feeling comes, just as visceral—*do they belong here?*

The comfortable nature of the gathering collided with the harsh facts of the setting, just as the harsh facts about our hosts' crimes collided with their utterly humane presence. At one point, David introduced me to a man who, upon learning of my allegiance to Auburn University football, told me confidently that the team was overrated that year. Across the room from us, a man named Derrick Quintero was sitting with a visitor, showing her a large painting. I knew that Derrick was one of the men who'd spent a lot of time painting with Billy in the months before his execution. But I didn't know that most of the people in the room didn't know him as Derrick. They called him Taco.

"You know those old Taco Bell ads that said, 'make a run for the border'?" David said, leaning over toward me. "Well, he did that."

I learned later that Derrick was one of eight men who'd escaped from the Kentucky State Penitentiary in June of 1988. After several weeks on the run, he was caught in Mexico, just across the border from El Paso, Texas. He and two of the other escapees—Billy Hall

and James Blanton—were later convicted and sentenced to death for
the murders of Myrtle and Buford Vester, a couple living in Middle
Tennessee. Authorities said the men robbed and killed the Vesters
after committing a series of other burglaries in the area. Attorneys
and advocates for Derrick, and Billy Hall, had spent decades raising
issues with the case and arguing for the men's innocence. Blanton
died on Tennessee's death row in 1999.

On the wall above where Derrick and his visitor were sitting,
there was an almost cartoonish red button with a sign that blared
PRESS FOR HELP. Months later, I asked Terry about it, and he told
me a story about a time when he was sitting near it with a few new
visitors. One of them asked about it just like I had, and he launched
into an animated monologue about how certain he was that the
thing didn't even work. To emphasize his point, he reached up and
hit the button. To his surprise, a group of guards came rushing into
the room.

Seated closer to us was David Duncan, a tall and slender Black
man whose thinning hair was in tight cornrows. He was one of
Terry's best friends and had grown close with David Bass over the
years. He had a visitor of his own sitting next to him, an older white
woman named Barbara Sullivan who had been coming to see him
regularly for several years.

The men on the row knew David as Slim and by that night
he'd been on death row for thirty-five years. In 1983, when he was
just eighteen years old, he was convicted for the rapes and murders
of two Middle Tennessee women—fifty-four-year-old Evelyn Ruby
Burgess and sixty-six-year-old Annie Malone. He was tried for the
killings separately, and for the first, a jury had sentenced him to
death. But even though he was still living on death row, David was
no longer living with that death sentence. I didn't know it on the
night we met, but a federal judge had vacated it three years earlier,
citing ineffective assistance of counsel during the sentencing phase
of his 1983 trial. Rather than pursuing another trial, prosecutors

agreed to a new sentence that would take him off death row and make him eligible for parole in 2027. By then he will have served 44 years in prison.

But in the fall of 2018, he was still in Unit 2 and spending a great deal of his time caring for Charles Wright, the cancer-stricken man whose longtime visitor, Demetria, had first introduced me to the community of regular death row visitors. Charles' condition had been getting steadily worse, but he was still living in his cell. He and the men who were close to him wanted him to be able to stay there as long as possible. They knew eventually he'd be taken away to the infirmary where he would be largely alone. But for now, David and a couple other men in the unit had been nursing Charles themselves, helping him change and bathe and use the bathroom. David leaned toward me as he talked about caring for his friend, and his passion for the task radiated from him. He said he was just doing what God put him here to do, to serve others, and that he could not live with the thought of a guard or someone else walking by the cell and seeing Charles a mess.

Charles was not out in the gallery that night. By then, he was often too weak to come out for visits. The state was seeking to schedule an execution date for him, but his attorneys and loved ones were certain he wouldn't live to see the death chamber.

But another execution was looming, and I could tell the last one was still weighing on Terry. He told me that days after overseeing Billy's execution, the warden had come back to the unit and stood quietly in Billy's old cell for a moment.

"He's gone," Terry said of Billy, grief and irritation evident in his voice. "He's not there anymore."

At some point later that night, after our visit, a team of guards would come to empty another cell. Ed Zagorski was scheduled to be executed in the next seventy-two hours. First, he would be taken to death watch, to a cell near the execution chamber. He would wait there to be killed.

Ed had agreed to answer some written questions from me through his attorney, and I'd published them in the *Scene* earlier in the day before coming to the prison to meet Terry.[4] I asked how he was feeling and, at sixty-three years old, he said he was "relieved it's over."

"I feel good," he said. "I have no resentment against anybody. I am glad that I get to go out in good health instead of rotting away in prison."

He referenced his love of motorcycles and, in response to another question about books and music that had been important to him during his time in prison, he talked about his love of classic rock.

"The song that I have been thinking about and will be in my head when they take me over there is 'Flirtin' With Disaster' by Molly Hatchet," he said.

Ed never had a regular visitor in all his years on death row, but he was beloved among the men who lived there alongside him. He was another of Terry's closest friends on the row, only he didn't call him Ed. He called him Diamond Jim, another nickname born of the dark humor shared among the condemned men. Diamond Jim, Terry explained, had been the nickname of a man who helped the authorities catch Ed.

Just before coming out for our visit, Terry had seen Ed, possibly for the last time. He was amazed at how upbeat his old pal had remained as the date approached. The warden had come to talk to Ed recently, Terry said, and Ed had looked at him and said, "Well, if you've got time, let's go do it right now."

Terry had typed up a letter for Ed the night before, and he pulled out a copy for us to read.

Diamond Jim,

I wanted to put a few of my thoughts on paper for you.

First, I want you to know my heart is sad concerning you. For reasons I may not be able to tell you in this letter (because I don't have the vocabulary) and most certainly I can't muster the words in person but my heart is just completely broken and I am struggling to find the words to say that "I MISS YOU RIGHT NOW" even though you have not gone anywhere.

You need to know that this ENTIRE unit is having a difficult time accepting the possibility that the state may kill you this Thursday. I am trying to think of ways I can help you.

I want you to know that I have drawn strength from you by witnessing what a strong man you are. This afternoon I watched as you went to Cpl. Amazon and thanked him for allowing you to go around the unit speaking to different folks. Watching you interact with others I get a quick look into how you seem to be handling everything. Seeing first hand the peace and resolve you have gives me hope.

I was recalling today when you and I used to order ice cream at the old prison. You ordered it one day and I ordered it the next so we could have ice cream twice a week. Do you remember that? smile

I have enjoyed our conversations over the many years. Has it been 33 years? That sure is a long time. I also recall when you would say "Terry can you hook me up with one of those Disney movies?" I just ask you to wake me up when you were done watching them, remember? smile

Well I guess I will close this out and no matter what may come PLEASE KNOW I will have you in my prayers always. Also I wanted you to know my family is praying for you.

Take care and stay strong my brother. I love you my friend.
GOD BLESS YOU,

Terry King

On the day of their execution, a condemned person is offered a final meal of their choice (with a twenty-dollar limit). But Ed was going to forgo his, Terry said. Around a dozen men in the unit had gathered various ingredients from their personal stashes and made pizzas for a last supper together with him.

There was one other thing, Terry told us. No one outside the prison seemed to have heard yet, but Ed had chosen to be executed in the electric chair. Because he was sentenced before the state made lethal injection its primary method of execution in 2000, Ed was legally entitled to choose the way he would be put to death. When the warden had come to him thirty days before the execution date to make his decision official, Ed had declined to make one because of ongoing legal challenges to the state's lethal injection protocol. But just hours before our visit, the Tennessee Supreme Court had upheld the protocol, prompting Ed to make his choice.

I wasn't too surprised. Another one of the questions I'd asked him through his attorney was whether he was afraid of what would happen later that week.

"No, not at all," he said. "I don't want to be tortured with those drugs, but I am not afraid of death."

When our time was up, we said our goodbyes to Terry and the other men. We retraced our steps through the prison grounds and back out to the parking lot and I felt, as I have many times since, the visceral relief that comes when you walk out of a prison. What I had just experienced complicated that feeling, though. Now, along with the relief that came with leaving, there was a deeper awareness of the fact that there were people we were leaving behind. People with whom we'd shared popcorn and conversation and laughter and hugs. Over the following days and weeks, I would tell my wife and family and friends about what I was certain had been a transformative experience. As I did so, I felt like a child playing Pictionary, pointing over and over again at the sketch I'd drawn, urging them to understand it fully. I began to see why David and Al felt compelled to invite so many people out to the prison, to let them see for themselves.

In the car, as we drove away from the prison, I texted attorneys trying to confirm what Terry had told us about Ed choosing the electric chair. I had never seen the chair in practice—no one had in Tennessee since Daryl Holton chose to sit in it for his execution in

2007, and before that it had been out of use since 1960. But I was familiar with the dark and strange history of what *Tennessean Magazine* in the 1930s had once called a "gruesome piece of furniture."[5] Two years earlier, I'd written a story for the *Scene* about the chair, marking the 100th anniversary of its first use in an execution and considering the possibility that it might soon be making a comeback.[6] Now it was, and bringing with it all its memories and ghosts.

6

Before the executioners turned to electricity and pharmaceuticals, they relied on a rope.

For more than a century, the primary method of execution in Tennessee, as in most of the country, was hanging. Condemned people died wearing a noose. Like the execution methods that would come after it, it was an otherwise useful tool for life conscripted into service as an instrument of death.

There is no official record of the people hanged at the gallows that were erected by local officials around Tennessee during those years. But researchers have worked to uncover this history, excavating a long list of state killings that goes back to the days before Tennessee became a state. In *Legal Executions in Tennessee: A Comprehensive Registry, 1782–2009*, Nashville attorney and Tennessee State University professor Lewis Laska draws on newspaper accounts and local records to document the state's full death penalty history, detailing what is known about the crimes and executions of the condemned.

The first recorded executions in the territory that would later become part of Tennessee were carried out on September 10, 1782, under the authority of North Carolina. On that day Judge Spruce McCay—an "irascible" jurist who, Laska writes, had lost a hand and had it replaced with a brass ball which he would slam down on a table like a gavel during proceedings—had sentenced three men to hang following their conviction by a jury. They went to the gallows without delay. The men, Isaac Chote, John Vann, and William White, were white and of unknown age. Their crime was horse stealing.

The theft of a man's horse—a source of labor and transportation—was taken especially seriously in those days, and even after North Carolina removed it from the list of capital crimes a few years later, it was still punished harshly.

Horse thieves were thereafter sentenced to "one hour in the pillory, 39 lashes on the back well laid on, ears cut off (cropped) and nailed to the pillory, and branding on the cheek the letters 'H' and 'T,'" Laska writes. "However, for the second offense, the punishment was death without benefit of clergy."[1]

Many men felt the whip on their back and the brand on their cheeks in the years that followed, and there were more than a few second offenders. In 1799, Laska writes, the young state of Tennessee made horse stealing a capital crime again, and it remained one until 1809. The record of early executions in the state includes numerous men put to death for making off with another man's valuable gelding or mare.

The first person to be hanged after Tennessee became a state was a white man of unknown age named Robert Parker, a laborer who'd been convicted of stealing "five hundred Spanish milled dollars" and was walked to the gallows on April 28, 1797.[2] Hundreds more would follow. Laska records the hangings of 386 people in the state between 1782 and 1913. More of them were Black than white and a number were enslaved Black men convicted of crimes against the white men who owned them.

There is a painful and convicting truth revealed by which of these hangings have been remembered and which have been left for lonely historians to dig out of a mass grave of the past.

One of the most famous hangings in Tennessee history came

during the Civil War. Sam Davis, a twenty-one-year-old Confederate soldier and slave owner who was acting as a courier, was captured behind Union lines in 1863 and charged with espionage. He denied the charge but was hanged after he refused to give up the names of Confederate spies. Davis was quickly mythologized, known as the Boy Hero of the Confederacy. He became an icon of the Lost Cause, which recast the defeated Confederacy as valiant and justified. Today, a monument marks the place where he was hanged on the Public Square in Pulaski—the small Tennessee town where the Ku Klux Klan was later born—and a statue of Davis stands outside the state Capitol in Nashville.[3]

Despite his romanticized image, Davis was not a boy. But there were indeed children hanged at Tennessee gallows. In 1809, a twelve-year-old enslaved Black boy named Jesse Ward was executed for arson after a whipping—he'd burned the home and several barns of the man who owned him.[4] In 1833, a thirteen-year-old enslaved Black girl was hanged after she was convicted of drowning a white man's five-year-old son.

For much of the 1800s, hangings were far from private. Large crowds often gathered to listen to gallows sermons and the final words of the condemned before the noose was fitted around their neck. On May 24, 1872, a crowd of 8,000 to 10,000 people gathered in the courthouse square in Smithville for the hanging of eighteen-year-old John Presswood Jr., who'd murdered a thirty-six-year-old housewife named Rachel Billings with an axe.[5] Laska's book describes another hanging several years later, at which people erected reserved seating near the scaffold and prepared barbecue.

These macabre fairs did not always go as planned. There were a number of botched hangings. In some cases, it was the rope that broke rather than the neck of the condemned. In others, human error and the fallibility of the method led to nightmarish scenes in the hot light of day. When William Rea was hanged in 1882, Laska writes, he had to be dropped three times before slowly choking to death.[6]

In 1883, the state legislature changed the law, permitting outdoor executions but forbidding "the drop" from taking place in public view. To comply with the law, Laska notes, some sheriffs obscured the gallows with a large drape or built a wooden stockade around the execution site. Others carried out hangings inside the jail yard or inside the jail itself.

But there were other killings drawing crowds then too. Tennessee's official executions were shadowed by those carried out by racist lynch mobs. The Equal Justice Initiative (EJI) has documented more than 4,000 lynchings of African Americans in the United States between 1877 and 1950, including 236 in Tennessee.[7] As EJI founder Bryan Stevenson has said, capital punishment is the stepchild of lynching, and the ropes of the lynch mob and the state have never been fully disentangled. It wasn't until 1885 that Tennessee first executed a white man for killing a Black man. Today, death rows in the United States are disproportionately Black, and Black defendants accused of murdering white people have historically been more likely to receive a death sentence.[8]

■ ■ ■

The officially convicted and condemned in Tennessee died at the end of the rope until 1913. But in the late 1800s, a new execution method arose—the electric chair.

The innovation in state killings was, as Craig Brandon puts it in *The Electric Chair: An Unnatural American History*, midwifed by greed.[9] Brandon's book, and Richard Moran's *Executioner's Current*, details how the chair was born out of a bitter rivalry between Thomas Edison and George Westinghouse, who were fighting for control of the burgeoning electric power market.[10] At the same time, the state of New York was considering adopting electrocution as a more humane alternative to hangings. Edison saw an opportunity.

The famed inventor was pushing direct current for use in powering cities, while Westinghouse had developed the alternating current. The two had been engaged in a public relations battle over which was safer. So, when Dr. Alfred Southwick, a dentist from Buffalo and a leading advocate for using electrocution as an execution method, wrote to Edison asking for advice on the best way to kill a human with electricity, Edison—who had initially denounced the idea in the name of abolishing capital punishment—heartily endorsed his rival's machinery, which used alternating current.[11] What better way to make sure direct current was seen as the safe option for electric power than to make alternating current synonymous with the electric chair? Brandon writes that Edison even suggested that executing a person in the electric chair be known as "westinghousing." He also quietly funded the construction of the chair.

Westinghouse tried to fight Edison's campaign legally, but his lawsuits against Edison were bogged down in the courts. So, when the state of New York sentenced William Kemmler to die in the electric chair in 1890 for murdering his wife with a hatchet, Westinghouse hired a prominent lawyer to oppose it on the grounds that it was cruel and unusual.[12] The world's first electric chair execution, then, was a proxy war between feuding capitalists.

Alternating current ultimately won the war of the currents, becoming the primary method of powering businesses and homes across the country. But Westinghouse failed to stop it from powering the first electrocution. On August 6, 1890, Kemmler was led into the death chamber at Auburn Penitentiary, reportedly wearing a suit and polished shoes that had been provided to him for the day of his experimental death. He did die, but the experiment did not go well. The chair had been tested on dogs, cats, and horses, but a man proved more resilient. A report in *The New York Times* the following day described the execution as "a disgrace to civilization." After a first round of current was sent through the chair and into Kemmler's body, he fell still. "He is dead," a doctor attending the execution declared. But then, other witnesses saw Kemmler's chest rising and falling. "Great God, he is alive!" someone shouted, while another yelled to "turn on the current!" A media witness fainted. The current was turned back on, and the job was finished, with a foul stench overtaking the death chamber.[13]

After the execution, the *Times* reported, New York's deputy coroner W. T. Jenkins was asked how the electrocution compared to a hanging.

"I would rather see ten hangings than one such execution as this," Jenkins said. "In fact, I never care to witness such a scene again. It was fearful. No humane man could witness it without the keenest agony."[14]

Nevertheless, other states were soon building their own electric chairs. In Tennessee, the state legislature approved Senate Bill 125 on September 27, 1913, making the electric chair the official method of execution. The bill stated that "whenever any person is sentenced to punishment by death, that court shall direct that the body of such person be subjected to shock by a sufficient current of electricity until he is dead." It appropriated $5,000 "or so much thereof as may be necessary" for the construction of a death chamber and electric chair, which would be housed at the Walls in Nashville.[15] Going forward, as then–state representative Lonsdale Porter McFarland Sr. phrased it, the state of Tennessee would be "burning the poor devils to death instead of strangling them."[16]

Whatever debate there was over the adoption of the electric chair in Tennessee is likely lost to history. Transcripts of legislative debates would not become available until many years later. But the roll call was preserved. The electric chair was approved by the Tennessee Senate by a vote of 27 to 4 and the Tennessee House by a vote of 64 to 2. The state's records show the last names of the six men who voted against: Cecil, Fitzpatrick, Fulton, Hare, Emmons, and Shaw. Then Governor Ben Hooper signed the bill into law.[17]

It was widely seen as a move toward a more humane manner of execution, and some hoped it would hasten the end of the death penalty. In an editorial published two weeks after the law's passage, the *Lawrence Democrat* praised the adoption of the electric chair as "a short step it is true but nevertheless a step in the direction of juster, less horrible, less barbaric penal laws." At the same time, however, the paper concluded that "the killing of men for crime is illogical, and out of harmony with saner instincts of civilization." Although the state's new law preserved "this ancient horror," the editorial ended on a note of optimism that the electric chair would ultimately "help bring man to a realization of the futility and hurtfulness of the age-old error of killing to punish killing."[18]

Three years later, a twenty-two-year-old Black man named Julius Morgan was accused of raping a nineteen-year-old white woman named Lura Sutherland in Dyer County. The county earns a mention in the introduction of Margaret Vandiver's *Lethal Punishment: Lynchings and Legal Executions in the South* as a place with "a well-established tradition of lynching by 1915."[19] As soon as word of the alleged rape spread, Morgan was apprehended by a mob intent on stringing him up. The county sheriff, both Vandiver and Laska write, managed to seize Morgan from the townspeople and moved him from jail to jail as the lynch mob repeatedly demanded that he hand Morgan back over to them. Morgan was ultimately convicted of the rape, and Laska writes that he later confessed. At the time of the crime, he'd been a fugitive after escaping from an Arkansas prison where he was being held for an attempted rape. His execution was set for July 13, 1916.

"Several times during the night and early morning Morgan began crying and trembling, especially when he first saw the electric chair," Laska writes. "He was practically carried to the chair but became calm when seated."[20]

The hopes of the *Lawrence Democrat*'s editorial board would not be realized. The state of Tennessee electrocuted 124 more men over the next forty-four years, strapping them into the chair to be subjected to shock by a sufficient current of electricity until they were dead. The overwhelming majority of them were Black. Between 1916 and 1960, eighty-five of the men executed in Tennessee's electric chair were Black, while forty were white.

The chair's use peaked in the 1930s, a decade which saw forty-seven men electrocuted, often in quick succession. Twice that decade, the state carried out triple executions—strapping three men into the chair on the same day—and in the spring of 1937, eight men were executed in less than two months.[21] The last triple execution in Tennessee's history came on August 31, 1948, when three Black men—James Scribner, William Turner, and Thomas Taylor—were electrocuted one after another for the rape of a young white college student named Mae Pullum. At the time of the execution, the three men were also charged with the rape of another woman, Wanda Poston, during the same attack. Although the men initially confessed and implicated one another, Laska writes, they later said that their confessions had come after beatings and mistreatment by police.[22]

On November 7, 1960, William Tines—a Black man convicted of rape—became the 125th man to be executed in Tennessee's electric chair. It marked the end of an era in the history of Tennessee's death penalty. The state would not execute another person for forty years.

The run of killings scarred some of the people closest to it. Governor Frank Clement oversaw six executions during his two terms as governor in the 1950s, all of them coming in a two-year period. He visited the men on death row before each execution—even bringing Billy Graham along once—and was said to have agonized over their deaths to a point which contributed to the severe alcoholism that ruined his marriage. In *Lead Me On: Frank Goad Clement and Tennessee Politics*, Lee Seifert Greene writes about Clement's visits to death row, including one in which the governor broke down weeping while speaking to the family of a Black man set to die. A devout evangelical Christian, Clement would later say that the condemned men he visited with "gave their heart to God before they died."[23] Six of the eight times the governor was faced with a pending execution, he allowed the executions to proceed. But during his farewell address in 1959, he urged the state legislature to abolish the penalty, reportedly departing from his prepared text to make a direct plea.

"When I became Governor, I had no idea what it was like to look a man in the eye and know I had to decide on this man's life," he said, as quoted by the *Knoxville News-Sentinel.* "Eight times I faced this decision. Six of those men are dead. I don't believe capital punishment solves anything."[24]

He reiterated that position after he was elected to a third term as governor in 1962 and acted on it. He stayed the executions of condemned men and later commuted all five men remaining on the state's death row after a bill abolishing the punishment passed the state Senate but was narrowly rejected in the House.[25]

Among those voicing support for Clement's efforts to bring about the end of Tennessee's death penalty was the Reverend Pickens Johnson, who had spent thirty-one years as the prison chaplain at the Walls. During that time, he'd been present for eighty-four executions, standing in the death chamber and praying as men were readied in the electric chair. After retiring from his role at the prison, the reverend spoke at legislative hearings in favor of abolition.[26]

The state would continue to claim the right to kill the citizens it had condemned. But a series of governors either refused to see the penalty enforced or saw legal appeals delay pending executions. As the state neared thirty years without an execution though, it decided to update its equipment.

In 1989, as the state prepared to close down the Walls and move death row and the execution chamber to Riverbend, Tennessee officials contracted a former military surveillance equipment dealer and self-made execution equipment manufacturer named Fred A. Leuchter Jr. to refurbish the chair. He hadn't really set out to become the go-to expert on electric chairs; he told *The Atlantic* in 1990 that he "just kind of slid into it." He'd been pursuing electrical engineering projects unrelated to killing human beings when, the magazine reported, the warden of a New England prison called him up for help repairing an electric chair that had been damaged during a riot. That one-off job led to others, and soon his services were in high demand.[27]

In Errol Morris' 1999 documentary *Mr. Death: The Rise and Fall of Fred A. Leuchter, Jr.*, the eponymous Mr. Death discusses his work on Tennessee's electric chair and reveals a dark bit of lore surrounding it.

"Tennessee contacted me with the construction of their new prison," Leuchter says. "I was asked to inspect the equipment at the old facility and make a determination of what could be salvaged. The only consideration was that they wanted to maintain the electric chair, which they have had in place since 1898. The reasoning being that the wood from the electric chair not only had the tradition of all of their electrocution executions, but it also formerly served as the wood of their gallows."[28]

The film includes footage of Leuchter receiving the chair in a large box at his Massachusetts home, opening it in his front yard and sitting in it for photos. He delivered back to Tennessee an updated electric chair built from new wood as well as wood from the original.

In 2016, when I was working on my story about the chair for the *Scene*, I asked former Riverbend warden Ricky Bell about its supposed connection to the old gallows. Until Tennessee resumed executions two years later, Bell was the only warden to oversee executions in the state in the modern era.

"I can say this," he told me. "That wood is old in that chair. Because when we drilled into it to put the restraints on it, you can tell it's old. It's hard. It's real hard, and it's old."

Bell told me that he spoke to Leuchter on several occasions and that the execution engineer gave him a warranty on the chair: "five years or two executions, whichever came first."[29]

Around the same time he was working on Tennessee's electric chair, Leuchter was becoming involved in another eccentric and toxic pursuit: Holocaust denialism. On behalf of the German neo-Nazi publisher, Ernst Zündel—who was facing trial for charges stemming from his publication of denialist materials in Canada—Leuchter compiled a report asserting that structures identified as gas chambers at Auschwitz and Birkenau were not used for mass killings by the Nazis. His report was widely discredited and Leuchter was disgraced.[30]

But his engineering would soon be put to use. In 1998, Tennessee's state legislature adopted lethal injection—first used in the United States in Texas in 1982—as an execution method.[31] Soon after, as it prepared to start killing condemned prisoners again, the state made lethal injection its primary method.[32] The protocol then called for one drug—pentobarbital, a barbiturate. But people convicted before the change was made would be given a choice: The gurney or the chair.

In the spring of 2000, Robert Coe became the first man put to death in Tennessee since 1960. He chose the gurney. So did Sedley Alley, in 2006, and Philip Workman, who was executed in May of 2007. But later that year, when Bell went to see Daryl Holton thirty days before Holton's scheduled execution, the forty-five-year-old Gulf War veteran made a different choice. Holton had been convicted of murdering his four children by shooting them execution-style with a rifle in the garage. He and his ex-wife had been in a dispute over custody of the children. He was sentenced to death, and with the punishment approaching, he chose the chair.

Three days before his execution, he explained his choice to Dan Barry of *The New York Times*.

"It's not very intellectual," he said. "At the time of the commission of the offense, that's the punishment that was in place. That was the law."[33]

Eleven years later, a new warden came to Ed Zagorski asking him the same question. Ed and his attorneys believed that Billy Ray Irick had been subjected to a slow and torturous death by Tennessee's three-drug lethal injection. Electrocution would not be painless by any means, but it would be quicker. So, Ed chose the chair, whose arms had held 126 condemned men before him and would hold more after him too.

7

Ed Zagorski was on death watch, the way station between death row and the execution chamber. Just a few hours after David, Al, and I had finished our visit with Terry, a group of guards had come to take Ed from Unit 2 and move him to an eight-foot by ten-foot cell adjacent to the small room where he would be put to death. There are four such cells at Riverbend—the building's design allows for the possibility of several people waiting their turn.

Thirty-four years had passed since Ed was sentenced to death for the murders of John Dale Dotson and Jimmy Porter, two men who'd met him in the woods of Middle Tennessee for a large drug deal. Now he was due in the execution chamber in less than three days.

He had been scheduled for execution more than once in recent years but never gotten this close, and he had every reason to believe this date would stick. A little more than a month earlier, Ed's attorneys had sent Governor Bill Haslam an application for clemency—the formalized way in which a condemned person pleads for mercy.

"Dear Governor Haslam," Ed said in a note accompanying his application. "Thank you for your time. I just wanted to let you know that I regret everything that happened. I feel really bad for [the] victims' families and the vast impact it caused. I [know] their lives would have been so much better in so many ways and not a day has gone by I haven't thought about it. If you spare me I will continue doing my best."[1]

The governor rejected his request, "after careful consideration."[2]

So now, Ed waited for his execution in a cell with a metal desk with a metal stool, a toilet, a sink, a shower, and, according to the Department of Correction, a small window that "provides a limited view of one of the prison's grounds." Death watch is suicide watch, really. Special measures are in place to ensure that a person does not kill themselves there before the state can do it in a different room nearby. The condemned person is kept under twenty-four-hour supervision by guards working twelve-hour shifts. They are allowed to have basic hygiene items and a dozen sheets of paper. But the single pencil they have access to must remain in a guard's possession when it is not being used.[3]

Ed didn't have much use for a pencil anyhow—he could hardly read or write. But he did want to send some final messages of gratitude to the people who had helped him over the years. So, as he waited in his death watch cell, he spent much of his time dictating farewells to be delivered on the day of his execution. He also did push-ups—thousands of push-ups. Ed was built like a bulldog, stocky with a round head and a belly, and even at sixty-three years old he threw himself into the physical challenge. Guards counted as he did 12,001 push-ups over the course of three days in his cell, and he was delighted by the fact that he could do so many more than the men watching him, many of whom were ex-military.[4]

Otherwise, he spoke to his lawyers about the legal disputes swirling around him or visited with Joe, who had agreed to sit death watch with him as a spiritual adviser. The two had first met back at the Walls, when Ed was struggling with an injured wrist and Joe helped get a doctor in to see him. They'd never been particularly close. But Ed had no regular visitors or close family who would be with him in his final days, so Joe had agreed to do what he had done so many times before—sit with a person as their violent death at the hands of the state drew near. They'd spent the past several weeks visiting regularly, talking about Ed's life and his coming death. Like Terry, Joe was struck by how equanimous Ed remained as his date approached.

It was still unclear, though, what would happen when the date arrived. That is, how the state would kill him. Soon after Ed had informed prison officials that he wanted to be executed in the electric chair, they'd told him that it was too late for him to make that choice. In a letter to Ed's attorneys, the Department of Correction's general counsel argued that his decision needed to have been submitted by two weeks before the execution at the latest.

This put Ed and his attorneys—led by a tireless Nashville-based assistant federal public defender named Kelley Henry—in the unusual position of arguing for their client's electrocution. The affidavit Ed had signed when he made his choice explicitly stated that he believed both the electric chair and Tennessee's three-drug lethal injection protocol were unconstitutional. But if the state insisted on executing him while he and other men on death row were still challenging the lethal injection protocol in court, then he wanted to sit in the chair. Kelley, a veteran of death penalty fights who represented numerous men on Tennessee's death row, filed an emergency motion in federal court the day before the execution was to take place.[5] In it, she asked the court to block the state from using lethal injection to kill her client and to order the use of the electric chair if the execution did proceed. But she began the motion by emphasizing the horror of having to make such a choice at all.

"Secrecy, evasiveness, and a rush to execute on the part of State actors have forced Edmund Zagorski to make a terrible choice: either allow the state to subject him to an execution by lethal injection where the evidence establishes the last 10–18 minutes of his life will be spent in utter terror and agony, or request to be electrocuted which will end his life by burning his organs causing his body to be mutilated and experiencing excruciating pain for (likely) 15–30 seconds."

Later, she dismissed the notion that the executioners weren't prepared to use the chair.

"The prison practices the electrocution protocol every month," she wrote. "The electric chair is examined by an electrician every year. The idea that the chamber requires two weeks for reconfiguration is ludicrous. Unless the prison loses power, they can carry out an electrocution."

On Thursday, October 11, the day that was supposed to be Ed's last, his case and the manner of his death were still at the center of multiple legal disputes. Around noon, U.S. District Judge Aleta Trauger released an order blocking the state from using lethal injection to execute him, meaning Tennessee officials could appeal to a higher court or honor Ed's preference for the electric chair.[6] The day before, the U.S. Court of Appeals for the Sixth Circuit had granted a stay of execution citing the merits of Ed's claim that he'd received inadequate assistance of counsel during his trial and sentencing.[7] He was also asking the U.S. Supreme Court to stay the execution and hear legal arguments against the legality of the state's lethal injection protocol.[8] But just as a stay of execution can be granted with the stroke of one judge's pen, it can be lifted with the stroke of another's. The final days and hours of a condemned person's life can see hope and despair batted horribly back and forth.

So as evening approached on that Thursday, prison officials were proceeding as if the execution would go ahead. Many of the farewell letters Ed had dictated had already been delivered.

Around 4 p.m., Ed and Joe were sitting in a small booth in the death watch area having what they thought may be their final visit when a guard interrupted to say that Ed's attorneys needed to speak to him. They were supposed to have about an hour left together, but another guard indicated to Joe that time was up. They looked at each other and Ed said what they both were thinking—that the stay must have been lifted and he was about to be executed. The two men shared a quick prayer and said goodbye. Ed went to call his legal team, which was huddled together in a downtown office.

Kelley answered his call and put him on speakerphone.

"Ed," she said, "the governor has given you a reprieve until October 21."

In light of the federal court's order that Tennessee must honor Ed's choice of electrocution, and with the execution set to take place in a few short hours, the governor had announced a ten-day reprieve to "give all involved the time necessary to carry out the sentence in an orderly and careful manner."

"I don't understand what that means," Ed said. "Does that mean I'm not gonna die tonight?"

"You're not going to die tonight," she said.

He responded, characteristically, with gallows humor.

"Make sure these people know that."[9]

■ ■ ■

Ed grew up in the 1950s and '60s in a disturbed and disturbing home on the poorer side of Tecumseh, Michigan, a small factory town sixty miles southwest of Detroit. He spent the better part of his youth seeking refuge and peace in other places.

The details of his childhood, at least those that stained the memories of the people who knew him then, are sketched out in more than two dozen signed declarations collected by attorneys and investigators working on his case. Some of the statements were given only months before Ed's execution date, by people who were only just learning that a person they'd known as a boy more than fifty years earlier was now on death row. They were sent to the governor's office along with Ed's application for clemency, and to read them is to confront the life that might have been yours if not for the accident of birth.[10]

The jury that sentenced him to death never got to confront that fact, which is just as Ed had wanted it. Ahead of his 1984 murder trial, he told his lawyers that if he was convicted, he preferred a death sentence to life in prison. To that end, he forbid them from gathering mitigating evidence that might convince the jury he deserved something less than execution.[11] But over the years, he had pursued appeals and subsequent attorneys uncovered facts about his life. In the months before his execution, investigators working for Ed's legal team discovered more and the attorney working on his clemency effort, Robert Hutton, compiled them, revealing how Ed was never truly allowed to be innocent as a boy before he was found guilty as a man.

The home he grew up in was not so different from the Walls, but for the fact that Ed could come and go.

"I remember it being very dirty—there was more dirt on the walls than on the ground outside," his former high school shop teacher recalled in a handwritten statement. "[Ed's] room was like the unfinished attic—it had no insulation, only rafters. The floors were wooden, but the floor didn't even extend across the whole room. Ed's bed looked like a wooden box—I'm not even sure he had a mattress."[12]

A former childhood friend remembered being intimidated by the house, where mice could be seen running around the floors.[13]

But when Ed left the house, he wasn't just looking for relief from the conditions but from his parents too. His father, Ed Sr., was a large man who could often be seen walking to work at a nearby factory, carrying his lunchbox and the remnants of past traumas.[14] He was a World War II veteran who, according to his sister-in-law, had fought in Iwo Jima and had been in Japan when the United States dropped two atomic bombs on the country. As a younger man he'd also been in a serious car wreck in which his fiancée was killed. He swore off driving for the rest of his life.[15]

In the recollections of Ed's childhood friends and neighbors, Ed Sr. is a figure who provoked fascination, sadness, and fear. One marveled at how the old man had no teeth, and never wore dentures, but could still eat a whole apple.[16] Others seemed almost to admire how, although he was an emotionally absent father, he did the best he could to provide for the family.[17] There was a different word about town too, though. One of Ed's former classmates described it as "common knowledge" that Ed Sr. was a "complete ass drunk" who "beat the shit out of Ed."[18]

Whatever was true about Ed's father, all of the people who knew the Zagorski family in those years agreed that his mother, Jeannie, was unwell. She came into parenthood plagued by demons and afflictions of her own. When she was two, one of her sisters said, she suffered a fall that led to surgery in which part of her brain was removed. As a fragile child, she had no soft place to land. Her father was a severe alcoholic and an impatient man who mistreated Jeannie, her sister said. She never finished school.[19]

Ed inherited this neglect, abuse, and illness like a family heirloom. His mother's abusive behavior, and his efforts to escape it, left an indelible mark on the memories of the people around him.

"I can see her now yelling, trying to hit Ed, and chasing after him," one of Ed's boyhood friends remembered. "Ed used to dig holes in the yard to slow his mom down when she ran after him. Once, I saw Ed's mom chase Ed through their backyard trying to hit him and trip a fall into one of those holes that Ed had dug. Ed helped her out of the hole, but I knew he had dug that hole to slow his mom down."[20]

Jeannie Zagorski was, in the memory of that same friend, "a big Polish woman" who was "dirty and had the hairiest legs I have ever seen." Another remembered her as "kind of like a kid in an adult body" with "bad body odor and terrible, terrible breath."[21] She was also said to be a hoarder, filling an already filthy home with various collections.[22] Her unkempt appearance and poor hygiene might've been less disturbing if not accompanied by her frequent violent outbursts. A cousin remembered that Ed's mother had once broken his arm in a fit of rage.[23] A friend said she used to destroy her son's prized possessions when she was mad at him and once smashed a beloved guitar of his.[24] Another friend remembered being at the Zagorski home when Jeannie threw hot coffee at Ed and recalled how she would scream at him—calling him "stupid ass" and "stupid son of a bitch."[25]

One of Ed's cousins said she "always believed that it was my Aunt Jeannie's fault that Eddie ended up on death row."[26]

For Eddie—or "Junior" as his mother could often be heard screaming—there was no peace in the middle of the storm. Around the age of nine, his aunt recalled, he developed a stutter, which she believed was "directly related" to the outbursts of his mother who "would yell and scream at him all the time."[27] He didn't always find relief when he left his parent's house. One of his childhood friends remembered him being taunted for his stutter at school, where he struggled with an apparent learning disability.

"We used to play 'cowboys and Indians' and when Junior tried to say 'bang,' he couldn't get the word out so he would always lose," he said.[28]

By that age, Ed had already suffered abuse far worse than school-yard bullying.

A man who knew Ed in elementary school said that when they were about eight years old, he and Ed were sexually assaulted by a friend's older brother. They'd gone to the friend's house to play, when the older sibling called the young boys into his room and forced them to masturbate him.

The abuse escalated, and the abusers multiplied.

"The sexual abuse was like a big loop that formed around us," the man said. "These older boys and men found out that they could sexually abuse us, and they took advantage of our innocence. As a young boy, it felt like they were everywhere in our small town."

The man said he had never told anyone about the abuse until the investigator working on Ed's case came to see him just months before

Ed's execution date. Thinking back on it, he said, he felt lucky that he at least had a loving father at home.

"I had someone that cared for me," he said, "but Ed had no one."[29]

Ed found solace at nearby gravel pits where he would go to ride dirt bikes, swim, and camp for days on his own, even through cold Michigan winters. When I sent him a list of questions through his attorneys before he went to death watch, I asked him to tell me about a happy time in his life. He told me about going to the gravel pits, which he described as his "paradise."

Friends and neighbors remembered him as loyal and kind, a boy who looked out for younger kids around him. Other families looked out for him, at times urging him out of his campsite and into their homes on harsh winter nights. Ed spent a lot of time in one neighbor's garage, learning how to build motorcycles, and he regularly helped another older man in the neighborhood do chores around his house.[30] He smoked a little pot from time to time, but he never caused any trouble or got in any fights.[31] He had two Doberman pinschers, and he cared for them well.

As a teenager, Ed dropped out of high school, and in the summer of 1972, he spent four months living with one of his aunts and her family. It was a different Michigan town, a different family, and a brief glimpse of a different life. He spent evenings in the basement playing pool with his uncle and took care of his young cousins when his pregnant aunt went to the hospital in labor.

"I have no doubt that Eddie's life would have turned out very differently if my husband and I had taken him into our home," she told his attorneys, in April of 2018. She said she had "cried many, many tears thinking about my nephew" and that she would "give anything to change his circumstances."

Ed went back to Tecumseh and spent a year or so working at the same factory as his father before leaving town. To many of the people who knew him growing up, it was as if he'd just disappeared. The last time his aunt saw him was when he was twenty or twenty-one. But years later, after corresponding with him in prison—often through audiotapes sent in the mail—she learned why her beloved nephew had gone missing from her life.

"Eddie had told me at one point that the reason he stayed away from me and my family for so long was because he was involved in the drug scene," she said. "He said he wanted to distance himself from us to protect us from anyone that might want to hurt him by harming us."[32]

■ ■ ■

It was the spring of 1983 when Ed started hanging around a Hickman County trout farm run by a man named Jimmy Blackwell. It was there that he met John Dale Dotson and Jimmy Porter, only they didn't know him as Ed. He'd introduced himself as Jesse Lee Hardin and claimed to have spent time working as a mercenary in Central and South America. At the very least, he looked the part, carrying weapons and survival gear. At some point, he made arrangements for the two men to meet him in the woods where they would exchange $23,000 for 100 pounds of marijuana that was to be dropped from an airplane.

The deal was to take place on April 23. Almost two weeks later, on May 6, the decomposing bodies of John Dale Dotson and Jimmy Porter were discovered in a wooded area near the interstate. They'd been shot multiple times and their throats had been cut. Investigators found items later identified as Ed's, and a cartridge that matched his semi-automatic rifle, at the scene. Three weeks later, Ed was arrested in Ohio after a shootout with police, during which he shot a deputy five times and was wounded himself. He'd fled Tennessee in Jimmy Porter's Datsun truck, according to court documents, and was carrying the dead man's .357 Magnum.

After his arrest, Ed offered authorities differing accounts of the events that left two men rotting in the Tennessee woods. In one statement, he said he'd been one of four mercenaries on the scene that night and that while the other men had gone into the woods, he'd been posted at a welcome center at the Kentucky border keeping watch for cops. Later, while he was in jail, he told visitors he'd only been there to "blow away FBI agents." In a separate statement to law enforcement, he said he'd been hired to kill Jimmy Porter. He never confessed to killing the two men but also refused to name any of the other people he said had been involved.[33]

In any case, two indisputable facts had been carried out of the woods in body bags. John Dale Dotson and his wife Marsha had been married for eight years and were raising three children from previous relationships together—none older than thirteen.

"His death ruined me, it turned my world upside down and I just lost it," Marsha Dotson told *The Tennessean* in October of 2018, as she rode out the emotional storm that came after the governor's eleventh-hour reprieve delayed the execution she'd been preparing to witness.

Jimmy Porter had owned an area bar where the Dotsons spent their last night together. His family declined to speak to the media as Ed's execution date approached, but his nephew told *The Tennessean* about how he'd learned of his uncle's murder when he saw the bodies being recovered on the news.[34]

On March 2, 1984, a Robertson County jury found Ed guilty and sentenced him to death in the electric chair. In the courtroom, Ed, then twenty-eight, showed little emotion and said "thank you" after his death sentence was read. Members of the jury found the sentence more upsetting. The next day's *Tennessean* noted that at least two women on the jury were crying openly as foreman Bill Clay read it aloud.[35]

Over the years, Ed's attorneys pursued appeals in which they argued that his trial had been unfair. In a filing opposing the state's request for an execution date for Ed in 2018, his attorneys at the federal public defender's office in Nashville made the case again.[36]

They argued that his incriminating statements before trial—which came during interrogations after he initially said he wouldn't speak to authorities without an attorney—were the direct result of "inhumane conditions and unconstitutional coercion." While being held in a county jail, a court filing said, Ed had been "placed in solitary confinement in an unventilated metal hotbox for seven (7) weeks during the heat of the summer, which decimated him physically and mentally, made him mentally ill and suicidal, and led him to give statements in order to end the unbearable conditions." He attempted suicide more than once.

They also raised serious doubts about Ed's guilt. They pointed to Jimmy Blackwell, himself a major local drug dealer who later cooperated with authorities and whose nickname—Diamond Jim—later became Ed's on death row. The original and since-deceased Diamond Jim had been implicated in a similar drug-related killing in the area.

Even if his guilt was certain, though, Ed's case was a stark example of the utterly arbitrary nature of the death penalty. Even prosecutors themselves did not initially believe that justice required an execution in his case—they offered Ed two life sentences in exchange for a guilty plea but pursued the death penalty when he declined. That put him in a rare demographic. In a 2018 report published by the *Tennessee Journal of Law and Policy*, attorneys Bradley MacLean and H. E. Miller Jr. examined what they called "Tennessee's Death Penalty Lottery." Among their findings was the fact that over a forty-year period, the state of Tennessee had convicted more than 2,500 defendants of first-degree murder, only eighty-six of whom received a sustained death sentence and only six of whom had been executed.[37]

Ed's attorneys emphasized how he was far from *the worst of the worst*, for which execution is supposedly reserved. They wrote that at "at least 20 (twenty) other persons convicted of drug-related double homicides (or worse) have not been sentenced to death, but to life imprisonment" including people convicted of killing as many as five or six people.[38]

But also among the people arguing against Ed's death sentence as his execution date approached were members of the jury that had handed it down. Thirty-four years after he'd read the sentence aloud in court—looking "pale" and "shaken" as he did so, according to *The Tennessean*—jury foreman Bill Clay was among six jurors who supported clemency for Ed and said they would've chosen a sentence of life without parole if only it'd been an option in 1984. Today, every state with the death penalty gives jurors that option.

Ahead of Ed's original execution date, as I reported on his case for the *Scene*, I spoke to several of the jurors, including Clay, who hoped the governor would overrule their decision. One of them, a man named Michael Poole who was only a few years older than Ed when he voted to sentence him to death, told me that the jury struggled mightily with the decision. Decades later, he was certain that an execution wouldn't accomplish anything.

"There's two gentlemen that have already lost their lives in this ordeal, if another person loses his does that make the world a better place?" he said. "I don't think so."[39]

Ed's clemency application noted that Marsha Dotson, the widow of John Dale Dotson, agreed.

"Even though Zagorski ruined my life and those years have been hard," she said, according to the application, "it would be OK with me if he wasn't executed and spent the rest of his life locked up in prison."[40]

But Ed would be executed. The governor's reprieve was only temporary and on October 22, the day after it expired, the Tennessee Supreme Court gave him a new date, scheduling him to die ten days later.[41]

■ ■ ■

On the same day the court released its order rescheduling Ed's execution, David arrived at Riverbend expecting to make a normal visit to death row.[42] He went through security, pulling his pockets inside out as he walked through the metal detector and making friendly banter with the officers. But when he met Terry back at the visitation gallery in Unit 2, Terry told him something he never had before.

"We're going to have a visitor tonight," Terry said.

"Who?" David asked.

"Diamond Jim," Terry replied.

David was confused. He'd never seen Ed in the visitation gallery; for more than thirty years, Ed had never had a regular visitor. But sure enough, Terry left for a moment and walked back into the room with David Duncan and Ed, who looked as if it could be any other Monday night, not one less than two weeks before his execution.

Ed plopped down in a chair next to David and they hugged before Terry began introducing him to others in the room. Soon, Ed was holding court as other men from the unit and their visitors sat and listened in quiet awe. His complete aliveness made his imminent killing almost incomprehensible.

He told a story from his life before death row. Before he appeared in Tennessee as Jesse Lee Hardin, he said he'd been relatively settled on the gulf coast of Louisiana, where he captained a boat that ferried people and supplies to and from an oil rig. One day, he said, there was an explosion at the oil rig, and Ed and two other men went speeding back toward the flaming platform where they helped rescue more than twenty people. When David said he was shocked they saved that many, Ed acknowledged that he'd probably only saved sixteen people by himself.

I wasn't able to confirm Ed's story with certainty, but the details matched an incident in 1980, in which an explosion at an oil platform operated by Pennzoil and staffed, in part, by Poole Offshore Co.—the company Ed said he'd worked for—killed at least five people and injured twenty-nine.[43] The selfless act he claimed was also consistent with the way childhood friends had described him—and with the testimony of former prison officials who'd come to know him on death row and supported his request for clemency. At least two prison guards recalled how he'd helped them break up violent altercations, noting how they'd trusted him with their lives.[44]

Soon, though, Ed was taken back to death watch, knowing this time that he would not be coming back. He started doing push-ups again, this time stopping after 22,000. He also kept visiting with Joe. They'd grown painfully close, and Ed had shared more stories of the short life he lived between his troubled childhood and his arrival on death row. During the years he was living in Louisiana, he told Joe, he'd spend the summers riding out to the Sturgis Motorcycle Rally in South Dakota on his Harley-Davidson and was known to bikers across the country as "Renegade." He spent months beneath the Black Hills, living amongst the Lakota people there.

Now October was coming to a close, and Ed would only see one day of November. But on one of his last days on death watch, he sat down in the visitation booth with Joe, vibrating with excitement.

"Do you remember Laurie?" Joe recalled him saying.

Laurie was the one woman Ed had truly loved in his life. They could have had a relationship, maybe a life together, but Ed had ended up driving away on his motorcycle, knowing his outlaw life-style wouldn't allow for it. He'd asked his attorneys to track her down, and they discovered that she'd died. They sent him a picture of her gravestone.

He'd been with her again, though, in a dream, and he eagerly told Joe about it as they sat mere feet from the execution chamber.

"I'm on green grass," he said. "And Laurie's there. And she's holding my hand, telling me everything's gonna be all right. I'm just looking at her. And she says 'hold on tight.' We came up off the ground and all of a sudden we're headed into some woods and we're not high enough to get over it. But we went right through the woods and came out the other side and landed."

"Ed, I don't think that was a dream," Joe told him. "I think that was a vision."

The electric chair, Ed was convinced, would transport him to that place where there was peace.

■ ■ ■

On the night of November 1, a cold wind whipped north from the prison and encircled the men and women holding a vigil under floodlights. Joe was there. He'd sat death watch with Ed twice now and there was nothing more for him to do. David was there too, along with many of the other regular death row visitors who had done this once before for Billy and had come now to do it again, to stand as testimony to the fact that the condemned man was known and cared for. Along with them were anti–death penalty activists, some local and some from out of state. They huddled together, they prayed, they denounced the death penalty and they waited.

On the road leading into the prison, armed officers had stopped each car, leaning in to ask, "for or against?" as if they were separating guests at a wedding. Under a small tent near the makeshift grass parking lot cordoned off for the night's event, more officers met each person who arrived and made them sign their name on a sheet of paper indicating whether they were "for," "against," or "media."

Only two men were there to cheer on the execution, and they stood in their fenced-in area, occasionally shouting taunts at the vigil.

"It's not gonna make a difference!" one of them yelled. "We're gonna kill your boy tonight! He's got five minutes left!"

Later, one of them hurled another verbal brick over the fence: "I hope he catches on fire!"

It was grotesque and also a real possibility. Twice in the 1990s, executions in Florida's electric chair ended with flames bursting from the condemned men's headpieces.[45] Tennessee's chair was supposed to be tested regularly, but it had only been used in an execution once in nearly sixty years. No one knew for sure what would happen to Ed.

As the execution hour approached, the group holding vigil prayed. They were doing this, heads bowed under the buzzing floodlights, when one of the men in the other field shouted yet again.

"Pray for the victims!"

He didn't know that only seconds earlier, the large group had done just that, remembering John Dale Dotson and Jimmy Porter by name and praying that their families would find some kind of peace.

The execution had not taken place yet, but the men and women gathered there were already mourning. They waited, shifting and pacing in the cold.

Joe told the group about Ed's final days on death watch, about his thank-you notes and his thousands of push-ups. David spoke too, sharing the story Ed had told him of his life-saving efforts in the Gulf of Mexico. They insisted that he be remembered for more than the crimes that sent him to death row.

Then, at 7:30 p.m., I received an email from the Tennessee Department of Correction. I had been checking my phone constantly and I didn't need to read the subject line to know what it was: ZAGORSKI DEATH ANNOUNCEMENT.

"The death sentence of Edmund Zagorski was executed by means of electrocution on November 1, 2018, in accordance with the laws of the state of Tennessee," it read. "The sentence was carried out at the Riverbend Maximum Security Institution in Nashville. Zagorski was pronounced dead at 7:26 p.m."[46]

I leaned over to David, who was standing near me, and showed him the news. He passed the word on to Joe, who announced to the crowd that the execution was complete. They started singing "Amazing Grace."

As I drove away from the prison, I looked at the cars around me and wondered if their drivers were even aware of what had just been done in their name. I knew they were no safer for it, and if the state they were driving in was now more just as a result, I couldn't see any evidence of it.

When I got home, I sat at my dining room table with a micro-waved plate of dinner and watched a video of the witnesses' press conference.[47] After the media witnesses gave their accounts of the execution, Kelley Henry, Ed's attorney, came up to speak.

I'd come to know Kelley as the state started revving up the death machine and I'd seen how she and her colleagues resisted it, throwing themselves into what experience told them were likely to be losing fights. Kelley seemed to combine a meticulous legal focus with a palpable personal connection to the people she repre-sented. It had been almost thirty years since the first time she lost a client to the executioner, and there had been many more since. Later, she told me that her life was like a "tapestry of executions."[48] Memories in her personal life were interwoven with memories of the work; when her son crawled for the first time, she was writing a brief for Arizona death row prisoner Walter LaGrand, who was executed in 1999.

Days before the execution of Billy Ray Irick, whom she'd also represented, I'd sat in Kelley's office discussing the upcoming lethal injection. As we talked, I asked her how much longer she thought she could do this punishing work, how she'd know when the cost was more than she could pay. But Kelley was more worried about growing numb to the trauma than being overcome by it. She told me that if there was ever a night when one of her clients was executed and she didn't cry, that's how she would know.

As head of the office's capital habeas unit, which represents peo-ple who have already been convicted and sentenced to death, Kelley had long maintained a policy that she and the attorneys who worked under her would not witness their clients' executions. She knew of at-torneys who had fallen into substance abuse, or died by suicide, after seeing their clients put to death. She worried the experience would so traumatize her staff that they would be unable to go on represent-ing the living clients who needed them, and she didn't want young attorneys seeking to prove their dedication by volunteering to act as witnesses. But she'd abandoned that policy, in part because of the ongoing legal fights surrounding execution methods. For the sake of the condemned men she represented, someone who knew the protocol step-by-horrible-step needed to be in the witness room.

So, on this night, she'd watched as Ed was electrocuted to death. Standing outside after the execution, bracing against the bitter wind, she described what she had seen. She fought back tears as she spoke.

First, she described the moment around 7 p.m., when she'd watched as a team of guards extracted Ed from his death watch cell. As the guards approached him, she said, Ed spoke to them. She looked down at her notes to read exactly what he'd said.

"First of all, I want to make it very clear, I have no hard feelings," he told the execution team. "I don't want any of you to have this on your conscience. You are all doing your job. And I'm good."

Emotion tried to choke her voice as she repeated his words.

Following the protocol, the guards had rushed into the cell and restrained Ed with handcuffs, a belly chain, and leg irons. Kelley got in line and walked with the procession into the execution chamber. The electric chair was there, waiting, and they asked Ed to sit down in it. The guards started strapping him into the chair, tightening a restraint across his lap and criss-crossing straps over his shoulders and across his chest. His wrists were also strapped down tightly on the arms of the chair. At one point, Kelley said, as the guards were strapping a saline-soaked sponge onto each of his ankles, Ed told them that one seemed a little loose and perhaps they should tighten it. More than once as the guards readied him in the chair, Ed looked up at her and smiled, telling her, "Chin up."

In his final days, she said, Ed wanted everyone around him to be at ease. He kept things light during his time on death watch, and when she talked to him about the last thing he wanted to see, he told her he wanted to see her smiling.

"So, I tried very hard to do that," she said.

Looking at Ed through the witness room window, she said she caught his eye and placed her hand over her heart—a signal they'd discussed that meant she was holding him in her heart. She tried to smile.

Then Ed spoke his last words: "Let's rock."

8

The line had moved again, and it was hard now to see what would stop it. If Billy's execution brought the shock that state killings had returned to Tennessee, Ed's brought the weight of realization that they were almost certainly going to continue. The courts had not intervened, and the governor's prayerful consideration had not led him to show mercy.

Many of the death row visitors had become regulars at the prison during a period of relative calm. They'd seen the state schedule executions only to have them called off amid legal challenges and reports of difficulty acquiring lethal injection drugs. But the state's efforts eventually bore this terrible fruit. Two men had been put to death now, and another was scheduled to die in a month's time. Why should there not be more?

There would be. A little more than two weeks after Ed's execution, the Tennessee Supreme Court set execution dates for six men, four in 2019 and two in 2020. The killing calendar extended more than a year into the future. The Monday night gatherings inside the prison would continue, but so would these occasional Thursday night vigils outside it.

Joe would not be there, though. For him, Ed's execution was a falling boulder that shook loose a mountainside of resting trauma. It had been nearly forty years since the execution of John Spenkelink, what he called his "baptism in blood into the death penalty." There had been so many more executions over those years, so many times when he found himself sitting with another human in that emotional vise as it clamped shut. After sitting death watch twice with Ed and standing outside in the cold prison field as news came that he'd been executed, Joe broke down. He told the death row visitors that he would be stepping back, and he started intensive trauma therapy. He could not go back to the prison grounds, and it would be many months before we were able to talk about his work and relationships there at all.

For David, the death row visitation gallery had become a sacred space, and now a second man he'd met there had been killed. Terry had been in Knoxville for a court hearing, held in a jail there on the night of Ed's execution. He found out the next morning that his friend of more than thirty years, Diamond Jim, was dead.

"While I knew they most likely had put him to death," he wrote to me in a letter, "I didn't know for sure until 11/2/18 @ 7:55am when they put me in the back the police car I asked one of the officers to look on their smart phones and they told me they killed him. The closer I got to the prison the more emotional I got. When we were on Cockrill Bend Blvd. I began to cry and when we pulled in the parking lot I got pissed off because the tent was still up. To me, that represents murder. We all know why they put it up. I asked myself why was it still up at 9:35am the next day?"

I'd be standing under that tent again soon. The state's original schedule put around two months in between the three executions scheduled for 2018. But Ed's brief reprieve and rescheduled electrocution meant there was only about a month before the next man, David Miller, was due in the execution chamber. A few days after Ed's execution, the Department of Correction put out its call for media witnesses, and I faxed in my application.

Earlier in the year, an Associated Press reporter named Michael Graczyk had retired after witnessing more than 400 state killings. I wasn't looking to break any records. But I thought the experience of having witnessed one execution would be useful in witnessing another. Beyond that, a group of my colleagues in the local press corps had taken their turn witnessing Ed's execution while I reported from the outside. It was mine again. Tennessee was going to keep killing prisoners, and most of us were going to have to watch them do it more than once.

9

The prison was draped in darkness, a shroud for the evening's plans. Winter had chilled the air and shortened the days and it felt right for the world to turn its back on the sun.

I'd underestimated how disturbing it would be to feel familiar with the process, to know how to check in with an official at the top of the prison driveway and to feel a muscle memory as we milled around beside the white tent in the parking lot for another official to lead us inside. I did not need to be led. I knew to go to the conference room where we would be served bitter government coffee, and I knew the route from there to the execution chamber. I wished I didn't.

There were changes inside the prison and things I hadn't noticed before, though. Gone was the smell of fresh paint that had greeted us for Billy's execution—these nights were not new anymore. On the desk at the security checkpoint, there was a sign that read YOU CAN'T HAVE A GOOD DAY WITH A BAD ATTITUDE, AND YOU CAN'T HAVE A BAD DAY WITH A GOOD ATTITUDE. Near the back of the room, a Christmas tree stood draped in holiday rainbow lights. Several weeks later, Governor Bill Haslam and many of Tennessee's other leaders who see themselves as Christians would celebrate the birth of the Lamb of God who takes away the sins of the world. Haslam could not take away David Miller's sins, but he did have the power to show him mercy. After "careful consideration," however, he declined to spare David's life, just as he had refused to spare Ed's or Billy's.[1]

As we worked our way through security, I stepped up onto a platform and waited for the guard to start it moving through the body scanner. A warning label on the scanner disclosed the radiation we were exposed to while passing through. I was learning just how true it was. The prison was a toxic place, and contact with it could change a person on a cellular level. There was life and grace to be found inside, but getting to it meant being exposed to trauma that seeped through your skin. The men inside were confined within poison walls. An execution was just the most acute version of what the place was trying to do to them all the time.

Once we were through the checkpoint—and supplied with our coffee, notepads, and pencils—we started making our way to the execution chamber.

■ ■ ■

Helen Standifer was not at the prison that night. She was eighty-four years old, living more than 1,600 miles away in Chandler, Arizona, and that's where she'd decided to stay. One violent death in Tennessee was enough.

"I don't see that it accomplishes anything at all," she told me when I spoke to her on the phone two days before the execution and asked her why she'd decided not to witness it. "It's immaterial. It doesn't bring my daughter back; it doesn't accomplish anything. Frankly, I don't see any reason to be there."[2]

Her daughter was Lee Standifer, the twenty-three-year-old woman who went on a date with David Miller in May of 1981 before he murdered her in an eruption of long-simmering rage. Helen was still in her early forties then. As I spoke to her on the phone thirty-seven years later, the strain of the decades evident in her voice, a surreal and heartrending effect of the decades-long interlude between the murder and the execution occurred to me for the first time. Lee was unjustly frozen in time while the years accumulated for everyone else. Now, Helen was the eighty-four-year-old mother of a twenty-one-year-old daughter who would never grow any older, just as Kathy Jeffers had become the aging mother of a seven-year-old little girl who would never know adolescence.

Helen recalled the paperwork she'd received in the mail every time there was a new appeal or update in the case. But just as she did not see any reason to attend the execution, she had no interest in discussing what the thirty-seven years since her daughter's murder had been like for her.

"I don't want to get into the soap opera stuff," she told me. "Of course, it's been extremely difficult for the whole family, but that has nothing to do with—that's not something that needs to be gone through with anybody else but me. The only reason I'm doing this at all is because I know there's no advocate there for her. And because it was so long ago, I've been startled when I talk to so many of you people back there—some of you were not even born at the time this happened."

She and her family had only lived in Tennessee for a brief period, she said. They'd made wonderful friends during that time, but most of them were long gone now. She was speaking to affirm her daughter's existence, to insist on it.

Lee had been an upbeat child who loved school, undeterred by slight brain damage and a learning disability.

"She didn't let that bother her," Helen said. "I think it bothered other people, but it didn't bother her in the least."

As she spoke about her daughter's childhood, the timing of the execution seemed to trip her up, her voice stumbling over the words.

"She loved the holidays, and I guess this makes it terribly tough because she loved the holidays, she loved her family. We always got a bit of a tickle out of the fact that she always had to—she started this when she was probably in grade school—she started putting jingle bells on her shoelaces around the holidays."

Helen laughed at some of the memories she still carried with her. Once, when Lee was a little girl, she was having trouble tying her shoe. Her father told her to "use your head." So, Lee bent down, pressing her head against her shoelaces.

When the family lived in Colorado, they did a lot of camping, fishing, and hiking. Lee was involved in 4-H and won a gold medal for swimming the backstroke in an early state-level iteration of the Special Olympics. When she was older, after her family moved to Knoxville, she got a job at a food-packing facility in the area. The repetitive nature of the work made her feel comfortable. She took the bus to work in the mornings and home in the evenings. She loved the work, and her bosses loved her, Helen said, because she never missed a day and was always on time.

Soon, her parents let her move out of the house for the first time. She spent a year living with her sister and some friends who were students at the University of Tennessee. When they moved on, Lee's parents struggled to find a place for her to live that could accommodate her needs. Eventually, she moved into the local YWCA. That's where she was living when she met David Miller.

■ ■ ■

The stories start to run together, of boys whose bodies and brains were beaten and bruised before they became the violent men who were sent to death row. David was twenty-four when Lee met him, a man buckling under the weight of trauma and abuse that started before he was born and had rarely been interrupted for more than two decades since. Court documents, records from his childhood, and expert testimony gathered by his attorneys in the months before his execution recount the "continuous hellish nightmare" of his childhood.[3]

His mother, Loretta Winkelman, conceived him in a one-night

stand in Ohio when she was seventeen and drank heavily throughout her pregnancy.[4] It was a fitting introduction to a mother who
would only ever poison him. When David was eight months old,
she began living with the man she would quickly marry, an alcoholic ex-Marine named John Miller, a violent man who spent the
next ten years physically abusing Loretta and their children.[5] He
targeted David, subjecting him to beatings that made up some of
the boy's earliest memories.

Summarizing the attacks recalled by family members who witnessed them, Dr. Pablo Stewart, a psychiatrist who evaluated David
in 2003, wrote that John Miller "knocked David out of a chair, hit
him with a board, threw him into a refrigerator with such force it
dented the refrigerator and bloodied David's head, dragged him
through the house by his hair, and twice ran David's head through
the wall." Other times, Stewart wrote, John Miller resorted to more
traditional methods—kicking, punching, slapping, and strangling
his stepson. David's mother—who was later diagnosed with brain
disease after exposure to toxins while working on an assembly line
at a plastics factory—provided no refuge.[6] She would whip him with
whatever happened to be around—a belt, an extension cord, a wire
coat hanger, or an umbrella. She also allowed him to believe that the
man who beat him mercilessly was his biological father until after her
marriage to him ended.[7]

By the time he was ten years old, David had attempted to kill
himself twice. His mother and John divorced, but while that meant
the end of his stepfather's sadistic attention, it was only the beginning
of David's suffering. In his preteen years, he started experiencing sei-
zures and dissociative episodes and around the same time he began
drinking beer and liquor, layering it on top of a variety of pills. Not
surprisingly, he struggled in school. The substances dulled an ever-
present anxiety but could not spare him from the pervasive trauma
of his childhood, which included not just physical abuse, but sexual
abuse as well.[8]

In interviews with psychiatric experts, David said his first sexual experience was when a cousin sexually assaulted him at the age of four or five. Later, he said, he was sexually assaulted by one of his grandfather's friends, who had taken him fishing. His own mother— who was by then drinking heavily, exacerbating her mental illness, and inviting a revolving cast of men into her home and her bed— sexually abused him too, he said, raping him on several occasions before he was fourteen years old.[9] His family reportedly disputed this account.[10] But Dr. David Lisak—a clinical psychologist who specifically studied the long-term impact of childhood sexual and physical abuse on male development—found David's allegations "extremely credible."[11] David had disclosed the abuse in a fit of rage after Lisak confronted him about his mother's allegation that David attempted to rape her when he was sixteen.

"When I confronted Mr. Miller about this incident, he immediately became extremely agitated and tense," Lisak wrote in a subsequent report. "When I pressed him for an explanation of why he assaulted his mother, of why he would attempt to rape her, he began to literally vibrate with anger, his face turned a vivid red, and he seemed very close to simply exploding with rage. Instead, he blurted out the following words: 'I bet she didn't tell you who started all that!' I asked him what he meant by 'all of that.' He yelled, 'It was she that started all that, not me!!' I again asked him what he meant by 'all of that.' He then became even more agitated, began to get up out of his chair, and finally started demonstrating something with his hands while his face was contorted with rage and pain, and he couldn't find words to say. Finally, he said, 'having me dance with her, and putting my hand here (he demonstrated his hand at his mother's breast) and putting my hand there (he demonstrates his hand at his mother's genitals).' At this point Mr. Miller's breathing was so fast and his face so flushed that I gave him several moments to calm down."

David went on to share more details of the abuse before saying that he was done talking about it.

In his report, Lisak concluded: "This incestuous abuse, by far the most damaging abuse suffered by Mr. Miller, scarred him to his core, and instilled in him a rage at his mother that endures to the present day. His rage has also been enacted on many other innocent 'stand-ins' for his mother."

Reading all this, it was impossible not to imagine what David's life might have been like if he'd had a mother like Helen Standifer, who fought to preserve her daughter's dignity long after Lee was dead, instead of one like Loretta, who stripped him of his dignity and innocence. Still, though, another thought crept in. What would a clemency application for Loretta Winkelman look like? Surely Loretta was not born wanting to become a battered wife and a mother who would damage her son so deeply. Surely the woman she became was nothing at all like the girl someone once knew. It was easy, too easy, to see her as the most vile of creatures, just as easy as it was to see the men on death row as *the worst of the worst*. But I'd spent enough time with the documentation of their lives to know that their stories were nesting dolls of trauma and pain.

David left his mother's toxic orbit at the age of fourteen, when the state removed him and his siblings from her home. When he was seventeen, after spending time in foster homes and a poorly run juvenile facility, he joined the Marines. He made it through boot camp but became disillusioned when he learned that he would not be deployed overseas to Vietnam. He went AWOL more than once and was dishonorably discharged. He returned to Ohio and to the bottle and was soon arrested for stealing a car. After a year in jail, he was released into a halfway house, and after some schooling he got a job as a welder, the same trade his stepfather had plied when he wasn't brutalizing David and the rest of the family.

"This period of Mr. Miller's life was, in retrospect, his last chance at making a successful adaptation to adult life," Lisak wrote. "For a brief period, he had the ingredients in place, but the vulnerabilities that were the legacy of his abusive childhood ultimately undid him."

When David left the halfway house, he moved in with his elderly grandfather, the only person from whom David could ever recall hearing the words "I love you." He continued working and even started drinking less. Until one day, he came home to find his grandfather dead. The loss sent David into a spiral and back into substance abuse.

Around this time, he met a woman named Laurie, and their brief time together produced a daughter named Stephanie, with whom David would have one of his only lasting, loving relationships. Reports from the doctors who interviewed and evaluated David present different accounts of his relationship with Laurie—with one describing it as a tempestuous union that included drug-induced violent assaults by David—but in any event it did not last. Laurie married another man, and David, after a brief interlude in Texas, left Ohio for Tennessee.[12]

He was hitchhiking through the Knoxville area in 1979 when a fifty-year-old Baptist preacher, the Reverend Benjamin Calvin Thomas, picked him up. The reverend took David in and gave him a place to live in exchange for sex, trapping David—then in his early twenties—in yet another toxic relationship with a would-be caretaker. He was often violently and publicly drunk, and he was twice accused of rape by women who declined to prosecute, citing their fear of him. In one of his interviews with Lisak, he continued to deny one of the allegations but confessed to another.[13]

That was the man Lee Standifer met while she was living at the YWCA, trying to make her own difficult transition into adulthood and apparently doing well. On Wednesday, May 20, 1981, she and David went out on a date. They were seen at a downtown bar, the public library, and a cafeteria before David hailed a cab, which dropped them off near the preacher's home where David was living.[14] David had already been drinking heavily earlier in the day and had taken LSD.[15]

David later told authorities pieces of what happened next, although he said then and maintained decades later that his memories of the night were fragmented. While he and Lee were in the house, standing in the living room near the fireplace, he said that he told her he was going to go back to Houston. She grabbed his arm, he said, and told him she didn't want him to leave. He hit her and she fell to the ground. After that, investigators said, he bludgeoned her with a fireplace poker, killing her, and then stabbed her dead body at least six times. One stabbing appeared to have occurred with such force that the state's medical examiner suggested the knife might have been driven into Lee's body with a hammer.[16] In his assessment, Stewart pointed to the brutal nature of the murder and David's chaotic and irrational behavior following it as evidence that was not premeditated but rather a violent explosion resulting from the mixture of severe posttraumatic stress, alcohol, and acid.[17]

At trial, prosecutors insinuated that David had also sexually assaulted Lee before the murder. But while a medical examiner found evidence of sexual intercourse, there were not clear signs of sexual assault.[18] After his arrest, David told the authorities how he'd used a rope to drag Lee's body out of the house, through the yard, and into the woods some sixty feet from the home.[19]

When the reverend returned home from church that night, he found David cleaning the basement floor and discovered blood in the kitchen. David told him he'd gotten into a fight, and according to his testimony at trial, the reverend kicked him out, driving him out to I-40 and leaving him there with twenty-five dollars. A day later, the reverend called the police to report that he had found the body. David was arrested in Ohio on May 29.[20] He was convicted the following year and sentenced to death. After the Tennessee Supreme Court ordered a resentencing in his case in 1987, a second jury handed down the same penalty.

In his clemency application, David's attorneys argued, "If this case were tried today, David would not be sentenced to death and it is likely he would not even be convicted of first degree murder."[21] His original trial, they wrote, took place before a landmark U.S. Supreme Court decision stating that it wasn't fair to try an indigent and mentally ill person for a capital crime without giving the defendant the assistance of a mental health expert. They noted that David's trial attorney tried to obtain such assistance but saw his request denied because the law at the time did not require funding for a defense expert. David's clemency attorney also emphasized that when he was resentenced five years later, David's post-conviction attorney failed to obtain such assistance as well and later conceded that his representation of David had fallen short.[22] The juries heard very little about David's horrific childhood and never saw expert testimony that would come years later, testimony asserting that the fatal rage he directed at Lee Standifer was forged by a lifetime of abuse, mental illness, and substance misuse.

When I asked Helen Standifer about David's case for clemency, she referred to the two juries that heard his case—"24 people made a decision." She did not insist on his execution, only that he be prevented from harming anyone else.[23] Like Ed Zagorski, David was convicted in the early 1980s, before states gave juries the option of sentencing a person to life without the possibility of parole.

"All along my only reason for anything is that this could not happen to another family, OK?" she said. "That's the one thing that I'm very strong on is that he could never be out. At the time of the trial— and I have no idea, I have not been back there for many years, I don't know whether that's still the situation—but at the time of the trial, they basically said if they give you a life sentence it means about thirteen years in jail before you're out. That was not acceptable for me."

"As long as he wasn't out and nobody else had to go through this that's all that matters."

■ ■ ■

On the same day I spoke to Lee Standifer's mother, two days before the execution, I also spoke to David's daughter, Stephanie Thoman, who was living in Ohio. She was just two years old when he was sent to death row and didn't have a memory of meeting him until she was twelve.

"I remember meeting him," she said. "I was happy. I was glad to meet my father."[24]

They maintained a relationship over the years, with David "always trying to give me fatherly advice." On two occasions, she'd taken her three children to see their grandfather.

"I think that he's a kind person," she told me. "He's quiet. He kind of stays to himself. It's hard to imagine him getting mad."

Her most recent visit with him had been in August, prompted by the scheduling of his execution. It was the first time she'd gone to visit him alone and they bonded during the quiet time together.

"I'd never really just sat there and looked at him," she said. "And he did the same thing with me. He was like, 'Are your eyes hazel?' I'm like, 'Yeah.' And he's like, 'Mine are too!' I'm like, 'Yeah, I think I have your eyes.'"

They didn't talk about anything too emotional then, she said. Now, with his execution just days away, she found it hard to believe it was really happening. She said she had not gotten deep into the details of his case, but she felt bad for the Standifer family. She wasn't sure if she'd be able to talk to her father again.

"I talked to his lawyers today and told them to tell him that I love him," she said.

■ ■ ■

From the dark witness room, we heard the sound of a handle bouncing off a plastic bucket, a bucket for the saltwater solution and the sea sponges that would be strapped to David's head and ankles.

A voice came through the speaker: "Sound check."

In my notes from that night, an entire page is blank except for the time stamps I'd scribbled in pencil down the left side, the white space recording the silence we sat in, waiting.

7:00
7:01
7:02
7:03
7:04
7:05
7:06
7:07
7:08
7:09
7:10
7:11

The curtains opened at 7:12 p.m. David was strapped in the electric chair, wearing his beige Tennessee Department of Correction uniform. His head was shaved, and his eyes were cast down at the tile floor. It occurs to me now that he might've been able to see his reflection.

He'd dreamed of this night. It was a recurring nightmare he'd described to Lisak during one of their interviews.

"I'm at my execution, strapped to the gurney so I can't move at all, and my stepfather is present," Miller told him. "I see him sitting in the viewing gallery. I don't see any expression on his face, but I hear him say this to me: 'I hope you have nightmares about this, you sorry bastard!'"[25]

He was awake now, with the gurney replaced by the chair. I don't know if his stepfather's curses were echoing in his mind.

The warden asked him for his last words, and he mumbled something we could not understand. The warden asked him again, and David said: "Beats being on death row."

With that two guards moved toward the chair, placing a wet sea sponge onto his head, fastening a leather helmet on top. Saline solution from the sponge poured down David's forehead, and one of the men wiped him with a towel before they attached a thick dark-gray veil to the helmet, covering David's face. Then another man picked up a large cable and plugged it into the chair.

Less than a minute later, an exhaust fan kicked on, followed quickly by the first cycle of electricity. It was quieter than I expected, a humming, like a guitar amp turned up to full volume.

David's body jolted up out of the chair, pushing against the thick leather restraints as 1,750 volts raced through his body. He stayed that way, stiffened above the chair, for around 20 seconds before he fell back into the chair. A brief pause, then another cycle. His body shot from the chair again. It looked like some invisible force was trying to extract the last of his soul. Another 20 seconds. And then he fell back into the chair again, still. We stared ahead in the silence. The exhaust fan continued running and the veil across his face gently rippled.

We looked at his apparently dead body for a little more than five minutes before the curtain was closed. We heard voices in the execution chamber. Then the warden's voice came through the microphone: "That concludes the execution of inmate David Miller. Time of death 7:25. Please exit at this time."

Back outside, we stood in the cold under the white tent in front of a cluster of television cameras and reporters who were waiting to hear about what we'd seen. The Tennessee Department of Correction's spokesperson, Neysa Taylor, read her statement announcing David's execution and time of death and then read another, from a woman who only wanted to be identified as "a victim from Ohio."

"After a long line of victims he has left, it is time to be done. It was time for him to pay for what he has done to Lee."

We each took our turn describing the electrocution. Then David's longtime attorney Stephen Kissinger, an assistant federal public defender from Knoxville, stepped up to the podium.

"I think we've probably all heard the minute-by-minute accounts of what happened, so I just want to say a few words about what we did here tonight," he said. "David Miller was a friend, a father, and a grandfather. During our last conversations, one of the things he talked about was the opportunity he had to make just a handful of close friends. He mentioned Nick and Gary and Leonard, and if those guys get a chance to hear this, I want them to know that they were with him until the end. He talked about his daughter, Stephanie, and his grandchildren."

Until his execution, David had been the longest-serving prisoner on death row. In those thirty-seven years, people had come to see him on occasion, although he didn't have any regular visitors in his final years. He did indeed have friends among the men in Unit 2. The visitors who'd gone to the prison earlier in the week, on Monday night as David was preparing to be taken to death watch, heard about a line that had formed outside his cell earlier that evening. He gave postage stamps and a paint-by-numbers kit to friends before he left.

His attorney continued: "And if any of you have been reading what we submitted to the governor, what we've been saying to the courts for the last twenty years, you'll know that he cared deeply for Lee Standifer, and she would be alive today if it weren't for a sadistic stepfather and a mother who violated every trust that a son should have. I know I came up here promising to tell you what we did here today, but I think maybe what I should be doing is ask you all that question. What is it we did here today?"

Later that evening, after I got home from the prison, I got a text message from David Bass, who had been at the vigil outside the prison once again.

"No TV cameras at all with us," he wrote. "No yelling from the protester. Seems like it is getting routine. Scary."

10

David Bass sat in my living room looking over the list of the soon-to-be-dead. It was two days after David Miller's execution, and now David was looking down at his phone where he kept the grim roster of men who would be put to death over the coming months. The scheduled executions now stretched into the spring of 2020.

Next on the list, set to be executed in a little more than five months, was Don Johnson, a "very religious man" known to David and others on and around death row as Donnie. David didn't know him well, but he knew of him, as did many of the other regular visitors. After that came a man named Stephen West and then after him, Charles Wright, whose visitor, Demetria, had led me into the death row community months earlier.

David had come to care deeply for Charles, and this is why he hoped he would die soon. Charles' cancer had worsened to the point where he'd been moved out of Unit 2 and to the infirmary, away from the men who'd been caring for him on death row. Weeks earlier, Demetria had told me she thought she'd gone to visit him for the last time. But Charles had lived on long enough to see the state schedule him for an October 10, 2019, execution. When I wondered aloud whether I hoped he would die before that date, David cut me off.

"I do. I do."[1]

Next on the executioner's calendar was Lee Hall, one of Terry's closest friends whom David had met once. A little more than two months after that, Nicholas Sutton would be due in the chamber. Nick had been in the visitation gallery on the night of my first visit, and David saw him there often. Two months after Nick, Abu-Ali Abdur'Rahman, the man known as Abu whom David had met on his first trip to death row, was scheduled to be executed. He'd come close to the execution chamber before, only to see his death called off, but the state seemed especially determined now. David assumed that Abu's date would attract more attention than usual. He was well known and beloved among the death row visitors, but also more familiar to the general public—his case and its many flaws had received quite a bit of media coverage already.

For David, a troubling dichotomy was taking shape. With each execution that was carried out, and each additional one that was scheduled, he sensed that the broader public was becoming inured to the killings and the few headlines they produced. At the same time, though, they were growing only more traumatic for him.

He'd spent years imagining that his friend Terry might never be executed. But now he no longer could. Terry had been on death row longer than some of the men who'd already been brought to the death chamber or scheduled to go there. His own date wasn't coming imminently—he still had multiple legal challenges pending in the courts. But soon his appeals would run out. When David, Al, and I had visited him two months earlier, Terry had guessed he had about two years until that happened. But that could change.

"The thing I can't get out of my mind is this is real," David said to me, looking up from the list of names. "Somebody who's arguably my best friend now is gonna be put on the list one of these days. And I just really freak out."

■ ■ ■

In early January, three months after we met during my first visit to death row, I wrote Terry a letter and apologized for how long it had taken me to do so—the truth was I hadn't been sure how to begin. But I was quite sure that the few hours we'd spent huddled together, sharing popcorn in the visitation gallery, had changed my life and left me unable to see Terry or the other men on death row merely as a reporter's subjects. I had entered the prison that night as a writer and person opposed to the death penalty. But just that one evening, just that brief experience of proximity, had turned me from someone who believed The State should not execute The Condemned, to someone with a disquieting awareness that Tennessee meant to one day kill Terry, a man who had given me a hug, shared his snacks with me, and listened warmly as I talked about my newborn daughter. It would be my experience that there is no coming back from that.

"For now, how about this," I wrote. "If I am going to ask you all about your life, seems only fair that I tell you more about mine."

I told him how I'd grown up on the east coast of Florida, in a small beach town that everyone I knew, foolishly, wanted to leave; that I'd met my wife, Mallory, at Auburn before moving to Nashville, where we started our life together and had our two daughters. I asked him what he was reading and told him, somewhat awkwardly in hindsight, that I was eagerly devouring a book about the infamous Boston gangster Whitey Bulger's life and crimes and eventual arrest. I also thanked him for trusting me enough to let me into his life. By then I had told him and David that I hoped to write about the community they'd introduced me to, and Terry had agreed to keep in touch with me and tell me his story. Over time, letters, and phone calls, he did.

Terry Lynn King was born to Paul and Billie King on June 14, 1962, at Knoxville's Baptist Hospital, a nondescript collection of rectangular buildings that loomed over the Tennessee River looking not so different from a prison. I think of the other babies that must have been born in that hospital on that day and wonder where they ended up. On that day they were all guilty of nothing, and they would grow up to be capable of terrible and beautiful things.

To hear Terry tell it, his childhood was mostly free of the horrors that filled the files I'd read about many other men on death row. He did not share the history of horrible physical and sexual abuse that had plagued the youths of so many around him. But as we talked about his life, tragedies and traumas emerged.[2]

Once, long after we first met, he asked me if I told my two daughters often that I loved them. I told him I tried to tell them as often as they'd listen. He couldn't recall hearing those words from his parents as a boy.

"I don't have no memory of them telling me they loved me when I was young," he said. "I only remember it after I got older. Maybe I just don't remember. That's kind of crazy. So, it's great that you do that."[3]

The Kings lived in Corryton, a small unincorporated town about fifteen miles outside of Knoxville. They were a family of five that should've been a family of six. Terry had a brother, Gary, who was two years older and a sister, Donna, who was two years younger. Another child, a girl born about a year before Terry, died as an infant. Terry's maternal grandmother also lived with the family, and Terry recalled how she used to set aside five dollars every week from the meager wages she received from her job at Knoxville's Standard Knitting Mill, saving it up so she could afford Christmas gifts for her eleven grandchildren at the end of the year. Terry's father, Paul, was a roofer and a heavy drinker who liked to share with his son. On rainy days, when he and his crew could not work on a roof, they would gather at the King house, killing the day with cold beer. Sometimes Terry would be there, six or seven years old, huddling between his father's legs among the group of men. Often, his dad would lean over and say, "Get a sip of this, boy," laughing as he poured beer into Terry's mouth.

It wasn't the only one of the father's sins that would be visited upon the son.

According to family members, Paul King had previously been involved with the Ku Klux Klan in East Tennessee. By the time Terry was around six years old, his father had fallen out with the organization and had started serving as an informant for the FBI, traveling to Nashville to report about the group's activities. Their violence, though, would follow him home. Late one night, in 1968, something woke Terry from his sleep and led him to look out the front window of his home. Outside, he saw his father's white Ford Fairlane haphazardly pulled up into the yard with a line of four or five other cars lined up on the road in front of their home opening fire. Someone inside yelled at Terry, yanking him back from the window. The shooting stopped, but not before Paul King, who'd been pinned down inside his car, was shot in the head and shoulder. He survived, and Terry spent days sitting on the side of his bed, looking up with confusion and concern at his gauze-wrapped head. With a boy's naive curiosity, he would later stick his fingers in the bullet holes that pocked the inside of his father's car. Years later, he would wonder why his father, with the Klan chasing him, had driven home to his wife and children.

There were good times, though. Many decades later, Terry would still remember the silver artificial tree the family would put up at Christmastime and the way it included a color-changing light that made the tree appear to change colors too. His mother and her sister had married brothers, and his aunt, uncle, and cousins lived in the house next door to the Kings. They would get together often and stay together late into the evening, before the adults would carry sleeping children back to the proper house. From a young age he was very close with his cousins, and they loved to play cowboys and Indians in the wooded area behind the families' homes. Once, Terry's father brought home ponies and built a fence so the family could keep them. Another time, when Terry was around eight years old, his father brought home several beagle puppies. All of them died except for one, which Terry kept and named Jim. It was the last gift he ever received from his father, a man who'd brought both danger and joy into his life.

In March of 1971, Paul King died at the age of thirty-five from a massive heart attack brought on, at least in part, by his alcoholism. Terry, who had already failed the first grade at Clear Springs Elementary School and was struggling with a then undiagnosed learning disability, walked home from school one day to find his mother and grandmother crying in the front yard.

"When I learned what it was about I remember going out in the backyard standing there crying and telling God that I hated him for allowing my daddy to die," he wrote in a letter to me. "I can remember being so angry and sad. I was so mixed up and lost."

■ ■ ■

For Terry, the death of his father was a bomb that went off in the middle of his still-new life, and its fallout would linger like a cloud over the rest of his youth, darkening normal childhood activities.

His now-single mother worked to provide for Terry and his siblings. His father's brother, Terry's Uncle Bud who lived next door, tried to step in as a father figure to his distraught nephew and even coached Terry's baseball teams. Terry was a lefty with a natural curve—a fact he noted to me with some pride—and for a time the sport provided him with some distraction from grief.

But as a young hurting boy, he resented attempts to fill the void left by his father's death, and a deep sadness always lurked just below his sensitive surface. Terry's uncle frequently invited him to tag along with him and his own son on trips into the woods to hunt squirrels and rabbits. On one such trip, which would stick like a thorn in Terry's memory, they were standing in a field when Terry started to weep uncontrollably. He stood there crying until his uncle came over and picked him up.

Despite his difficulties in school, Terry was mechanically inclined from an early age, curious enough to take things apart to see how they worked and always confident he could put them back together again. When he was eleven, his mother and grandmother bought him a go-kart for his birthday. One Saturday when his family went out on a shopping trip, he decided to stay home with the new vehicle. But instead of racing around the neighborhood streets, he set about taking the whole thing apart, inspecting its Briggs & Stratton engine and spreading its dozens of pieces all around the driveway. When his family came home, they came apart. But he assured them he'd put it back together and it would start right up without a problem. It did, and from then on when a family vehicle needed a tune-up, an oil change, or new brakes, they called on Terry to do it.

Not long after his father's death, though, Terry started pursuing another interest to which he seemed almost naturally inclined—drugs and alcohol. He started drinking beer and hard liquor with older boys in the neighborhood, which soon led to experimentation with other substances. He'd sworn off smoking, having been repulsed by the overwhelming odor that filled the King family car on road trips as his parents smoked cigarettes in the front seats. But he was more drawn to substances that could obliterate his reality anyway. He would remove the gas cap from his go-kart and inhale the fumes straight from the tank, fading away into the mental haze they induced. What he found there wasn't always pleasant.

"As the fumes overpowered him, he would lie down on the ground, writhe, and cry out 'the snakes are crawling all over me!'" according to one court filing. "On other occasions he would place a photograph depicting his deceased father lying in his coffin on the bed in his room. After inhaling large amounts of gasoline fumes, he would kneel before his father's photograph and sob uncontrollably."[4]

By his early teens, Terry was huffing the fumes from gasoline, paint, glue, and Pam cooking spray, and he'd started adding LSD, Quaaludes, and Valium to the mix. A neurologist would later explain to one of his attorneys the effect that all these substances had on Terry's young brain, likening it to a brand-new paper clip that had been straightened out and could never really be bent back into place.

Trouble found him, and when it didn't, he went looking.

When he was thirteen, he was skipping school and hanging out at a friend's house when they found the .25 automatic pistol that belonged to his friend's dad. They played with the gun, drawn to the danger of the thing and oblivious to its lethal power at the same time. Terry looked down its short, stout barrel, assuming it wasn't loaded. Moments later, pointing the gun at the wall, he pulled the trigger and it fired, missing him and his friend but putting a hole in the wall. They shoved some cotton in the hole and painted over it. Around a year later, while his mother was at a neighbor's house getting her hair done, Terry was with another friend. This time they were messing around with a .12-gauge shotgun, waving it around and pointing it at one another. At one point, acting as if a bird was flying overhead, his friend whipped the gun upward and pulled the trigger. It blew a hole in the ceiling.

It was around the same time that he first got in trouble with the law, arrested for drinking on school property when he was fourteen.[5] After his freshman year of high school, he dropped out and started working various jobs around town. He blurred his days with booze, pills, and noxious fumes. For his sixteenth birthday his grandmother had bought him a Chevy van, and to a teenager in the 1970s, it was a dream vehicle. It had a custom bed in the back, a sunroof, a shag carpet, a cooler, and a booming stereo system. Terry was always on the move and his van was often full of people going with him. On the spur of the moment, he would drive down to Daytona Beach, Florida, where he rode a whirlwind of drink and drugs before spinning back up to Tennessee.

He careened through his teenage years, under the influence of substances and the older men with whom he used them. When he was seventeen, two adult men stood watch while he robbed two convenience stores with a sawed-off shotgun. He was arrested again and did a short stint at a juvenile detention center.[6] But the law wouldn't see him as a juvenile much longer. He was like a car speeding recklessly down a highway, passing exit ramps that might lead to a better life. Sometimes he took them, only to get back on the lonely highway he'd been headed down all along.

For a couple of years starting when he was nineteen, he found a job he might've been happy doing for a long time. He worked for a man who salvaged airplanes, buying wrecked airplanes for parts or to rebuild. Terry's job was to go to wherever the grounded plane was being stored, take it apart, and haul it back to Knoxville. He was that kid in the garage with his go-kart again, only now he got to drive all around the country, towing a thirty-three-foot goose-neck trailer with an entire airplane on it. Despite his previous forays into criminality, he was a trustworthy employee, handling tens of thousands of dollars of cash or airplane parts on his own. The job kept his hands busy and kept him on the move. He loved it.[7]

Still, he never fully freed himself from harmful entanglements, the booze, the pills, and unhealthy relationships. Around the same period when he was traveling and working on airplanes, Terry started seeing a woman named Lori, a single mother whose own struggles mingled dangerously with his own. He had a taste for toxic things and their relationship fit the pattern. In his recollection, they were suited for sex and fighting and not much else. They lived together for stretches and even after breakups, for each other they were yet another bad habit that couldn't be kicked. One night after making a visit to Lori's house while she had another boyfriend, Terry recalled, he came outside to find two of his car tires slashed. Still, he kept coming around and she kept having him.

In 1982, when Terry was around twenty years old, he moved to Daytona, and Lori came with him. It was, he hoped, an escape from the damaging cycle of his life in Tennessee and a new start for him and Lori. But by going south together, they all but ensured many of their problems would make the trip too. Soon after they arrived in Florida, their relationship deteriorated further, and they broke up. Years later, Terry's attorneys would note that it was during this time that he came to believe Lori was mistreating her daughter and that, after she left him for another man, he cooperated with the authorities in having the child relocated to live with Lori's sister.[8] Once again, there appeared to be a possible exit from the road Terry was speeding down. He was offered a job at an airport in Daytona, which might've provided stability and kept him in Florida. But around the same time, only a few months after he'd left Tennessee, a cousin of his drowned in a lake near Knoxville. Terry returned for the funeral and ended up staying to work with his uncle, a roofer who needed the help after losing his son. It was a decision Terry would come to see as a tragic turning point in his life. He returned to town and to old patterns which he'd hoped to leave behind.

It wasn't long after he resettled in Knoxville that he started hearing from Lori again. Terry did what he'd done so many nights before. He went to the Foxy Lady, a popular bar where he'd been a Friday night regular and met Lori for a few drinks before they left to drive up to an overlook above the city. But while they were there, Terry would recall, Lori started acting strangely. Her behavior made him wonder if she'd taken drugs and concerned him so much that he contacted his cousin and they both took her to a nearby hospital. He was there, waiting for an update on her condition, when the police showed up. They said Lori had accused him of assaulting her. Terry denied it. Hearing his side of the story and noting Lori's apparent toxication, the police let Terry go. It wasn't long after that, though, that he learned there was a warrant for his arrest. He turned himself in and was released on bond.

The case seemed to recede, but he found trouble elsewhere. One night that same year, he and a cousin were headed to the house of a man who owed Terry some money. It was late, as they'd arranged to meet the man before he left his house for a job where he worked the overnight shift. Terry drove a Buick Skylark, in which he'd just put a brand-new engine. The car could fly, and its driver liked to find its limits. That night, driving fast down a dark county road, they passed a police cruiser. The officer sped out onto the road after them and Terry hit the gas, fleeing for no particular reason. He sped on, veering off onto an old country road until he saw what he thought was a motorcycle up ahead but turned out to be an oncoming car. Swerving to avoid a head-on collision, he pulled the car off the road and into a ditch, still hurtling forward at more than 100 miles per hour. No sooner had he raced off the road and into the ditch than a concrete culvert appeared in his headlights. He wrestled the car up out of the ditch and slammed on the brakes, but at those speeds there was no way to avoid the collision. The car skidded straight into a large tree.

Terry woke up in the hospital, relieved to find he and his cousin were still alive. He hadn't been wearing a seat belt and when the car hit the tree, and he'd been thrown into the steering wheel, crushing his chest and slamming his head against the windshield. His heart was bruised, and a serious concussion left him seeing double out of one eye, requiring him to wear an eyepatch for more than a month. His cousin had broken an arm and a leg. They had no idea how they'd gotten out of the car, which caught fire soon after the crash.

Terry was charged with reckless driving. He told me, with some apparent pride, that he'd represented himself and convinced the judge to dismiss the charge. But he was running out of road. Somewhere in his mind, though he'd dismissed them at the time, were the words of his grandmother who'd warned him that he would one day reap a bitter harvest.

"Boy, the good Lord is going to allow you to end up in a place where you are going to have to cry out for him, for he is the only one who can help you!" she'd told him. "You are out of control and can't be told anything, but you will have to fall down on your knees someday and cry out to him."

11

Demetria Kalodimos' introduction to the death penalty came in 1984.[1] She was twenty-four years old, a promising-but-green reporter who'd just moved from Champaign, Illinois, to take a job as a weekend co-anchor for WSMV in Nashville. It was a major career move, bringing her to the city where she would become a household name. It also gave her the chance to reclaim that name. The news director at her previous station in Champaign had made her use the name Demetria Kaye on air, fearing that her Greek surname sounded "too ethnic."[2]

But although the grim drama of state executions was foreign to her, she was already familiar with some of the harsh realities of crime and punishment. When she was eleven, a cousin of hers was shot and killed by the police during an armed robbery. His brother, another cousin with whom Demetria had played childhood games, was sent to prison for his role in the crime. She learned then how it felt to mourn a loved one's violent death and to have another loved one, someone who shared her name and some of her memories, on the other side of a prison's walls. She saw how people looked at her family when they learned these facts, how they subtly recoiled at them. But she'd never fully considered the business of killing the condemned until she started preparing to cover an execution about six months after she moved to Nashville.

In the summer of 1984, Tennessee was gearing up to use its electric chair for the first time since 1960. A thirty-three-year-old white man named Ronald Harries was set to be executed for the 1981 murder of a convenience store clerk named Rhonda Greene. Harries had shot the eighteen-year-old girl, and fired at another employee, during a robbery in Kingsport.[3]

While many modern-era capital cases drag on for decades before an execution, Harries had made the unusual choice of ordering his attorneys to stop fighting the case in court. Instead, he skipped right to asking then Governor Lamar Alexander to spare him and commute his sentence to life in prison. The governor said no.[4]

In the run-up to the planned execution, prison officials offered reporters a tour of the Walls, showing off the electric chair whose return to duty seemed imminent. It was Demetria's first time inside the wretched facility. At one point during the tour, she spotted the prison's most infamous resident, Martin Luther King Jr.'s assassin, James Earl Ray, doing curls alone in the rec area. As soon as she left the prison, Demetria rushed to call her parents and tell them about the sighting.

Harries was due in the electric chair on June 13, having failed to persuade the governor to intervene on his behalf. Demetria was sent to interview the Greene family about the impending execution of their daughter's murderer. She flew to Kingsport—a small town in the northeast corner of the state—on the station's small plane, and the ride made her almost as anxious as the assignment itself. Later, she was sitting in the Greene's living room when they got the call that a federal judge had stayed the execution and ordered a hearing to assess Harries' competency. The judge wanted to know if the stresses of prison life, and the heavy doses of anti-anxiety medication Harries had been taking, had significantly affected his ability to make decisions for himself.[5] After a federal appeals court upheld that stay and ordered that Harries be resentenced, he agreed to a deal with prosecutors that got him off of death row. He died in prison in 2012.[6]

But on that summer day in Kingsport, with Demetria and a camera crew in their living room, the Greene family was appalled to learn that Harries would not be executed. The experience of sitting on their couch when they got the news stuck with Demetria. Mostly, she would recall it as the first time she felt a deep internal uneasiness about this thing called capital punishment and the way some people who weren't even victims seemed to yearn for it. On the flight back to Nashville, even some of her colleagues seemed let down by the news that there wouldn't be an execution.

■ ■ ■

Some thirty years later, unbeknownst to most of the Nashvillians who'd spent those decades watching her on the nightly news, Demetria spent around nine months conducting her interviews with men on death row and planning to speak to them further on camera for her planned documentary. One of those men was Charles Wright, a stout Black man who stood around five foot ten and had a lazy left eye.

After a few brief interviews, Demetria had started writing letters to Charles, looking to fill in some gaps in her notes. But their correspondence soon led to something more, an unexpected friendship that went beyond the reporter-subject relationship. Charles urged her to fill out an application to be one of his approved regular visitors. She did, although she was skeptical about her chances of being approved. Prison officials had carefully restricted her access to the men on the row, and she was as well known as anyone in the local press. She assumed that her name on an application would not go unrecognized. But, although it took a while, her application was eventually approved, and she was cleared to sit with Charles in the visitation gallery and talk to him away from the glare of the department's press handlers.

That didn't mean she was free from the various slights and indignities of passing through the prison's security checkpoint.

"I have had many, many, many encounters with 'your skirt is too short, you have tights, your shirt is see-through,'" she told me after years of visiting. "I mean, I've gone out to my car in the summer and put on my dirty laundry that I happened to have in my trunk just so I could go in that day."

But that didn't surprise her as much as Charles did, the way his humanity shone through such dehumanizing surroundings. Preparing for her first visit, she steeled herself for what she expected might be a serious and even bleak couple of hours. But sitting in the visitation gallery, amidst the echoes of other conversations, she quickly found herself laughing. She was surprised to find that the appearance of execution dates on the calendar, while unwelcome, had not seemed to disturb Charles as much as it did her. "I've had a date since the day I came here," he often told her. Charles was funny and eager to talk about chopper motorcycles, the blues, and the seventies funk and soul music he used to dance to in Nashville clubs. She noticed his appearance too. Even after decades on death row, she could tell how important it was to him. He insisted on keeping himself groomed, and his cell, she would learn, was always neat and tidy. Once she found out about where he'd come from, she understood why.

Charles had been born into squalor in 1955's segregated Nashville. He was the second of what would eventually be ten children who were not raised so much as tolerated at best and neglected or abused at worst. Their mother was named Johnnie Mae, and she was fifteen when she had the first of them. Their fathers were men who either left them or made their life hell. Charles' father left the family when he was three, having given him his lazy eye and little else.

Charles' siblings described their childhood to his defense team in 2018, sharing details and stories of his formative years that his jury never heard. While Charles was young, they lived like squatters and strays, bouncing between more than a dozen dilapidated rental homes that protected them from neither weather nor vermin. In one of their homes, Charles' older sister R. remembered, some rats which had infested the place got into bed with their younger sister and attacked her, biting her so badly that she had to be hospitalized.[7]

They were the descendants of enslaved people, living in immense poverty in a city still organized by the logic of Jim Crow. Charles' grandmother, who the children called Mama, told the children stories about how her mother had been forced to pick cotton on a plantation.[8]

The children's mother, whom they called Johnnie, mothered them sporadically.

"I would not say Johnnie had a drinking problem," R. said in a signed declaration. "I would say she had a problem being home with her kids."

When she was at home, some of her children later recalled, she did the best she could. Trouble was she often wasn't at home. When Charles was young, Johnnie would stay out running the streets and hitting the city bars for days at a time. She had a habit of using whatever money she had on a given day to buy food for that day only. She never kept groceries in the house. During her long absences, her children were left hungry at home. R., who was often left to care for her siblings—which then included Charles and two other younger children—remembered nights when she and Charles would go out looking for their mother.

"If we found her in a club, we cried for her to come home; told her we was hungry," R. said. "Sometimes she would come; sometimes she would not."

They were children on their own in the dark bad world. On one such night, R. went out looking for Johnnie by herself and was gang-raped by a group of boys.

Charles' introduction to crime came in this context of survival. Sometimes their mother would send them out to steal welfare checks out of mailboxes, planning to cash the checks and buy food. (A similar scheme later got her arrested when she was caught with a stolen government disability check.) Other times, the kids would dig food out of dumpsters or steal from stores themselves. Even at a young age, R. remembered, Charles sought to protect his siblings. When they got to a store knowing what they planned to do, he would make her stay outside while he went in to steal some food.

"He never wanted me to have to do anything wrong," R. said.

They all seemed to agree that the worst of their youth came when Johnnie started messing around with a man named Jesse Maples in the early 1960s. He was, in their unanimous estimation, "lowdown and mean." Johnnie by then had five children already who were nearly taken from her on more than one occasion. Soon she had two more with Jesse, an angry and lascivious drunk with a wandering, predatory eye. After having two children with Johnnie, he raped and impregnated a young girl. He went to prison, but when he got out after only a few years, Johnnie reunited with him and was soon pregnant again.[9] They got married, and that's when, as Charles' younger brother D. remembered it, "life went to shit."[10] Charles was around thirteen.

Jesse's violence took many forms. He and Johnnie's fights blew through like daily storms and he beat her often. Once, one of their daughters remembered, he grabbed her by the hair and held her face down over the flame on the gas stove. She grabbed a knife and stabbed him. They both ended up in the hospital.[11] Charles would often intervene, stepping in to protect his mother and shouting threats at Jesse. But Johnnie would always call off her son.[12]

Jesse also directed his petty dictatorial impulses toward the children. He insisted that no one ate dinner before him. But sometimes, they remembered, he would come home in a drunken rage and throw the food out into the yard as the hungry children went chasing after it.[13]

One source of tension between him and Johnnie was his irritation about paying for the care of his children as well as those she'd had with other men. But he drew no such distinction when it came to his perverted sexual proclivities. He harassed and molested the girls in the house, whether they were stepdaughters or his own biological children. One of his daughters said she spent her childhood "trying to get away from Jesse," and started sleeping with "six, seven layers of clothes, everything I could put on to protect me from him touching me."[14] But his abuse continued. One of Johnnie's daughters received his sick attention too, and she also tried to protect herself. She would push her dresser in front of her bedroom door to try to keep Jesse out; once she even tried to kill him by mixing cleaning solution in his gin. He only got sick, though, and her other defenses were in vain. When she was thirteen, she said, he raped her, and she got pregnant. She had the baby and never found out whether the child's father was her father or a boy she'd been seeing at the same time.[15]

When he didn't have his eyes on the girls in his own home, Jesse was prone to running around with other women as well. Later, in 1976, Johnnie shot and killed a woman during a fight over him. She got five years' probation.[16]

At home, Jesse was a brute to the boys too. His son was gay and knew it from an early age. But Jesse would beat him and threatened to kill him if he was ever caught with a boy. The abuse was so bad, the son recalled, that he contemplated killing his father or killing himself.[17]

Charles could not hide his antipathy for the man who beat on his mother, preyed on his sisters, and generally menaced his family. But he was not the man of the house. When he was around sixteen, Jesse threw him out and he went to live with R.[18]

It was then that Charles started running with an older crowd. He was often sent to do the crew's dirty work, breaking into homes or warehouses. And it was R.'s boyfriend, Vernon, the dope man in the housing project where they lived, who first gave Charles a needle. Vernon, who also spoke to Charles' defense team in 2018, said he used Charles as a tester. He would cut heroin with sugar and then have a tester use some to tell him whether it was strong enough.[19] Charles quickly became an addict, but at the time he was just a user, not a dealer.

"Whatever he got," one of his sisters remembered, "it went right into his arm."[20]

■ ■ ■

By the summer of 1984, not long after Demetria arrived in Nashville, Charles was, perhaps improbably, alive and staying in Murfreesboro, around thirty-five miles southeast of the city. He was approaching thirty and making a living by fixing cars and selling marijuana. His criminal record by then included numerous arrests and convictions for burglary and grand larceny.

In the late afternoon of July 18, he rode into Nashville with Gerald Mitchell and Douglas Alexander, two men he knew through the local drug trade. Of the three men who could say what happened next, two didn't live to see the next day. Prosecutors argued that Charles suspected Gerald Mitchell of stealing his marijuana supply and lured the two men to Nashville with a plan to kill them. Charles initially denied any involvement in the killings and later gave conflicting accounts of the events, according to court records, but eventually he testified that he had gone to Nashville with the men to buy drugs which they planned to sell. In Charles' version of the events, an argument between the men in a north Nashville park led to Gerald Mitchell shooting Douglas Alexander; Charles admitted shooting

Gerald, but said he'd done so in self-defense. Prosecutors, however, made the case that Charles first shot Gerald then killed Douglas to eliminate the only witness, the latter being a key part of their argument for the death penalty.[21]

On April 4, 1985, after a little more than three hours of deliberations, a jury found Charles guilty of two counts of first-degree murder. *The Tennessean* reported that the then thirty-year-old "showed no emotion" as the verdict was read. The following day, on Good Friday, Charles' attorneys and even his mother pleaded with the jury to spare his life.

"Please spare his life," Johnnie said to the jury through tears. "Please don't take his life."[22]

Charles' public defender, Jim Weatherly, appealed to the day's spiritual meaning.

"Nobody planned that this hearing would be today, the day that Jesus died, but it is today," he said, his eyes welling with tears according to *The Tennessean*.

"I'm not going to equate Charles with Jesus—that would be ridiculous—but Christ was a human being and Charles is a human being."

Later, he told the jury, "I know you're going to do the right thing, and I just beg you to let Charles live."[23]

But a few hours later, the jury handed down a death sentence.

Years later, Charles' attorneys would argue, as they did in Ed Zagorski's case, that his sentence was plainly arbitrary. While he would go to death row for committing two murders arising out of a dispute over small-time drug sales, other men had received life sentences after being convicted of five or even six murders.

They also argued that "something was rotten" in the Davidson County District Attorney's office during the period when Charles was convicted and sentenced. Between 1977, just after the death penalty was reinstated, and 1989, 70 percent of the cases in which Nashville prosecutors obtained first-degree murder convictions involved Black men. In that same period, prosecutors sought the death penalty for seven men—all of them Black.[24]

■ ■ ■

By the time Demetria met Charles, he'd been living on death row for nearly thirty years, starting at the Walls before moving to Riverbend. He'd replaced working on cars with working in the kitchen. He worked as a cook at Riverbend for more than twenty years and was known to whip up creative concoctions on death row using whatever ingredients happened to be around. On occasion, a guard might even bring in a homegrown tomato to share.

Although he'd had many run-ins with the law on the outside, his behavioral record on the inside was nearly spotless. He had two write-ups over the years—one for having an extra watch and another for having an extra washcloth.[25]

His family kept in close touch with him over the years and many of his siblings became regulars at the prison, loyally visiting him as often as they could. His conviction and sentence had dealt a blow to the family and especially to his mother. In the end, his siblings believed it was the abuse from her husband and her son's death sentence that finally killed her.

Charles' compulsion to protect those he cared for did not fade over the years. He was often concerned for his family's safety. When he spoke to his sister R. on the phone, he ended their conversations by urging her to lock her front door. He stressed over Demetria's safety too and always wanted to be sure that she didn't drive with her convertible's top down through bad parts of town.

The town she was driving through, of course, was much different from the one he'd grown up in. During their conversations, he would often ask Demetria what had become of old spots he remembered. Sometimes he got to leave the prison for a hospital visit and, if the driver was feeling generous, they'd take the long way home so he could see his old neighborhood, winding through the Nashville streets he used to walk when he was young and hungry.

As she got to know Charles, Demetria also got to know death row and its particular culture. She learned about how for a Super Bowl, say, or another big sporting event, some of the guys would all sit in their cells with their TVs turned up and watch together, yelling back and forth to each other. And she began to realize how much the hope of even a seemingly small kindness—like Popeyes chicken being brought in for Christmas dinner—could buoy a person in such dire circumstances. On some Monday nights, she would leave the prison and sit in her car in the parking lot feeling exceptionally free. The cold drink in her cup holder took on a new meaning, as did the fact that she could leave there and drive anywhere she wanted.

Demetria met Charles' family and he met hers. It wasn't too long after she started visiting him that he made room on his approved visitation list for her husband, Verlon, a songwriter who bonded quickly with Charles.

But as the state was working to resume executions, cancer came for Charles. It started in his prostate and spread like a brush fire to his bones. It was burning through his body so fast that in the summer of 2018 doctors predicted that he might only have weeks to live. He survived though, primarily under the care of men like David Duncan and Don Johnson who worked to keep him well enough to stay in the unit with them. It's both moving and unsettling to imagine him, ill enough to be hospitalized but cared for by friends in a prison cell. He couldn't last long like that, though, and by winter he was moved to the prison's infirmary.

Demetria visited him there and was reasonably happy with the care he seemed to be receiving. The prison medical team's evident personal connection with him moved her. Still, he was gaunt and bedridden. The staff had lost his dentures, leaving him without his top teeth, and his lips had become horribly chapped. After years of keeping himself well groomed, his hair had begun to grow unkempt, and he was despondent about it.

But when I spoke to Demetria in January of 2019, she had recently noticed some improvements in Charles' living conditions. He had new pillows and sheets and the lighting in the room was better. Now Charles even had lip balm on his lips. The doctors and nurses caring for Charles had been compassionate, but what she'd begun to see was a care that came from a closeness and a knowledge that only another man from the row could possess. She knew who to thank. It was Charles' old friend David Duncan.

■ ■ ■

The crimes that sent David Duncan to prison were horrific. Fifty-four-year-old Evelyn Ruby Burgess was found naked from the waist down with her throat slashed, lying in the aisle of the Short Stop Market where she worked as a cashier. Police said she appeared to have crawled out of the walk-in refrigerator where she'd been raped. Eighteen months later, sixty-six-year-old Annie Malone died from a heart attack after she was raped by her assailant. After David became a suspect in the second attack, police matched his fingerprints to a set found at the scene of the first.[26]

But these facts were not relevant to Barbara Sullivan when she went to Riverbend to visit David for the first time in December of 2014.[27] She was not indifferent to the pain of victims and their families. But the way she saw it, the man who'd committed those terrible crimes was not the man she was going to see.

Barbara hadn't been looking to befriend a man on death row. In fact, she had always been a supporter of the death penalty, seeing it as the other side of the Golden Rule. But she'd been sitting in a pew at St. Paul's Episcopal Church in Murfreesboro when she heard mention of a death row visitation ministry. Interested parishioners were invited to attend an orientation with Joe Ingle. And for reasons she never could locate, Barbara felt drawn to it. Her adult daughter did as well, and they were quickly paired with a man on the row, but he died of cancer before they could visit. So, they went to Joe Ingle to ask if they could be matched with someone else who wanted a visitor.

"You're in for a treat," he told them. It was David.

Barbara told me she never felt unsafe visiting the prison but admitted that David—who stands six feet, four inches tall—was intimidating at first. That feeling disappeared quickly, though, replaced by an admiration of his passion and his fiercely caring spirit. The man she came to know, she said, should be preaching somewhere.

"It's not pertinent to our relationship," Barbara told me when I asked about his past. "It's not who he is. That might have been who he was on one night or at one moment. It's certainly not who he is now, thirty-some-odd years later."

The men she'd met through David were no more murderers than they were painters and poets, Christians and Muslims.

David had suffered great loss during his years on death row. He kept living in the land of death while his loved ones in the land of the living were dying off. He was there when his stepdaughter died and Joe came to the prison, seeking to comfort him but unwittingly breaking the news.[28] He was there too when his wife died, as well as both of his parents.

But he lived on among the family he'd found on the row. In 2015, when David learned that his death sentence had been vacated, he and Barbara had only been visiting for a few months. Although he'd been optimistic about the outcome of his case, it was still a shock to his mind and body, which had spent every day for decades under the weight of wondering when his name would appear next to a date. His victims' families accepted his new sentence but were adamant that he should never leave prison.

"I want him to come to know Jesus Christ and . . . I want him to come to repentance, but that does not change the fact that he is a convicted first-degree murderer," Evelyn Ruby Burgess' son Charles Anderson told the *Gallatin News* in 2019. "He was a vicious criminal, and he really deserved that death penalty and should have gotten it years ago."[29]

When I spoke to David on the phone years later, he was indeed a man working out his salvation. He'd finally moved off death row into a new unit with the prison's general population. He'd left the only community he'd ever known in his adult life, including some men he'd known since their first days on death row at the Walls.

"I left a piece of me back there with them, but in the same sense I brought a piece of them with me when I left," he said.[30]

One of his several close friends on the row was Terry King. He and Terry had always looked out for each other and often spent time doing arts and crafts together. Once, Terry told me, when Terry hurt his shoulder and was unable to lift his arm, David had shaved his head for him.

Leaving death row also meant leaving Charles. But that was only temporary. Not long after he moved into the general population, David got a job as a caretaker in the prison's infirmary, allowing him to resume his passionate care for his old friend. He was once again fighting to preserve Charles' dignity.

When I asked David about the crimes of his youth, he spoke not dismissively but as if they'd been committed by a person he no longer knew. That young boy, he told me, was a "mouthy piece of shit."

"I hate what took place," he said. "I really do, I hate what took place. It's something that I can't change. But the only thing that I can ask is forgiveness from the family, from the community, forgiveness from everyone. It didn't have to happen, you know, but I'm not the same person that I was. I have grown."

■ ■ ■

By early 2019, Charles' lawyers and loved ones were all but certain that he would not die in the execution chamber. Their hope was that he might be able to die outside of prison, though. He was too ill to go home. But for months they'd been pleading with Governor Bill Haslam to grant him a compassionate release so he could at least die in a hospital surrounded by his remaining family.[31]

Among the people supporting the effort was former Nashville congressman Bob Clement, who'd gone to visit Charles at Demetria's urging. Bob was intimately familiar with the way a governor could handle such awesome power. His father was former Tennessee Governor Frank Clement, who visited death row himself, oversaw six executions, and later commuted the death sentences of five men. Bob had grown up at the governor's mansion and played basketball and football with the prisoners who were employed as workers there.

In the fall of 2018, Bob wrote a letter to the governor asking him to release Charles.

"Charles is not a threat to society. He has been a model prisoner during his 36 years on Death Row," he wrote. "I believe the length of time [he] has served facing execution is cruel and inhumane punishment. When I visited him recently, I asked him what he would do if he was ever released. He has dreamed he would someday live with his family and work on old cars and bicycles. In reality he would be going home to spend his remaining days among loved ones."[32]

Haslam would leave office without taking any action on Charles' case, leaving the decision to his successor. For Demetria, every visit with Charles felt like it could be her last.

She knew that Charles' faith had become important to him, and because of her own Greek Orthodox tradition, it became very important to her to get a cross around his neck. So, on presumably her final visit, she wore a leather cross she'd gotten during a trip to Greece. She made it through security without an issue, and when she got to Charles lying in his infirmary bed, she placed it around his neck. They both wept. As it happened, she would go on to visit him many more times. He just kept living. And every time he would proudly pull the cross out from under his shirt to show her he was still wearing it.

12

David Bass, Al, and I walked out of a Nashville meat-and-three and across the street to Al's car, where he reached inside to retrieve a white cardboard box. A sticker on the top identified its contents: Billy Ray Irick. Inside were the ashes of the man I'd seen executed eight months earlier, the man who'd brought the three of us together. On this April day, Al was transferring custody of Billy's remains to David.

The path to this moment had been anything but straight and nothing like David and Al had expected it to be when they volunteered to claim Billy's body after his execution. Once they'd gotten the money together for Billy to be cremated, Al told David that he'd pick up the ashes when they were ready. But when the call came from Music City Crematory Service that the job was done, Al was on vacation in Florida. He called David from the beach.

"So, Al calls me and goes, 'Could you run by and pick up Billy?'" David recalled.[1]

On his lunch break, David drove to the crematory to claim Billy once again. He took the box holding Billy's ashes and put it in his trunk.

"Then it dawned on me that I didn't know exactly what I was going to do with these ashes," he told me. "I had failed to tell my wife, who's a wonderful person, that I was even involved in this. We live in a 540-square-foot apartment, and I just didn't know how it was going to work. So, we decided that Billy could stay in the trunk until such time we got this worked out."

That turned out to be a while. Billy stayed in the trunk for some time. He even rode down to Alabama and back for a wedding David and his wife were attending, sitting quietly beside their luggage. Eventually, David passed Billy back to Al. One night, Al drove by David's apartment and David came out with the box, passing it through Al's window before Al drove off again. Ever since then, Billy had been sitting on a shelf in Al's house.

Now, Al was passing the ashes back to David, who was going to bring them to Hank, the death row visitor who planned to spread them in South Dakota. David and I were going to visit Terry that night, and David would pass off the ashes then. He worried about bringing them to the prison. The guards there could search a person any time, and if an execution was approaching, they would sometimes even search cars. Soon, though, we were laughing at David's concern. What would an officer think upon discovering Billy's ashes in David's car in the prison parking lot—that he was trying to smuggle Billy back on to the row?

■ ■ ■

After Billy's cremation, the visitors had been faced with the question of what to do with his ashes. Where could a man who'd known so little peace in his life be truly laid to rest? He'd spent most of his life incarcerated, but the prison grounds were not a happy place for him. Nor was the Knoxville area where he'd grown up and lived before he went to death row; horrible things had been done to him there and he'd done horrible things to others. But after learning that Billy claimed Lakota heritage and had adopted Lakota spiritual beliefs, Hank had an idea. South Dakota, the home of the Lakota people, was also home to him and his wife, Janet. His mind went to the Black Hills and the massive mountain carving—the world's largest—of Crazy Horse underway there. Perhaps if Billy's ashes were spread there, then a place that brought him spiritual enlightenment in life could bring him peace in the afterlife.[2]

Hank had started visiting death row through his church, St. Paul's Episcopal in Murfreesboro, and he had developed a close relationship with a man on the row named Jessie Dotson. Hank saw similarities between death row visitation and the work he did as a Court Appointed Special Advocate for foster children in juvenile court. He had seen kids languishing in an overburdened system, bounced through six foster homes and six different schools. He saw their needs going unmet. On death row, he met men whose needs hadn't been met on the outside and who were now languishing in prison. He saw their isolation. In both cases, he told me, he tried his best to build relationships and fill some holes in people's lives; to be a constant for someone who'd rarely known stability.

"Doing what I can even though it's not solving the big problem," as he put it to me.

The Crazy Horse Memorial had been a work in progress since the late 1940s, when Polish American sculptor Korczak Ziolkowski started blasting in the Black Hills at the behest of Lakota Chief Henry Standing Bear.[3] Hank had followed the mountain sculpture's progress with awe his entire life, and he hoped to honor it and Billy by spreading Billy's ashes there.

He wrote a letter to Monique Ziolkowski, the sculptor's daughter and CEO of the Crazy Horse Memorial, to tell her Billy's story and seek approval for his plan. He told her about his tragic upbringing, his mental illness and his horrible crime. He also told her about Billy's claimed Lakota heritage, which Hank said he believed even as he could not confirm it.

"Now that it is done there remains one thing we can do for Billy," he wrote. "That is, we can bring Billy home, the home of his Lakota heritage, and scatter his ashes in the Black Hills, specifically, on Crazy Horse Mountain. Right now, I can think only of the words of Crazy Horse, 'My lands are where my dead lie buried'. I believe this is where Billy should be."[4]

If the organization had hesitation, Hank wrote, he would find another place in the hills. But after several conversations over a period of months, they granted him permission to come to the mountain, hike to the memorial, and scatter Billy's ashes there.

Around a month after he got Billy's ashes from David in the Riverbend parking lot, Hank and Janet flew to South Dakota and drove to the Black Hills. Hank's telling of the story would be interrupted by tears. Months after the fact he would struggle to articulate what it was like to be there with Billy.

The staff at the memorial held back some other visitors so Hank and Janet could climb the mountain.

"We took him up there," he told me. "I walked out on the arm of Crazy Horse. This was the land of Paha Sapa, which was sacred to the Lakota. And even though it was stolen from them, it's still sacred. We took him there and said some words and then we spread him there down below the arm of Crazy Horse. So, he is on the mountain, and he is in the mountain."

He is not just in the mountain, either. As he worked to finally lay Billy to rest there, Hank had learned more about the goals of the Crazy Horse Memorial Foundation. He learned of a summer program through which thirty-two Native American teens who'd graduated from high school could work a job and take courses at the University of South Dakota, earning a full semester's worth of credits.

Hank and Janet would begin to feel a burden for the Native American youth they knew were facing long odds. For those Native American kids growing up on Pine Ridge, a Lakota reservation where the weight of unemployment and alcoholism is crushing, college was an opportunity that could also leave them saddled with debt.

Hank and Janet were not wealthy, but they decided to start a partial scholarship that would provide some tuition support for one Lakota student chosen by the foundation.

As he explained this plan to me, Hank spoke about Black Elk, a Lakota holy man who taught about the "sacred hoop," a visual representation of everything in life—heaven, earth, the Great Spirit, plants, animals. After the Wounded Knee Massacre in 1890, Black Elk said, "The nation's hoop is broken and scattered." But Black Elk also had hope. He was said to have had a vision as a child in which the seventh generation of Native Americans following their first contact with Europeans would rise to take a stand for their tribes and for the land to mend the hoop. It occurred to Hank that the seventh generation was growing up now and that maybe he and Janet, by helping them, could help mend the hoop.

They could not undo America's history of genocide any more than they'd been able to stop the state of Tennessee from executing men they'd come to know. But they could do this one small, good thing.

■   ■   ■

That night at the prison, after David and I had made our way through the checkpoints and barbed-wire fences and down the winding sidewalks to Unit 2, I was startled when Terry walked into the visitation gallery. He wore his normal white T-shirt and beige Tennessee Department of Correction–issued pants, but half of his face looked like a bruised fruit, yellow with black around his eye.

David had mentioned to me that Terry had been involved in an incident, but he looked worse than I was expecting. The week before, another man on the row had come up behind him without warning and attacked him, punching him in the face. As Terry told us the story, he clutched an incident report from the prison. He insisted he'd done nothing to provoke the one-sided fight and repeatedly invited us to read the report that said as much. We told him we didn't need to. We believed him.

Surprising as it may be, this sort of thing is rare on Tennessee's death row, which officials will tell you is the most peaceful unit in the prison system. (On future visits, I would look over to see the guard at the door of the visitation gallery asleep.) An attack like this was not only unusual but also a violation of a community that strived against all odds for togetherness and peaceful resolution of conflicts. Terry told us that several of his friends had approached him afterwards and offered to respond in a more forceful way, but he'd urged them not to do anything. The man who'd attacked him, he said, was severely mentally ill, and Terry wanted him to get help instead of just punishment. But that's not what they do here, he said. He told us the man would be medicated and put behind a door.

When I left the prison that night I thought of how bewildering and beautiful it was that I should meet such peaceful and gracious men on death row, and how distressing it was that they are condemned to live in a place built for the irredeemably violent. The very premise of death row is a lie and once you know the truth it is like a bruise whose soreness will not go away.

13

On the morning of May 9, 2019, a small group of death row visitors, a few lawyers, and a handful of reporters gathered at Riverside Chapel Seventh Day Adventist Church in Nashville. Among the attorneys were Kelley Henry and Reverend Charles Fels, who'd abandoned a lucrative career as a criminal defense lawyer to become an Episcopal priest but was now representing Don Johnson in his clemency effort. Those of us in the press sat in the front pews, beneath the altar, our notebooks and recorders ready to hear another pitch for mercy. A fifteen-minute drive away, at Riverbend, the executioners were preparing to do their job again in one week's time. Don was scheduled to be executed on May 16 for the 1984 murder of his wife, Connie. At the church, a group of people who had come to know and love him were making a final plea on his behalf.

The location was not random. Not long after he arrived on death row, Don had met a man from Riverside Chapel who was visiting Riverbend as part of the church's prison ministry. Don had been baptized and began leading Bible studies of his own on the row. In 2008, he was ordained as an elder at Riverside Chapel, and he'd been an active leader of the church's prison ministry, from the inside, ever since. He even preached the gospel on a radio broadcast from the prison on Sundays.

The men and women who'd come to the church to speak on Don's behalf hoped all this would make an impression on the state's new governor. Bill Lee, a businessman-turned-politician who made a fortune from his family's HVAC and plumbing business, had been in office for just four months after winning the race to succeed Bill Haslam. His campaign had emphasized his Christian faith and made frequent mention of his involvement with a Nashville prison ministry, so much so that some of the men on death row had been rooting for him to win. The three executions carried out in 2018 stood as testament to what could follow a governor's prayerful consideration. But everyone close to death row hoped that with this case and this governor, things might be different.

One at a time, the visitors stepped to the front to speak about their relationship with Don. Tommy Bugg had been visiting him for more than twenty years.

"When we visit on Saturday mornings, we hug and sit and then we have a conversation for about an hour or an hour and a half," he said. "And then we'll get his Bible, and we will read; if the day is the 23rd, Don will pick the 23rd of Proverbs and then I'll pick something in Psalms and read."

Thomas Lawrence was introduced to Don by a member of the church and used to visit him once a week. Their conversations, he said, were often about other men on the row and some help or encouragement they might need. He said Don offered hope to men who had none.

"It would be a shame to take that light out of a place that is so dark," he said.

Another visitor, John Dysinger, had made Don a member of his family. It'd been fifteen years since John, his wife, Pam, and their five children started visiting the man the kids came to know as Uncle

Don. It was an earlier execution date that had brought them all to-gether when John was asked by his church to serve as a spiritual adviser to Don as his date approached. Now, with a new date on the calendar—one that looked more likely to be kept—they were prepar-ing for his death. John said Don was intent on softening the blow for those around him. He didn't want them to mourn.

I asked John how he'd talked to his children, when they were young, about who Don was and why he was locked up.

"We never focused on who he was because we never knew him as who he was," he said. "We've only known him as who he has become. And who he has become is just an incredibly kind, compassionate, loving, thoughtful Christian man."

But some were skeptical. Don's son had been quoted in Memphis' *Commercial Appeal* a day before confirming that he planned to attend his father's execution and saying that his father was nothing but a "con man."[1]

The visitors, though, felt they knew Don as well as anyone. Richard Garner said he'd gone to visit Don 500 times in 10 years.

"When I read somebody says he's a con, I have to laugh," he said. "I think I would know after 500 visits."

Don didn't seem especially worried about all this. I'd sent him some questions through his attorneys, and in response to one about how he was feeling with his execution date approaching, he replied that he was "too blessed to be stressed."[2]

"I am at peace," he said. "I have surrendered to Him. My routine is a little busier, because of more attorney visits, but otherwise it is the same as it has been for years. I still start each morning in prayer and every day I set time aside for Bible study."

I also asked him if there was anything he wanted to say to the governor.

"I ask Governor Lee to pray and see how the Lord will move him, to do what he feels is best, to decide whether I should continue to fellowship and share the Love of the Lord, or whether my time and my work here is done," he said. "I trust Governor Lee, he has shown he is a man of faith and I trust he will decide as the Lord moves him. I am prepared to accept whatever decision he makes."

■ ■ ■

The application for clemency, submitted to the governor about a month earlier, started with a simple, profound request: "Please spare the life of Don Johnson."[3] Clergy members, men on death row, and regular visitors wrote letters of support, and Don's clemency attorneys sought to illustrate Don's "moral transformation." They also drew on interviews with his family members to convey the brutality of his youth. In their estimation, it was no shock that Don had ended up on death row. The remarkable fact about him, they argued, was that he'd become a sincere "man of God" during his time there.

Don's mother, Ruby, was just fourteen when a twenty-four-year-old married father of two named James Lee Johnson took an obscene interest in her. She was sixteen when she gave birth to their first child and eighteen when James Lee left his wife for her. The marriage that followed was as long as it was terrible.

"Throughout their forty-six years of marriage, James Lee treated Ruby like a whipped animal," the attorneys wrote. "She was slapped, beaten, and choked. She was emotionally abused, degraded, and demeaned."[4]

Don was conceived during Ruby's brief escape from that hell. While still a teenager, she ran off to Michigan where some of her family lived. During a brief fling with a man there, she became pregnant with Don. But she soon returned to Tennessee and the financial security, coupled with abuse, she had with James Lee. Don was born into their cold, unloving home.

James Lee routinely beat Don, a "frail little boy" who found only more bullying at school. Growing up, Don never knew that his real father was far away in Michigan. So, when James Lee reared back with a leather shaving strop, a switch, or a bare fist, Don thought it was his biological father who was attacking him. His mother became abusive too, inflicting pain on her children as her husband went out to prey upon other young girls just as he'd preyed upon her.

Don wrote about his life and his time in prison in 2015 when he responded to Hamilton Nolan's *Gawker* series, "Letters From Death Row."[5] In his seven-page letter to the site, he acknowledged that he was a thief from a young age. When he was around six, he would steal candy and toys. Later he graduated to armed robbery. By his own admission, his attorneys wrote, Don was a terror. Unable to stop the beatings at home and bullying at school, he would start fights on his own, purposely provoking his tormentors. Teachers gave him passing grades just to get him out of their classes. On occasion, Don ran away from home.

When he was fourteen, in 1965, he was sent to the State Vocation Training School for White Boys, better known as Jordonia, an institution for troubled juveniles. It was notorious for its prison-like conditions and referred to as a "Prep School for the Pen." There he faced beatings from guards as well as from other boys. In at least one instance he was the victim of an attempted rape. He told his attorneys that, while the abuse he faced at Jordonia was not necessarily worse than what he'd suffered at home, it was more stressful, because he never knew when he'd be assaulted next or by whom.

After spending less than a year there, Don was sent back home. Nothing had changed, though, in him or in the home. He went back to thieving and was soon sent to another state institution. This one, Pikeville, was worse than Jordonia. As his attorneys noted in the clemency application, the *Kingsport Times-News* described being sent to Pikeville as "like going to Hell."[6] A story on a report on the institution in Murfreesboro's *Daily News Journal* ran under the headline "Humans Treated Worse Than Animals, Report Says."[7] Pikeville was overcrowded and rat infested, a precursor to the Walls. Again, Don suffered attempted sexual assaults and physical abuse by guards and other boys.

Not long after Don returned home from Pikeville, at the age of eighteen, he left his parents' home and moved out on his own. As his attorneys put it, "He had learned very little in school, but his father and the State of Tennessee had given him a master's class in violence."[8]

■ ■ ■

More than ten years later, Don was living with his wife, Connie, near Memphis. They had a son together named Jason, and Don had adopted Connie's daughter, Cynthia. His inclination toward criminal activity had followed him into adulthood, but in his early thirties he had the appearance of a man who'd settled down. As he wrote to Gawker in 2015: "I had all that one could really ask for or want, I had a home that I rebuilt in 1981 myself after it had burned. I had off road 4 wheelers that we all rode them often on Sundays."[9] As Don would later tell his daughter, Connie loved romantic comedies, country cooking, and the Rolling Stones. She wore Chanel No. 5 perfume.[10] But if they ever had a calm country life, it wouldn't last long.

On the morning of December 9, 1984, Don started telling family and friends that Connie was missing. She'd gone Christmas shopping alone the night before, he said, and never came home. He even shared his seeming concern about her disappearance with his boss at the camping equipment center which he managed and filed a missing person's report. It was his employer who, after going out to help with the search, found Connie's van at the Mall of Memphis. Police found her body inside. A large green garbage bag had been stuffed down her throat, asphyxiating her, and she'd bled from her ears and her nose.[11]

Don denied any involvement in her death. But the police soon learned that he had signed a man named Ronnie McCoy out of a nearby penal farm for work release. Under questioning, McCoy told police that he and Don had been at the camping equipment center; Connie had been there too. He said he'd left the couple alone for a few minutes and that he came back to find Connie dead. McCoy also admitted to helping Don move Connie's body and clean up the scene.[12]

Police later found traces of her blood on a couch in the office where they believed the killing occurred; they also found the keys to her van and some other personal belongings in Don's truck. The motive remained murky, although *The Commercial Appeal* later reported some possible theories: a looming divorce or Connie's life insurance policy.[13]

Don was arrested, charged, and convicted. He did not initially testify during his trial, but during the penalty phase—as the jury prepared to decide if they would sentence him to death—he took the stand and wept as he denied killing his wife. He said that he'd left McCoy and Connie alone for a few minutes and returned to find her dead. He speculated that McCoy had tried to rob her—she was carrying $450 for Christmas shopping, Don said—and killed her during the struggle. Don admitted to helping move Connie's body, but said he'd done so because he was afraid of McCoy.[14] The jury didn't buy it—one called his testimony "lousy" while another said his performance on the stand alone should have "strapped him in the chair"—and they returned with a death sentence.

Don would later claim responsibility for his wife's murder. The opening words of his clemency application identified Connie Johnson as "the woman whose death Don caused," and later in the document, Don identifies himself as having been "a liar, a conman, a thief and finally, a condemned murderer." At the same time, by his account, his personal transformation began before he was even convicted.

"After my December 1984 arrest and while I was still in a shock as to being actually charged with the murder of my wife, I felt something moving me to attend various chapel services offered there in the jail and I did," he wrote in his letter to *Gawker*. "Then one morning in February 1985 it was as if the preacher was talking directly to me, and before I knew it I was in front of that large group of prisoners in front of the chapel on my knees praying for the Lord to help me, this is for the first time as an adult and realizing for the first time I was living my life wrongly."[15]

His arrest for his wife's murder meant that his children lost both parents at once. In 2014, his stepdaughter Cynthia told my then *Nashville Scene* colleague Amanda Haggard that she remembered her mother dropping her off at a babysitter's house on December 8. When her father picked her up, she said, he told her and her brother that their mother had "gone to live with the angels." Cynthia was seven.

"And the next thing I remember is all of my aunts and grandmother talking in low whispers," she recalled. "They told me to leave the room when a television broadcast came on, but I still remember hearing them—the people on the news—and wondering: 'Why are they saying my daddy killed my mama?' Then I was sent to live with one of my mom's sisters, and from then on out, it was very hard."[16]

Almost twenty-two years later, Cynthia was moved to go visit her father when she saw he'd been scheduled for execution. But her request was denied, seeing as she was also the daughter of Don's victim. The execution was called off. But in 2012, the prison reached back out to her to inform her that she would be allowed to visit her adoptive father. She went to Riverbend, she told the *Scene*, with a list of things she'd been waiting years to tell him—what her childhood was like without her parents and how it felt to be the daughter of the man who killed her mother. She did tell him all that, and he listened. And then something else happened.

"It just came over me that I couldn't keep hating him," Cynthia said. "And I realized that my hatred wasn't affecting him. It didn't, and wouldn't ever, change what happened. I told him that day I forgave him. I said: 'I can't keep hating you. I forgive you.' He started crying."[17]

■ ■ ■

Around seventy-two hours before Don's execution, I got a call from David Bass. It was Monday night and he and Al had just left the prison. Three times already the visitors had gathered on a night like this with an execution looming. But this one was different.

David started to tell me about the evening, how men from the row, including Don, had led the whole visitation gallery in a final prayer. But he was choked up and quickly handed off the phone to Al, who was able to relay the story.

"It was kind of holy ground," he said. "It made you want to take off your shoes."[18]

Don and his visitors had spent much of the night in a private room together but came out into the gallery toward the end of their time together. Terry encouraged everyone in the room to circle around. Kevin Burns, who'd become an ordained minister while on the row and was better known as KB, prayed that the governor would be moved to save Don and that Don would stay strong. Don prayed too, and Al noted how privileged he felt to be standing next to him and holding his hand during the prayer.

"Don prayed that we would be strong," Al said. "He thanked God for his life and thanked God that he'd had the opportunity to serve and hoped he could serve more. He said he wanted to serve until he took his last breath."

When they were finished, Don went around the circle and received a hug from everyone.

As we spoke, Don would've been preparing to be taken to death watch. There was still no news from the governor, and we weren't sure what to make of that. I'd assumed that if the governor was going to spare Don from the death chamber, he'd spare him from death watch too. That wasn't going to happen. But until the lethal cocktail started swirling in Don's veins Thursday night, there was nothing to stop the governor from calling it off. He was going to be in Memphis, where Don had been convicted, the following day. Maybe, we speculated, he planned to make an announcement there.

I thanked them for calling me, and Al sighed before offering a goodbye that might as well have been a prayer.

"I hope we don't see each other Thursday night."

■   ■   ■

We would see each other, though. The next day, the governor announced that "after a prayerful and deliberate consideration" of Don's request for clemency he would not be intervening.[19] Thursday came, and I drove out to Riverbend once more.

A large group was gathered in the now-familiar patch of grass designated for death penalty opponents—visitors, clergy, activists. Just as the visitors had done on Monday night with Don himself, they stood in a circle to pray. They prayed for Don and for the governor and for the men and women who would be putting Don to death. They also prayed for Connie and her family. And Al asked that they pray for someone else too. On the other side of the fence was the same man who reliably showed up to cheer on the executions. On this night he stood by himself. Al confessed that he'd always hated that man, but on this night, he just felt sad for him. With emotion weighing down his voice, he said that if he hated that man, he would be no better than him or the state which was about to execute him. Later, I stood with Al, and his gaze still seemed drawn toward the man on the other side of the fence.

"He seems so alone," he told me.

Next, the group took communion, with clergy members offering bread and wine. They didn't know it then, but inside, in the execution chamber, Don was matching the state's protocols with a liturgy of his own. Associated Press reporter Travis Loller, a media witness to the execution, later described his final words as a long prayer that "echoed the words of Jesus as he was crucified." Don asked for forgiveness for the people participating in the execution, saying "they know not what they do." And he prayed for all those he'd hurt. Then, once the drugs started flowing, he asked the warden if he could sing.

"Given permission by the warden, he sang 'They'll Know We Are Christians' and then 'Soon and Very Soon,'" Loller wrote in her account of the execution. "His voice trailed off in the middle of the second song after the words, 'no more dying there.'"[20]

It was still light outside when word came that the execution was finished. On the faces of everyone in the field there was a quiet distress. If Don could not get clemency from this governor, then who would? There were five more executions on the calendar and now no reason to believe they wouldn't be carried out. They spoke of hope and the "road to abolition" but also noted with grief that on this night the United States would see its 1,496th and 1,497th executions since 1976. Executioners in Alabama were on the job too.

There was one last thing to do for now, though. In lieu of a final meal, Don had asked that his supporters feed the homeless. And so, as he was being put to death, the men and women in the field had taken up a collection to buy pizza. At a vigil at the Riverside Chapel Seventh Day Adventist Church, supporters collected Kroger gift cards so the church could buy food to distribute.

Later, I spoke to Lindsey Krinks, a housing activist and tireless advocate for the people society ignores, and she told me what it'd been like passing out pizzas on the street on behalf of an executed man.

"When I told one man where the pizzas were from, he said 'no way' in disbelief and then took off his hat in reverence," she said.[21]

14

The following morning, I sat at the neighborhood coffee shop a few blocks from my house, writing my account of another night at Riverbend. It was the fourth time in less than a year that I'd found myself sitting with my laptop—in my bed, at the kitchen table, on my front porch, at the coffee shop—trying to shout and lament in text what had happened there the night before.

Seven months had passed since my first visit with Terry. We had exchanged letters and I was talking to David about finding a time for me to accompany him to another visit. For the time being, my trips to the prison were exclusively for the purpose of witnessing executions on the inside or waiting on the outside to hear that they were finished.

I was walking home from the coffee shop when I got a text message from Kelley Henry, the federal public defender who represented so many men on death row and had witnessed Ed Zagorski's electrocution, as well as Don's lethal injection the night before. She was reaching out to tell me that Charles Wright had died. Life had left him that morning in the infirmary, less than twenty-four hours after Don's execution and just a few buildings away from the chamber. He was less than five months away from his own date. Death had spared him from execution.

But it was a death still, a loss. Kelley was already in Florida for work on another case when she received the news from the prison doctor. She learned of one client's death while another's voice, singing from the gurney, still echoed in her mind. They were more than clients to her, though; something closer to family.

"I am heartbroken," she told me.[1]

She'd known Charles for nearly twenty years. He was one of the first men she was assigned to represent on Tennessee's death row in 2000. He was always kind, respectful, and easy-going, she said. When they first met, she was pregnant, and he would always ask after her and her family. Her thoughts that morning were with his brothers and sisters who had "faithfully visited him" since he went to prison in 1985. They were in a season of terrible loss. Charles died just a week after one of his younger sisters, Brenda, and a few months after his older sister Rosie.[2]

Kelley also worried for Charles' community on the row, a group of men enduring their own season of death and grief.

"I am sure that my guys are hurting today with the loss of Don and Charles in less than twenty-four hours," she told me.[3]

Later, in a written statement released to local media, she said that Charles "desperately wanted to one day touch the grass and eat his sister's cooking."

Eight days later, Charles' family held a memorial service for him at a funeral home north of the city. I decided to go, and I brought along my two daughters, then one and almost-three, as my wife was at work for the day, and I'd struck out on other childcare options. I told them we were going to a church service and our oldest was still too young to ask many questions. We arrived and sat with David near the back of the funeral home's chapel. He helped me keep the girls quiet and occupied. At the front of the chapel, Charles' body was lying in an open casket. The girls didn't notice.

He looked more peaceful than Billy had lying on the gurney in the execution chamber. More honestly, I should say, the image of him in his casket does not sneak into my thoughts the way the image of Billy does. I hoped that his loved ones got something like relief from the fact that the manner of his death was not homicide, that although he had endured the pains of cancer he had at least not been put to the gurney or the chair. I know it brought relief to Demetria. Knowing the end was near, she'd written to me in an email earlier that month about how grateful she was that "he will not have to lay in front of that glass window, with witnesses watching."

Seated in the pews around us were family members, friends, and members of his legal team. A large picture of Charles and his two recently departed sisters stood near his casket, while pictures of Charles as a younger man scrolled on a screen behind it. I sat with my daughters and looked at those pictures, and later it would occur to me that Charles had been denied that the type of childhood I wanted for my daughters. Whatever else was true of him and the choices he later made as an adult, he knew violence and neglect by the time he was their age, and he came to know heroin not long after that.

By the time he died, he'd spent thirty-four years on death row. His attorneys' requests for a compassionate release had been denied by two governors, but now his family was laying him to rest and praying for him to rest in peace.

A preacher stood over him delivering a sermon, punctuating words that echoed Don's final hymn.

"Earth has no sorrow that heaven cannot heal."

15

This is Terry King's confession. He has given it many times, and after he finished telling me the story, on a summer night more than a year and a half after we first met, he apologized for my having to hear it.

In June of 1983, a little more than a month before he got in trouble, Terry turned twenty-one and celebrated with a party he wouldn't remember.[1] A friend with a swimming pool and a Jacuzzi hosted some fifty people for a barbecue. They procured two kegs of beer and enough Quaaludes to dose the whole crowd. Afterward, Terry only had pictures as evidence.

But as it had for so long in his life, his wild and carefree attitude cloaked a deep sadness. In that summer in particular, Terry was in the grip of a fierce depression. He was regularly drinking cases of beer laced with Quaaludes or taking Quaaludes laced with Valium.[2] On some days, he would get up for work and leave his house only to pull his car to the side of the road, climb into the back seat, and sleep there for hours. He was fired from his job at Sea Ray, the large boat manufacturer based in Knoxville.

He spent a lot of time those days with Joe Sexton, a friend since childhood who lived two doors down from the Kings and with whom Terry used to get into a kind of righteous mischief. Once, when Terry was eleven or twelve, after seeing that a neighbor was mistreating his horse—starving it to the point that its ribs could be easily counted—Terry and Joe cut the fence and freed the horse. Another time, acting on weaker evidence, they became convinced another man who lived nearby was mistreating a handful of cows he kept in a barn. The two boys let the cattle out, took all the hay out of the man's barn, and threw it out in the field. They ended up having to pay for the hay. As adults, they remained close friends but had replaced juvenile antics with regular substance abuse.

On the night of July 2, 1983, he and Joe had been up for two or three days straight without sleep—binge drinking and eating speed to stay awake—when they walked into a dive bar across from a Greyhound bus station near downtown Knoxville.[3] It was there that they ran into a twenty-year-old soldier named Todd Millard, a Wisconsin native who was on leave with a Fourth of July weekend pass from Fort Knox in Kentucky. It was around 8 or 8:30 p.m., early enough in a night where it can still lead anywhere. Soon the three men were drinking together and shooting pool. At some point, Todd asked for a ride, and he offered to pay. He was trying to get out to White Pine, a small town around forty miles east of Knoxville. Joe and Terry had come in Joe's car, and they agreed to take him.

As they started to make their way toward the interstate, though, Todd asked if they knew anywhere else they could go to get some more drinks, maybe meet a few women. It wasn't hard for Joe and Terry to come up with a place like that. They headed for the Lower Level, another dive bar they frequented on Asheville Highway outside the city. There they drank more beers and shot more pool until they noticed Todd had passed out. The owner of the bar, who knew Terry well, asked him and Joe to get their unconscious companion out of his establishment. They complied by dragging Todd outside and laying him in the car, before going back into the bar to party some more.

A foul seed had already been planted in the men's minds. Earlier in the night, Todd had flashed a large roll of cash and now he was incapacitated. Terry raised the idea of robbing him.

When they came back out to the car later, Todd was still passed out. Joe got behind the wheel and drove to the house where his mother still lived, on the same street where he and Terry had grown up. He went inside, leaving Terry and Todd in the car, and returned with a rifle. Terry recalled a series of confrontational exchanges between he and his friend as their night escalated toward murder.

"What'd you go and get that for?" Terry asked.

"In case he wakes up," Joe said.

Terry insisted they wouldn't have any problems with Todd. He was passed out and unlikely to remember much of anything. They could take his money, drive him out to White Pine, and leave him there. Joe wasn't convinced.

They drove off again into the night, which by then was preparing to give way to morning. At some point, Todd woke up and Joe, wielding half of a pool cue he had in the car, started beating him brutally over the head. With blood splattering everywhere, Terry started yelling at his friend, telling him to stop.

"You're gonna kill him!" Terry said.

"We're gonna have to," Joe said. "He knows who we are."

Terry continued to protest, urging Joe to just put this man they'd met only hours earlier out of the car and leave. Again and again, Terry told him, "I'm not gonna do this."

Joe had gotten the rifle but didn't have any shells and so they drove on, with Todd now in the trunk of the car, to nearby Grainger County, where Joe's grandmother lived. It was 4:30 or 5 a.m. When they arrived and Terry started questioning Joe again, Joe told him to wait in the car. He went inside and returned this time with a pistol. They started to argue again.

"Man, we ain't gotta do this," Terry said. "I'm not gonna be a part of this. I cannot hurt him. We can put him out here, he'll never remember our names."

They were out in the country now, their raised voices cutting through the early morning stillness. Terry thought just maybe he'd talked his friend out of doing something they couldn't take back. But then, out of the dark and quiet, came Todd's voice from the trunk of the car.

"Please, Joe! Don't kill me!"

That, Terry recalled, is when Joe went ballistic. Terry, again, tried to convince him that Todd—beaten to hell and still intoxicated—would not remember their names or faces, that they could just leave him behind. But Joe ordered them back into the car and drove them out from his grandmother's and into a hay field. He grabbed the pistol, told Terry to keep the car running, and took Todd into a wooded area.

Terry was standing at the car, with morning threatening to dawn, when he heard the gunshots.

Joe walked out of the woods and up to the car.

"He's not dead," he said.

"What?" Terry asked.

"He's not dead," Joe repeated.

He told Terry to get in the car and to stay there, that he would be right back. He returned with two shells for the rifle. Terry, convinced now that Joe was going to kill him too, asked Joe to give him one of the shells. In hindsight he would see it was foolish; if Joe wanted to kill him, he could've easily done so.

Joe took the rifle and the shells and headed back into the woods, and from the car Terry heard a gunshot that he would remember as an explosion. Joe returned and they drove off.

Later that night, Joe called from his grandmother's house and told Terry they needed to bury the body. At first, Terry told him no, he didn't want any part of it. But yet another argument ensued. They were both guilty, Joe said, and Terry had to come help him hide what they'd done. Terry told Joe to come get him in the morning.

As families in East Tennessee rose to go to church, Terry and Joe rode out to the wooded area where Todd Millard's body lay. They dug a shallow grave. Terry refused to touch the body, although he did help cover it up with dirt again. He looked around and found a large stone, which he placed next to the grave.

"What are you doing?" Joe asked.

"He needs a grave marker," Terry said.

Joe looked at him, standing over the grave they'd just dug for the man he'd murdered: "Are you stupid?"

They left the scene of the crime again. Terry felt numb and burdened by what they'd done, so much so that later that day he told a friend of his named Eugene Thornhill everything that had happened. Eugene told him to forget all about it, illustrating his point by telling Terry to pick up a small rock and throw it. But Terry couldn't throw his thoughts far enough. He ended up telling his ex-sister-in-law what he and Joe had done too, and she told him to call an attorney. He had a lawyer from a previous case, and he called him, but the attorney wasn't in the office. If he had been, Terry would come to believe, that might've been the end of it.

■ ■ ■

Several weeks later, Todd Millard's body was still in a shallow grave in the woods, and Terry and Joe were still out in the free world. Terry spent July trying to stay high and drunk, hoping to blur the image of Todd's dead body and muffle the sound of their shovels digging into the ground. The Army had notified Todd's father that he was AWOL on July 6, and his uncle had come to Tennessee to urge authorities to list him as a missing person.[4] But his body had not been discovered. The people to whom Terry had unburdened himself had stayed quiet enough. No one else knew what they had done.

So, the morning of Sunday, July 31, started like many other weekend summer mornings, with Terry and his cousin, Don King, preparing to spend the day hanging out around Cherokee Lake, a large reservoir outside of Knoxville created by the damming of the Holston River.[5] They met up at the house trailer where Don lived and washed his T-top Corvette before grabbing a case of beer. First, they headed off to meet some friends at a public swimming pool in nearby Jefferson City. They hung out there for a while and then left for the lake.

Summertime at Cherokee Lake in those years was the high season for a pastime known as "cruising the dam." Cars and motorcycles lined the road near Cherokee Dam, as others drove up and down in between them, showing off their rides and looking for a hook-up, whether sex or substances.

Terry drank heavily throughout the day and took a few Quaaludes. They were cruising the dam when they saw a blue 1979 Camaro with the driver-side door open. Terry noted the woman sitting inside in a halter top and short shorts. She wore a small gold chain on her right wrist, one gold-chain earring, and on her left ring finger, a gold set of engagement and wedding rings.[6] Her name was Diana Smith. She was thirty-one years old, a decade older than Terry. Later, it was reported that she'd left her home in the small nearby town of Talbott, where she lived with her husband and ten-year-old daughter, to get some fast food. But now she was at the dam.

Don and Terry pulled up next to her and started talking. She drank from a McDonald's cup, into which she occasionally poured some clear liquid out of a half-gallon bottle. Soon, she'd gotten out of the car and was standing outside of theirs, leaning over to talk to Don and Terry and attracting the attention of other passersby. They chatted for some time, making small talk and inquiring about each other's plans for the rest of the day. At some point in the conversation, she said she liked to do acid and that it made her "horny as hell." Terry seized on her comment in the same way he'd locked on to the sight of her shorts. He knew where they could get some acid, and he knew a friend who'd probably like to join them. It was Eugene Thornhill, the same friend Terry had gone to for advice after he and

Joe buried Todd's body. He'd just seen Eugene near the lake, unloading his boat with his wife and two young daughters. Despite Eugene's status as a married father of two, he partied often with Terry and Don. It was not unusual for them to go out chasing women together, looking for willing partners for group sex.

So, when Terry told Eugene about the woman he'd met who said she was turned on by acid, Eugene was in. He'd drop his family off at home, he said, and meet Terry back at Don's house. From there, Eugene and Terry would go together to get the drugs.

Don and Terry hopped back in Don's Corvette and drove down to a nearby gas station where Diana had parked her Camaro. When Terry went to her and told her the plan, she told him to get in her car. They raced west on Asheville Highway, back toward Knoxville, following Don back to his trailer. There they started drinking liquor until Eugene showed up. He and Terry drove to another friend's house, where Terry got five or six hits of LSD. When they returned, they found Don—an avid amateur photographer—flipping through a photo album, showing off some of his pictures to Diana. Don and Eugene passed on the LSD, but Terry took two or three hits and Diana took a couple too.

Time blurred. At some point, Terry saw Don and Diana having sex. Then Eugene and Diana. Then they were all in a room together. Don had set up his tripod and was taking pictures.

After several hours, Terry and Diana left the trailer in her Camaro and drove into Grainger County, to a wooded area where Terry and friends used to go as teenagers to fool around with their girlfriends. They were only a couple miles from his friend Joe Sexton's grandmother's house and from Todd Millard's shallow grave. They had sex there, and then, according to a statement Terry gave to police after hours of interrogation, they left to go get gas for her car. At a nearby gas station, Terry told her to pump the gas, but when she got out, she grabbed the car keys. He ordered her back in the car and they left, driving back to the wooded area. They had sex again and

Terry took forty dollars that he knew she was carrying.[7] It was then, according to Terry's statements to police, that she asked him a question, although when he told me the story, he said she asked it while they were having sex.

"Why did you all rape me?" she said.

"What do you mean?" Terry said. "We didn't do that."

She questioned him again.

"Why did you take advantage of me?"

Thirty-seven years later, he would describe the feelings that overwhelmed him then as panic and fear. He ordered her to get in the trunk of the car. What happened next, he told me, would be unbelievable to many people but he insisted that it happened. He said he removed a crank, some pistons, and tools from the trunk and made a pillow for her out of a blanket before she got in without a fight. Years later, he said, he could see that her comprehension of the situation was probably just as disturbed by confusion, fear, and substances as his.

He got in her Camaro and drove straight to see his friend Joe. They gave different accounts of the interaction that followed. In his own statement to police, Joe said that Terry told him he needed help, that he had a woman in the trunk of the car, and he wasn't going to let her go because he was "afraid he would get into the same mess he got into with Lori" (his old girlfriend who he maintained had falsely accused him of sexual assault).[8] Terry told me that he didn't remember mentioning Lori at all to Joe, although he acknowledged that his experience with her may have contributed to his panicked reaction to Diana's statement. Although he made no mention of it in his statement to police, Terry told me that it was Joe who proposed the solution to his predicament and that they argued over it.

Then, Terry told police, Joe retrieved his .30-30 lever-action rifle, ammunition, and a shovel. They drove away, Terry in Diana's Camaro with her still in the trunk, and Joe following in his blue 1970 Audi. They headed back into Knox County, but they hadn't gone far when both cars ran out of gas. Terry pushed Joe's car to a nearby service station where they put five dollars of gas in it and five more dollars' worth of gas in a can to put in Diana's car, which was parked up the road. One wonders what terror was going through Diana's mind, lying in the dark trunk. Had the drugs and alcohol started to fade, bringing her situation into a more frightening clarity?

With the cars fueled up, Terry and Joe took off again. They drove down Old Rutledge Pike, the same road where Terry had nearly died in a wreck as he sped away from a police car years earlier. They made their way to an isolated area near a creek, where there was once an old, covered bridge.

Again, Terry told me, he and Joe argued over what to do, but at some point, he backed the Camaro down toward a wooded area near the creek. The car got stuck. Terry got out of the car and opened the trunk. It was daylight now and he had the rifle pointed at the woman he'd met by chance less than twenty-four hours before. Diana got out of the trunk and walked at gunpoint farther into the woods. Terry told her to lay down on the ground. He later told the police that she asked if he was going to kill her and that he said no, adding that more men were coming to have sex with her. To me, though, he said she didn't even ask why he had a gun. A friend Terry later confessed to told authorities that Terry said Diana had begged for her life and that he'd ordered her not to look at him.[9] This is how he told me what happened next:

"I pointed the gun at her head and closed my eyes and said, 'Oh my God' and I pulled the trigger. That's what I did."

They burned Diana's belongings and her ID.

As he told me what happened after that, I noticed Terry slip occasionally into a passive voice. He said that he and Joe returned to the scene the day after "she was killed" and he referred to Diana politely as "Mrs. Smith." It seemed to me a sort of dissociation of his present self from this horrible thing his past self had done. He accepted moral and literal responsibility for the murder, but as he told me more than once, he did not relate at all anymore to the man who pulled the trigger. Hearing him tell his story, I experienced something similar. I knew he was on death row; I knew he'd committed a murder. But the man I'd met all these years after the fact did not seem capable of what he was describing.

Initially after Terry killed her, he and Joe tried to dig a grave, but the ground was too hard. Terry told me he never went back into the woods where her body lay. He was still haunted by the image of Todd's dead body. But he knew they had to move Diana. He recalled that Joe got a tent and wrapped her body in it. After that was done, he and Terry put Diana's body in the trunk of Joe's car and drove to a quarry lake. They threw the body in the water, after weighing the tent down with cinder blocks. But it didn't sink and instead stayed floating near the water's edge.

Terry took off all his clothes and dove into the lake completely naked. He pulled the tent-wrapped body as far out into the water as he could and let it go. He climbed out of the water, dried off, and put his clothes back on. Diana's body floated in the still lake. On the bank, Terry and Joe got some beer out of the car. They drank and kept drinking for some time.

■ ■ ■

Terry spent the days after Diana Smith's murder in much the same way he'd spent the weeks after Todd Millard's.[10] He stayed drunk and high, covering the knowledge of what he'd seen and done in a thick coat of beer and LSD. He also told someone what had happened, just as he'd done before. He went to a friend to unburden himself about both killings and seek advice, but also to see if his friend knew anyone who might want to buy Diana's Camaro. He and Terry had previously collaborated on insurance fraud schemes, chopping up vehicles and reporting them stolen to the insurance so they could pocket the money. His friend didn't help him, though, and didn't offer him any advice except to ask what the hell he was thinking.

One night a few days later, Terry was at a Knoxville-area bar called Chippy's when he ran into two men he knew from other bars and parties. They drank together, and later, as Terry was going to leave, he saw one of the men getting into a van he didn't own. It turned out the van he was stealing belonged to the bar's owner. He and the other man took off in the van and Terry followed them in his car, eventually getting out and joining them in the van and taking the wheel. Wildly intoxicated, they drove into downtown Knoxville and into the parking lot of a Kroger. One of Terry's companions jumped out of the van and grabbed a woman, attempting to pull her toward the van. Terry jumped out too, and soon the woman was screaming. The men got back in the van and sped away, with Terry driving. But instead of getting out of Dodge, as it were, they drove down to Cumberland Avenue, a main drag lined with bars and restaurants in the heart of Knoxville near the University of Tennessee campus. Terry turned onto the street and into a swarm of police cars, blue lights on and sirens wailing.

They were all arrested and taken to the city jail. Terry knew he was in a world of trouble, but it had not yet dawned on him just how large a world that was. He was in jail for nearly a week, with his mom preparing to put her house up as collateral so she could get him out, when he called home to ask her to tell Joe to bring him some clothes for court. That's when he learned that Joe had been taken in for questioning by the police. Around the same time, he read in the newspaper, which was circulated in the jail, that Diana Smith's body had been discovered on August 6, after a woman went to the quarry lake for a swim and noticed a foul odor coming from a yellow tent floating near the water's edge.[11] Todd's body was discovered in Grainger County the same week.

It turned out that Terry's friend had gone to the police and reported what Terry had told him (albeit with some erroneous details, according to Terry). Terry and Joe were soon charged in connection to both killings. Around that time, Terry's mother, Billie, and his Uncle Bud—who'd coached his baseball teams and taken him hunting after Terry's father died—were allowed to come see him. They cried together, and Terry told his mother he was sorry for what he'd done. She immediately offered to sell her house and hire an attorney, but Terry refused to allow it. He later learned that his mother and his grandmother were so distraught that they were put on Valium.

Over the years, Terry and his attorneys have argued that, although his guilt is not in question, what followed his arrest was a series of improper actions by police and prosecutors that deprived him of a fair trial and sentencing.

After their arrests, Joe and Terry both gave statements to the police. However, although these would later be summarized by the courts as, essentially, confessions given after the men waived their rights to an attorney, the truth was more troubling. After the discovery of Diana and Todd's bodies, Terry was taken from the city jail to the Knox County Sheriff's Department where he was questioned by two detectives from the Tennessee Bureau of Investigation. They interrogated him all night and into the early morning without an attorney present. For hours Terry denied any involvement with the killings. His attorneys would later claim in appeals that their questioning continued after he asked to see a lawyer.[12] He was exhausted after spending days getting little sleep in a four-person cell in the city jail. He'd hardly had anything to eat.

The detectives told him that Joe Sexton was claiming Terry had been responsible for both killings. Skeptical, Terry told them to show him Joe's statements, and they eventually did. Although he would later admit the truth, Joe initially claimed that Terry had also killed Todd Millard. Having seen Joe's statement to police, Terry gave his own, incriminating himself after a relentless night of questioning and isolation that left Terry, according to his post-conviction attorneys, "so worn down that he could not sign his name correctly."

In May 1984, to avoid a possible death sentence, Terry and Joe pleaded guilty in Grainger County for the murder of Todd Millard. But Terry did so without knowing that Joe had admitted to police that Terry did not kill Todd and had stayed in the car when the murder occurred. Moreover, Terry was led to believe that if he pleaded guilty to Todd's murder, he would get a package deal in which he would also be spared the death penalty for Diana Smith's murder. In fact, his conviction in the first case ended up bolstering the case for a death sentence in the second.

In their petition for a writ of habeas corpus—effectively a request for a hearing at which a person can challenge their incarceration as unlawful—filed in federal court in 2000, federal public defenders representing Terry made the case that the next trial had featured a long list of compounding injustices and errors.

Terry and Joe went to trial for Diana's murder in 1985, and Terry's attorneys would argue that the serious problems undermining the trial's fairness started there, with the fact that the two men were tried together. This guaranteed that their defenses would be antagonistic to one another, they argued, and violated the Confrontation Clause of the Sixth Amendment. Terry was deprived of the right to confront one of the main witnesses against him, they argued, because that witness was also his co-defendant. Compounding this problem, Terry's post-conviction attorneys argued, was the fact that Terry's trial attorney was an inexperienced lawyer who had never tried a capital case. The jury never heard in detail about the trauma of Terry's childhood and the effects of that trauma and heavy substance abuse on his underdeveloped brain. Courts later rejected Terry's ineffective assistance of counsel claims.

Terry's future attorneys would also argue that prosecutors were allowed to improperly introduce testimony, allowing them to falsely suggest a pattern of behavior and paint Terry's killing of Diana Smith as premeditated. They cited Joe Sexton's statement that Terry had invoked his old girlfriend, Lori, and her assault allegations, on the night he killed Diana and said that he didn't want to get into the same situation again. They used that statement as a basis to call Lori to testify during the trial, over the objection of Terry's attorney. She told the court that Terry had attempted to kill her in October of 1982 and had asked her "how it felt to be dying, so that the next woman he killed he would know how she felt." She lost consciousness, she said, and claimed that when she woke up, she heard Terry telling his cousin that he had killed her and he needed help throwing her body in a quarry, an allegation Terry's cousin said was false. Lori's testimony differed from what she'd told police three years earlier when she first accused Terry of assault and her own sister testified against her. She told the court that Lori shouldn't be believed, even under oath.[13] Terry would later face charges stemming from Lori's allegations, but they would be dismissed. Still, her testimony buttressed the prosecution's case for a death sentence. Although courts would later agree that Lori's testimony should not have been allowed, they deemed it a "harmless" error.[14]

Terry's attorneys argued to no avail that it was the cumulative effect of such errors that fundamentally tainted his trial and led to a jury sparing Joe's life but sentencing Terry to death.

In a letter, Terry described to me what happened at ten minutes after 1 p.m. on Wednesday, February 6, 1985, the day his "entire world changed."

He watched as the judge asked the foreman of the jury to read the sentence they'd decided upon, and he listened as the jury said the words "death by electrocution." He scanned the room, looking for his family and found them weeping in the gallery. The judge asked him if he had anything to say.

"I'm very sorry for all that has happened," Terry recalled saying, struggling to maintain the composure necessary to speak. "I wish I could change them, but I can't."

The judge ordered him transferred to the custody of the warden at the state penitentiary in Nashville—the Walls—and read again the fate to which he had been sentenced.

"Your body shall be subjected to shock by a sufficient current of electricity until you are dead."

16

In the summer of 2019, Joe Ingle was still attempting to shelter from the storm of trauma brought on by Ed's execution. He'd been close to the machinery of death many times before. In 2012, he published a book called *The Inferno*, detailing Philip Workman's journey to the execution chamber, a journey on which Joe was a close companion. But sitting death watch with Ed twice in less than three weeks had left Joe shell-shocked. More than seven months later, he hadn't been back to the prison. At the urging of a trauma therapist, he was spending time doing things that put his heart and mind at ease rather than under assault. For Joe, this meant regular attendance at Vanderbilt University baseball games and tending to his field of blueberry bushes. In late June, six weeks after Don's execution, he invited me to join him in the latter.

He'd been introduced to blueberry farming by a man named Hector Black, whose daughter had been murdered. Hector had gone from wanting the man who'd raped and killed her in her Atlanta apartment to be executed, to learning about that man's own violent and traumatic upbringing, to finally deciding, along with his wife, Susie, that retribution would not heal their pain. They went to a Murder Victims' Families for Reconciliation conference in Boston where they met Joe, and together the three of them worked to spare their daughter's killer the death penalty. In the years that followed, Hector and his daughter's murderer, Ivan Simpson, exchanged letters and maintained a relationship. Years later, after buying so many buckets of blueberries from Hector's farm, Joe asked him how to plant his own.

I arrived early in the morning, as was necessary to beat the heat and the birds that would eat Joe's blueberries if we didn't pick them first. His humble home sits on twenty-seven acres of land. Tall trees line either side of the property like walls to keep out the quarrelsome world, and in the valley between are rows and rows of blueberry bushes. Joe met me at his porch and laughed at my attire. I'd worn a T-shirt and cut-off jean shorts, thinking of the heat, but he informed me I'd be eaten up by bugs, possibly carrying ticks, and scratched to hell by branches and briars.

Joe's longest-tenured blueberry bushes were seven years old by then. A few near the house had served as a test run before he expanded in stages into the field. He told me they'd last thirty years or so. He would sell some of the harvest and give away others to people who'd been kind to him over the years. He'd keep some to make blueberry jam or to put on his cereal in the mornings.

Outside the porch, birds flitted around the various bird feeders Joe had set up in his yard, and for a moment I thought that the execution chamber seemed so far away. The feeders were empty, though. One of the side effects of Joe's malady, as he called it, his trauma, was that he'd lacked the energy to keep the feeders full as he normally would. As we got up to apply bug spray and head out into the field, one of Joe's dogs started barking inside. Joe and his wife had two dogs, both of them strays that had wandered onto the property and ended up adopted.

Down at the first bush, Joe gave me a quick primer on our task. He gently pulled at a blueberry, rolling it in his fingers as he examined it on all sides. The first one still had some reddish-pink coloring, indicating that it wasn't quite ripe. He moved on. The next was all blue. He picked it and plopped it into his bucket. We kept picking and when a berry fell to the ground, he urged me to pick it up. "No blueberry left behind." Minutes later he grabbed a plump, ripe one. "Now that's a nice blueberry, right there." Plop.

More than once while we were in the field, I assured Joe that we didn't have to talk about anything related to death row if he didn't want to. I worried that my mere presence might be triggering to him. We'd rescheduled this outing at least once because he just wasn't ready for the conversations that might occur. But he assured me on this day that it was the context that made all the difference. If thoughts of Riverbend and death row and the executions there came up while he was in his blueberry field, it was OK.

"When I'm on death row and I have those thoughts, it's not good," he said.[1]

I told him that I couldn't help but imagine some of the guys from Unit 2 getting to come out to his field and pick blueberries with him. It was so peaceful and therapeutic.

"There's no reason they couldn't do it, it's such a joke," he said. "These guys are not a danger to anybody. They've all been out there for thirty years. They're totally rehabilitated. I mean, now we're killing 'em. I mean, it's insane. Yeah. Nobody wants to be judged on the worst thing. These guys have looked at themselves, they're not proud of it if they did it, and they've pretty much changed their lives if they're mentally able to."

As the state sought to kill these men one-by-one, the community of people close to them was feeling a tension that Joe was well familiar with. There were those who wanted to work within the system, pernicious as it was, using various connections to get close to the governor and other power brokers to advocate for their friends on the row. Joe had tried this approach himself. By this point, he'd sat in rooms with governors from Florida to Tennessee only to see them sign the death warrants of his friends. For him, and others

within the community around Tennessee's death row, Governor Bill
Lee's denial of Don Johnson's request for clemency was a breaking
point. Here was a governor who'd made heaps of hay out of his
professed Christian faith, allowing the execution of a man who'd
become an ordained deacon in the Christian church. Some in the
community felt it was time for civil disobedience but eventually
held off at Don's request.

But the outrage and pain remained. Bill Lee and Dylann Roof,
the Charleston Emanuel AME Church shooter, have one thing in
common, Joe told me—they both kill ministers.

"We've had two Christian governors and they've participated in
killing more people in Tennessee than any governor since 1955," he
said. "I'm ready for an atheist governor."

I asked him about the conversations he'd had with Lee's predecessor, Bill Haslam. He declined to share the details of those pastoral
conversations but couldn't hide his disappointment with the outcome.

"You look at their actions," he said. "That's how you determine
whether you're faithful or not. It's not what you say, it's who you are and
what you do. You know, Jesus was very clear about that. By their fruit
you shall know them. I mean, this is not hard, people. So, you know,
don't come to me with 'I'm a Christian,' and turn around and kill people
in the electric chair or on the gurney. I mean, give me a freaking break."

"It's politics," he added. "It's got nothing to do with justice or
mercy or Jesus."

■　■　■

At the prison that week, Terry had received David, David's daughter
Caroline, and Al for a visit. Al brought two friends from out of town
who'd been wanting to meet Terry, and the two friends—a man and
his son—brought a question. The question came from their daughter
and sister, a young woman named Katie who'd been paralyzed from
the waist down in a horse-riding accident at the age of twenty-two.

She wanted them to ask Terry how he could be at peace and feel free despite his confinement. The subtext didn't need to be elucidated. After an emotional visit, Terry sat down and wrote her a letter.[2]

> Dear Katie,
>
> Hope and trust this letter finds you doing well. As for me, I am doing great.
>
> As you may know last night I had the privilege of meeting your father and brother. We had an awesome visit. I wish you could have been there. I hope I get to meet you someday.
>
> I would like to begin this brief letter by saying I know what it is like to feel as if life is over with. When I was 22 yrs old I was sentenced to death. I have been incarcerated for 36 years this August.
>
> I know what it is like to be 22 and believe that life is over with. I know what it is like to be 22 and feel trapped and no where to go. I know what it is like to be 22 and hear about friends doing things that you can't. I know what it is like to be 22 and believe life is passing you by. I know what it is like to be 22 and feel everything you do seems hopeless. I know what it is like to be 22 and feel trapped in a prison. I know what it is like to be so depressed that it hurts to even get up out of bed. I know those things because I have experienced them but I have outlived them all.
>
> However, I am here to tell you that there is hope, joy, happiness, peace and freedom that awaits you. I have all that in spite of my circumstances . . . I write you from prison sitting on death row and my life is so blessed. I truly believe in my heart you will never meet a more blessed person than me. God is so good to me.
>
> Please believe me . . . I have never been more free and at peace in my entire life. I know without any doubt in my mind that I have been forgiven and I thank GOD for that.
>
> My prayer for you is that you find happiness and peace regardless of your current circumstances. I assure you that many blessings are right around the corner.

17

On a warm afternoon in early August 2019, Dan Mann stood on the marble plaza beneath the Tennessee State Capitol, holding a poster board that magnified a short note from death row.

> Dear Governor Lee,
> We understand you are a man of faith and we would like to ask you to please come pray with us.[1]

Beneath this invitation were the signatures of thirty-two condemned men. The first was Terry King's. Farther down the list of scrawled names was Stephen West, a man who was then just a week away from the execution chamber.

Dan and his wife Bethany had been visiting death row since 2011, and they were among the people whose acquaintance I owed to the state's spree of executions. They were also among the subset of people in the community around Tennessee's death row who were increasingly convinced that the time for private diplomacy was over. Whereas someone like David Bass was inclined to build relationships into a bridge that would connect him to people in power—and thus put people in power in relationship with his friends on death

row—the Mann's were the sort who would just as soon go bang on
the governor's door. Each approach had its strengths and flaws. The
relational approach could be slow, while the confrontational approach
risked pissing off the people who could stop the killing. The truth
was, no one had figured out how to get them to do that.

The men's invitation to the governor, Dan said, had first been
made privately after Don Johnson's execution in May. It had been
ignored. And so they were trying again, this time in public. Standing
with Dan on the plaza was Reverend Kevin Riggs of Franklin
Community Church, a congregation based in the governor's home
county. He pointed out that one of the men who'd signed the letter
was Kevin Burns, a death row prisoner who'd been ordained as a
pastor by Riggs' church. The reverend said he'd come out that day
"to ask my neighbor, my governor, to honor this request. He's a man
of faith and I believe that with all my heart. I admire his prison
ministry; he's been involved in prison ministry most of his adult life."
That was true, although it had not inspired the governor to spare Don
Johnson's life.

The men's request was powerful, and I had no reason to doubt its
sincerity. But its power, it seemed to me, came at least partly from
the near certainty that this governor would not honor it and that he
would be seen refusing to do so. In any case, he would not be able
to claim the invitation got lost in the mail. Dan and a number of
other death row visitors and death penalty opponents were planning
to march that Saturday from Riverbend to the capitol. There, they
would hold a vigil until Monday, just days before the next execution,
when they would deliver the letter to the governor's office.

■ ■ ■

Dan first understood the death penalty as an instrument of God's justice.[2] As a middle school student at his private Christian school—a
segregation academy—he did a class project on capital punishment,

creating a diorama that showed various execution methods. For the firing squad, he used little green army men and painted them gray. He explained to his class what he knew as the Biblical basis for putting convicted murderers to death, reciting the words of Genesis 9:6.

"Whoever sheds human blood, by humans shall their blood be shed."

In adulthood he remained entrenched in evangelical culture. If the church doors were open, he recalled to me, he was there and probably teaching something. He worked in the Christian music and publishing industries. In 2008, he and Bethany were married, and in 2010 they moved into a home not far from Riverbend. It was around this time that Bethany received her adoption papers, answering a question she had carried with her all her life—from where, and from whom, had she come into being? The answer, it turned out, was prison. Her mother had been incarcerated and her biological father was a guard. This truth shattered her long-held vision of her mother as a glamorous, Audrey Hepburn–esque figure, and it would alter her view of more than just that. In prisoners, she now saw her mother, and in prison she saw the place where she—were it not for her skin color and zip code, as she told me—should have ended up herself.

This all generally coincided with a spiritual crisis in Dan's life. He'd been questioning what he believed and why he believed it. They knew their Bible well. But at that moment in their lives, a passage from the Book of Matthew, Chapter 25, with its talk of sheep and goats, stuck to them like a bur.

> When the Son of Man comes in his glory, and all the angels with him, he will sit on his glorious throne. All the nations will be gathered before him, and he will separate the people one from another as a shepherd separates the sheep from the goats. He will put the sheep on his right and the goats on his left.
>
> Then the King will say to those on his right, 'Come, you who are blessed by my Father; take your inheritance, the kingdom prepared

for you since the creation of the world. For I was hungry, and you gave me something to eat, I was thirsty and you gave me something to drink, I was a stranger and you invited me in, I needed clothes and you clothed me, I was sick and you looked after me, I was in prison and you came to visit me.'

Then the righteous will answer him, "Lord, when did we see you hungry and feed you, or thirsty and give you something to drink? When did we see you a stranger and invite you in, or needing clothes and clothe you? When did we see you sick or in prison and go to visit you?"

The King will reply, "Truly I tell you, whatever you did for one of the least of these brothers and sisters of mine, you did for me."

Dan and Bethany gave to the poor. They fed the hungry. Dan could hardly keep cash on him because he was so prone to giving it away. Bethany was the sort who would later bring a homeless man back to their home. But they did not visit those in prison. "Whatever you did for one of the least of these brothers and sisters of mine, you did for me." To them, it was—to borrow from the evangelical lexicon—a calling.

Around this same time, as fate or the Lord would have it, they were at a farmer's market near their home when they met Joe Ingle. They found out he was a minister and, not only that, a minister to prisoners. They eagerly—perhaps over eagerly, they would later admit—told him of their calling to visit prisoners. Prisoners on death row? Even better.

Joe was not skilled at, or perhaps not interested in, hiding his skepticism. He was cautious about bringing people out to death row who might use it as an exercise in grim tourism. But Dan and Bethany did not stop asking him. For six months they inquired, until eventually Joe came back to them with good news. He had a man on Unit 2 named Larry McKay. Larry was a bit antagonistic, Joe told them. He said the F-word a lot. Joe wasn't sure they'd be a good match. But Larry had been asking for a visitor. So, Joe had Dan and Bethany write him a letter, and a few months later, on Valentine's Day 2011 as it happened, they went to visit Larry for the first time.

On their first visit, Larry told them, "If you're gonna sell me something, I'm not buying." He'd refused visitors for 15 years now because, as he told them, "I've had the Mormons, the Catholics, the Muslims, the Baptists, the Episcopalians. I've had everybody in here that has wanted to sell me something. And when I told them I wasn't buying it, they quit coming." Dan and Bethany told him they were there to get to know him, not to sell him anything.

With that settled, conversation with Larry came easily. They found that Larry was eager to dig into what would otherwise seem to be the most mundane details of their days, living a free life through them. Early on, before the prison prohibited friends and family from sending photographs, Dan and Bethany would take pictures in places like the grocery store and mail Larry images of fruits and vegetables he hadn't seen in decades.

Their children came to know Larry; for some of them, Larry's voice on the telephone around dinner time was a regular feature of their youth. By the time I met Dan and Bethany, they'd been visiting Larry for 10 years.

In 1983, Larry and another man, Michael Sample, had been convicted and sentenced to death for the murders of two convenience store clerks during a robbery two years earlier.[3] Larry has maintained his innocence and Dan and Bethany told me they believed him. But it also, ultimately, didn't make a difference to them.

"It's my understanding that it's for the guilty that Christ came," Dan told me.

Their lives had been overtaken by what they described as the gospel of proximity. After putting themselves in proximity to these condemned, marginalized men they couldn't help but see humanity—the image of God, one might say—in them. Questions of guilt or innocence, they'd found, were secondary to this core truth.

And as the executions mounted, this proximity had moved them to an activism they'd once shunned. Dan recalled rejecting offers to be interviewed at the prison before Billy's execution, because he was there to mourn, not to protest. Now, though, he and Bethany saw no other choice but to be loud and even confrontational. They acknowledged that everyone in the community around death row had to choose their own path. Theirs was leading to the streets.

On August 10, 2019, just days before Stephen West's scheduled execution, a group of twenty or so circled up in a parking lot near Riverbend. It was early morning still, but not too early for the heat and humidity that would follow them, intensifying as they got closer to the governor's office. Reporting for The Intercept, Liliana Segura quoted Dan's message to the marchers.

"We're marching to offer the governor a holy moment."[4]

Dan and Bethany and many of the others there had experienced such moments with the men on death row—moments of prayer and intimate friendship. They had prayed with Don Johnson on his final Monday night. They were challenging the governor, yes, but also inviting him into something that had changed their lives.

Yet even as they walked the invitation to his door, they must've known he would likely not accept.

18

Stephen West was weeping in the arms of the electric chair, and I was sitting in the viewing gallery on the other side of that awful window through which I had watched two executions before. To my left was one of his relatives, whose name I never learned. And next to her was Stephen's attorney, Justyna Scalpone, who had been in the execution chamber with him just minutes earlier. We'd heard her, sounding like she was fighting tears, telling him, "We all love you."

The curtains had opened at 7:15 p.m. to reveal Stephen, bald and barefooted, strapped into the chair and flanked by two prison guards. He scanned the room and seemed to lock eyes with his attorney, who mouthed something to him. Then the warden, standing in the chamber in his black suit for the fifth time in just over a year, asked Stephen if he had any last words.

"Yes, sir," Stephen said, holding back the emotion that soon overcame him. "In the beginning, God created man. And Jesus wept. That's all."

The tears came then. He was sobbing. I wondered then, why weren't we all?

■ ■ ■

The men on death row and the people who visited him there knew him as Steve. By the time I sat down to watch his execution, I had read the court records and his application for clemency. I'd become familiar with what one psychiatrist cited by his attorneys called the "waking nightmare that is his life." It was a unique terror, but one that rhymed with all the others.

Steve spent the overwhelming majority of his life in the custody of people who wished him dead. His mother, Wanda, attempted suicide by gas inhalation while she was pregnant with him in 1962. She gave birth to him in a mental institution where she'd been committed, and it was his aunt who named him after picking up the newborn from the institution. Another aunt told Steve's attorneys that Wanda once told her, "If I could kill him and get away with it, I would."[1]

His mother's mental illness was combined with alcoholism and her husband—who was actually Steve's biological uncle and would later admit that he and Wanda abused Steve in an affidavit[2]—was also a heavy drinker. They neglected their children when they weren't beating them. One of Steve's aunts remembered how he was often kept in a back room. His older sisters would sneak food to him and as a small child he would hide under the bed trying to determine what was coming through the door for him. If it was "little feet" he would get food but if it was "big feet," he'd get beaten.[3]

Steve's mother once hit him with a broom so hard that it broke, his aunt said; another recalled a separate incident when Wanda grabbed her son by his feet and slammed him against a wall, causing him to bleed and throw up.[4] After a trip to the hospital, he was back to the house where his mother continued to torture him, withholding food and even making him sit naked in front of their house in the snow as a punishment.[5]

At one point, when he was younger than five years old, Steve also told his aunt that he'd been raped by a man in the house.

His mental disturbances started to appear early too; his attorneys wrote that he recalled hearing voices in his head and experiencing periods of dissociation as a young boy. One way his posttraumatic stress manifested, they wrote, was that he would freeze in fight-or-flight situations. A psychologist who evaluated Steve in 2019 determined that he had nine of the ten Adverse Childhood Experiences (ACEs) identified as significantly contributing to poor outcomes for adults. The only reason he didn't have all ten is because his sexual abuse could not be entirely confirmed.[6]

The psychologist wrote that Steve's parents put him on a "trajectory that would lead to major mental illness . . . and trauma-related diagnoses . . . that would put him at risk for the circumstances of becoming involved in a horrific and senseless crime."[7]

And that's what happened on March 17, 1986, when Steve, then twenty-three, and a seventeen-year-old co-worker named Ronnie Martin finished their shifts at a McDonald's in Lake City, Tennessee. After hours of drinking and smoking marijuana, they ended up at the home of the Romines family. They went inside with Wanda Romines, fifty-one, and Sheila, her fifteen-year-old daughter. Steve didn't know the Romines, but Ronnie knew the family because he'd tried to date Sheila and been rejected. At some point that morning, they raped Sheila before Ronnie stabbed her and her mother to death. Wanda and Sheila were found with their arms tied behind their back; Sheila had been stabbed seventeen times.[8]

Steve was tried first and confessed to raping fifteen-year-old Sheila, although he said Ronnie had coerced him into doing so. But the two men were tried separately, with Steve going first. Steve's jury never heard a tape of Ronnie admitting that he was the one who stabbed Wanda Romines and her daughter to death.[9] When Steve was asked at his trial why he didn't try to stop the killing, he said only, "I couldn't do nothing."[10] Decades later, his attorneys argued that he froze up in that moment, just as he had during other violent, traumatic moments in his life.

The jury also never heard about the horrible and damaging abuse Steve suffered at the hands of his parents.[11] In the end, Steve was sentenced to death, but Ronnie was sentenced to life and will be eligible for parole in 2030.

Tennessee is one of twenty-seven states that allow the execution of people convicted of involvement in a violent felony that resulted in a victim's death, even if they didn't kill anyone themselves.[12]

■ ■ ■

Steve's first couple of years on death row were spent at the Walls just before the prison closed. Terry was already there. The two were never close, but Terry told me he cared about Steve and had some fond memories of him.

"My grandfather, grandmother, mom and other family members would visit at least once a month," Terry wrote to me in a letter after the execution. "Oftentimes [Steve's] wife Karen along with his little girls would be visiting also. My grandfather would [always] have a handful of coins for the vending machines. It never failed that my grandfather would take out all his coins and give them to those little girls that seemed to make them smile. About two weeks ago I asked Steve if he remembered it and he did. My heart aches for his children. I sure hope they are okay."[13]

Death row was also the first place that Steve's mental illness was ever diagnosed or treated. He was diagnosed with major depressive disorder with psychotic features, chronic paranoid schizophrenia, and schizoaffective disorder, according to court filings, and from 2001 until his execution he was treated with a variety of drugs that a psychiatrist hired by his attorneys described as "chemical straightjackets."[14] As Steve's execution approached, I obsessed over this fact, which seemed to me like a tacit acknowledgment that he should never be executed. If prison officials had taken him off of his drugs, surely his disturbed mental state would have been undeniable. But it was masked—straitjacketed—right up until he was strapped into the electric chair.

In the last year or so before his execution, Steve did have a regular visitor. Rudy Kalis, a former television sportscaster for WSMV in Nashville, started visiting men at Riverbend with the Christian prison ministry Men of Valor. And he'd quickly become close with Steve.

"The minute I walked in and was with him, I liked him," Rudy told me a few days before Steve's execution. "I wanted to be with him, and he became a friend. He's got a wicked sense of humor, he's a humble guy. He's a redeemed man."[15]

After decades in journalism, Rudy said he'd approached his early interactions with Steve with a reporter's skepticism. But when he asked Steve blunt questions about his childhood and his crimes, he was moved by the honest answers he got. And he'd wondered, as I had, what this man would be like without the powerful drugs he'd been on for nearly twenty years.

"I've asked him, I've said, 'What would you be like without those?' He said, 'You know, I don't know.' But he seems so normal with those, with whatever he is taking. There's a gentleness, there's a calmness about him, there's a thoughtfulness. He's very, very perceptive. If you even have a hint of a yawn, he says, 'Oh you've gotta go, you've been here too long.' He is so caring."[16]

Steve loved to talk to the old sports reporter about the Tennessee Volunteers, Rudy said, and had taken up drawing flowers.

On the day we spoke, he was still hopeful that Governor Bill Lee would make good on previous statements about his Christian faith and his support for criminal justice reform. Along with other members of Men of Valor—through which Lee himself had visited men in prison before becoming governor—Rudy had gone to speak to the governor about Steve's case.

"I could not pound him in any way," he told me. "I literally said it is such a huge, difficult decision, and he said that he takes it so very seriously, that he prays about it and wants to make the right decisions. That's all that I can ask. There's a proverb in the Bible that says,

Proverbs 21:1, it says, 'The king's heart'—or the governor's heart—'is in the hand of the Lord, and he turns it whichever way he wishes.' So all I did was say to him, 'I can sense that this is so heavy on you.' I said, 'If I, as a man of faith, if it was my decision, because I've gotten to know him, I would give him life. I can't beat you over the head as a governor, I just pray that you make the right decision.'"[17]

But the governor's heart was not turned. Two days before Steve's execution, he released a one-sentence statement announcing that he would "not be intervening."[18]

■ ■ ■

The saline solution—what would help conduct the fatal electric current—poured down Steve's face as the guards fastened a helmet on top of a soaked sea sponge on top of his shaved head. The salty accomplice mixed with the tears still leaking from his eyes. As the guards removed his glasses and wiped his face with a towel, I noticed that one of them had a tattoo on his forearm featuring the American flag and the words "We the People."

They attached the thick veil to the helmet, covering Steve's face. I have often wondered since then what it looks like from the other side of that veil. Did Steve look ahead or close his eyes and wait?

The guards soaked the sponges at Steve's ankles, then gathered their materials and left the chamber. Another man picked up a large cable and plugged it into the chair. Then, around 7:19 p.m., the exhaust fan kicked on. Did Steve know this was the last sound he would hear?

The executioner's ballet began with Steve's body rising from the chair. As the current coursed through him for twenty seconds or so, the fingers on one of his hands, gripping the arms of the chair, snapped back one-by-one into a fist until only his pinky was still pointing out. He fell back down, then rose again with the whine of the current. Then it was done.

We sat there, looking at the dead body that used to be Steve

West. The chair held him, and we leaned forward to be sure he was not breathing. He did not appear to be. I looked into the execution chamber and saw something I hadn't noticed before. There was another window over the chair's left shoulder. I saw my reflection in it, my face hovering there next to Steve's body. We the people.

At 7:25 p.m., the curtains were closed. Two minutes later, the warden announced the time of death and told us to leave.

As we left the viewing room and started to make our way out of the prison, Steve's attorney, Justyna, handed me a printed statement from Steve's legal team and asked me to read it at the press conference and share it with the other reporters.

We kept walking out, quiet, and I felt sad and angry and tired. What had we just watched? A man who grew up poor, hungry, abused, and mentally ill, put to a violent death by low-paid prison employees while the state's most powerful officials, Attorney General Herbert Slatery and Governor Bill Lee, stayed far away. Slatery sent a deputy to witness the executions he sought, and Lee had nothing to say when it was finished.

Most of the close relatives of Wanda and Sheila Romines, including Wanda's husband (Sheila's father) Jack, had died since their murders. But Eddie Campbell, Jack's nephew, had spoken to Knoxville's WBIR in 2018 about how painful the decades had been.

"Jack would have done it himself if he could," he said. "He was never able to get over it. It devastated him his entire life. And he had to relive his wife and daughter's death over and over his entire life, every time there was another appeal or delay in West's execution. If you're going to have the death penalty, have the death penalty. If you are not going to have it, don't have it. But just make it one way or the other. Leaving families in limbo for thirty years is not how the justice system should work."[19]

Outside under the white tent, the Tennessee Department of Correction's spokesperson Dorinda Carter read a statement from Campbell:

As for the execution of Mr. Stephen West, I am deeply sorry that
any of his family had to go through such a horrible experience. I
hope that he has made peace with God and has truly asked God for
forgiveness for such a heinous crime that he was a part of. One of the
worst things about this execution of Mr. West is that Mr. Ronnie
Martin was not also included in the same punishment. Our family
has suffered very deeply over the past 33 years through all the appeals
that we think is very unfair for anyone to have to go through, when
all the proof in the world was there for the case to be over in 24 hours
let alone 33 years. I realize there are other families going through
some of the same feelings and punishment that my family and I have
had to experience very needlessly. Something in our Judicial system
has to be done to put a stop to all this needless suffering for families
of prolonged justice. I just wish that my Uncle Jack Romines, the
father and husband of the two people that [meant] the most to him
in his life and [were] so brutally murdered on March 17, 1986, could
have lived long enough to know that the State of Tennessee finally
brought justice in part for his loss. Uncle Jack passed away with a
massive heart attack on February 25, 2008, he was only 69 years old
and had to live without his wife and daughter for the last 22 years of
his life, but told me almost every day how he missed them. I realized
that 1 day or 22 years without a loved one is horrible enough, but
having to go through all the reminders of the Court of Appeals and
not knowing if justice will ever come or not is just too much for
victims' families to have to deal with. I just hope and pray that our
Judicial system in Tennessee will consider the feelings of the victims'
families that are still living in such a horrible situation and try and
bring a speedy and correct justice to not only the families, but to the
State of Tennessee as well. Most of our family is now deceased, but
I have forgiveness in my heart for Mr. West and Mr. Martin, but I
don't think that justice should be ignored. On behalf of my Uncle
Jack Romines and the remaining members of our family I hope this
statement will be published in its entirety and not just in parts.[20]

When it was my turn to speak, I read the statement from Steve's legal team.

"We are deeply disappointed that the State of Tennessee has gone forward with the execution of a man whom the State has diagnosed with severe mental illness; a man of deep faith who has made a positive impact on those around him for decades; and a man who by overwhelming evidence did not commit these murders but has nevertheless taken personal responsibility for his involvement in these crimes. We don't believe the decisions of the courts and ultimately the Governor reflect the forgiving and merciful citizens of this State."

I shared a few observations from the execution before answering a couple of questions. I'd not really thought about what I was going to say, but after answering one question about the differences between witnessing a lethal injection and witnessing an electrocution, I went on:

"The only other thing I would say is, I don't think I'll be coming out to another one of these. I think it's very important that people bear witness to these and that's why it's meant a lot to me to do it and why I've felt strongly about it. But I think I'll probably be taking a break. Maybe the governor or someone can take my seat if they want, but I think I'm probably done for now."

In that moment, I wished I could erase the nightmarish knowledge I had acquired, and I felt like the people who'd decided these killings were necessary should be the ones holding it. I felt what I deemed a righteous indignation—manifested in a somewhat smart-ass comment—at a multi-millionaire governor who had traded on his faith in a redemptive Christ during his campaign for office, only to sign off on the executions of men claiming that same redemption or suffering from profound mental illness. Was he even awake to watch our press conference?

Later in the month, Kimberlee Kruesi, a local Associated Press reporter who had witnessed one execution and would soon witness another, asked the governor about witnessing one himself.

"I've certainly thought about if I would, but I have not felt compelled to do it," he said.[21]

But if I'm honest, I was wrestling with more than just the governor's distance from the executions his signature approved as I left the prison that night. I felt uneasy about the compulsion I'd felt to voluntarily witness these state killings. I believed what I'd said about the importance of bearing witness, but I'd also started to question my motives for raising my hand. There is something in the reporter—the writer—that drives them to see something dramatic, something significant, something violent, and to be the one who gets to tell everyone else about it—to get the big assignment. I felt unsettled about the fact that this drive, which was, I suppose, a positive professional attribute, had led me here.

My wife had been upset with me when I told her that I'd volunteered to witness a third execution. I had done it without thinking more than twice, and I hadn't told her beforehand. But she had seen the toll these nights were taking on me more clearly than I could at the time and, I think, had begun to see it as a sort of psychological recklessness on my part. When that bill came due that night outside the prison, it did not occur to me that its cost was in large part due to the proximity I had gained to the people facing execution; that I was becoming more than just a reporter in relation to the men on death row and that this had intensified the trauma of seeing and anticipating their executions.

I had been to Riverbend on Monday night, for visitation, and on Thursday night, for executions, and I was now absolutely convinced that someone who had experienced one would see their worldview shattered by the other.

19

Less than two weeks after Steve's execution, a rare victory came in a Nashville courtroom.

The city's district attorney, Glenn Funk, stood before a judge and declared that he could not stand by a death sentence won by his predecessor. Seated to his left at the defense table was Abu-Ali Abdur'Rahman, one of the men David Bass had met during his first visit to death row, who was then facing an execution date less than eight months away. He wore glasses, a silver cross around his neck, shackles around his arms and legs, and the same Tennessee Department of Correction uniform he'd be wearing to the death chamber if he made it there. He'd come close before, even going to death watch in 2002. But now a prosecutor was saying he shouldn't go back.

In some ways, Abu's story, depressingly, blended in on death row. As a boy—born James Lee Jones Jr.—he struggled with mental illness and suffered brutal physical and sexual abuse. Once, his half-sister would later testify, his father hanged him in a closet by tying a wet piece of leather around his penis and attaching the other end to a clothing hook.[1] He spent most of his life in mental health institutions or prisons. In 1972, during a stint in a federal prison when he was in his early twenties, he killed a man who'd allegedly raped him and threatened to do it again.[2]

It was in the mid-1980s that Abu moved to Nashville and joined a radical Black religious group called the Southern Gospel Ministry. Among other things, the organization took an aggressive approach to cleaning up the neighborhood. Amidst the nationwide crack epidemic, they were particularly focused on ridding the community of drug dealers.

"We were trying to get a list of thorns in the black community—the drug dealers, the pimps or the numbers runners," Abu told the *Nashville Scene* in 2001. "Once we found out who they were, our intention was to run them out of the community."[3]

In February of 1986, Abu and a man named Harold Miller went out with a plan to run off a drug dealer named Patrick Daniels who'd been selling to area teens. Daniels ended up stabbed to death and his girlfriend, Norma Jean Norman, was attacked too. Her daughters, then eight and nine, hid in a bedroom and would later recall their mother crawling in with a knife still in her back and asking them to call for help.

Abu conceded to authorities that he'd been at the scene, but said he had no memory of the attack—not an implausible claim given his history of dissociation and blackouts. From then on, his attorney Bradley MacLean would later tell me, as I covered the looming execution for the *Scene*, "Everything that could go wrong in a capital case went wrong in Abu's case."[4]

The most glaring was the stunning inadequacy of his defense, which his trial attorney, Lionel Barrett, would later admit. He told the *ABA Journal* in 2011 that he did "everything I could have done wrong."

"Abu-Ali is on death row because of me," he said. "I failed him. I have no excuse. This is the only case in my entire career that I would do anything to be able to do over again."[5]

So heavy was the weight of that failure that it led Barrett to leave the law altogether. It also led a federal judge to set aside Abu's death sentence, although that decision was later reversed. Crucially, MacLean would later argue, it allowed the prosecution to get away with misconduct, including suppressing evidence the defense was entitled to.

In a 2016 motion, MacLean singled out the jury selection process. There, he said, prosecutor John Zimmermann relied on "false, racist stereotyping" of Black people to strike two Black prospective jurors. Bolstering the notion that Zimmermann would bring racist ideas to jury selection, MacLean pointed to a 2015 letter from Funk to the Tennessee District Attorneys General Conference in which the current DA disavowed comments he said Zimmermann made at an annual conference.

"Specifically, Mr. Zimmermann described prosecuting a conspiracy case with all Hispanic defendants," Funk wrote in the letter. "He stated he wanted an all African American jury, because 'all Blacks hate Mexicans.'"[6]

In response to MacLean's filing, Nashville Criminal Court Judge Monte Watkins had granted a hearing. A court date had never been scheduled. But now there had been a breakthrough.

I sat in the jury box with several other reporters watching as MacLean made his case, one which Funk did not dispute when he addressed the court. In the gallery sat victims' family members, death row visitors, and other observers.

"Overt racial bias has no place in the justice system," Funk said, going on to add that "the pursuit of justice is incompatible with deception. Prosecutors must never be dishonest to or mislead defense attorneys, courts or juries."[7]

With that he announced that he was proposing an agreed-upon order that would vacate Abu's death sentence but keep him in prison for the rest of his life. He went on to explain that he'd discussed this resolution with the family members of the two victims in the case.

"Last week and yesterday I spoke with George Daniels, the brother of murder victim Patrick Daniels," Funk said. "He advised that he would still like to 'burn his ass' and in a separate comment he stated that he wants this case to be over to finally have closure. He vowed 32 years ago to honor his brother by seeing this case to the end. I also spoke with Norma Jean Norman last weekend and yesterday who was the victim, in count two, of the stabbing. Her position is that she is at peace and has forgiven Mr. Abdur'Rahman but she does not want him to ever be released from prison. I spoke with [Norman's two daughters] and they still bear the emotional scars of being children cowering in a bedroom and hearing the murder of Patrick Daniels and then having to see their mother crawl into their bedroom with the butcher knife still stuck in her back . . . These women do not exactly share their mother's forgiveness of Mr. Abdur'Rahman but they are supportive of her position."[8]

Several days later, after the judge signed off on the order, Katrina and Shawanna Norman spoke to reporters outside the courtroom. For many years, Shawanna said, she and her sister wouldn't even keep knives of any kind in their homes. Although they weren't as forgiving as their mother, they did feel relief that the case—which had dragged on for three decades, reaching out to grab them over the years by way of notices from prosecutors in the mailbox—would finally be over. And they reserved some anger for the prosecutor whose misconduct had led to so much legal back and forth.

Also, among those in the courtroom to see Abu's death sentence removed had been Linda Manning, a Vanderbilt University professor who'd been visiting Abu for nineteen years. When she'd first started going to see him back then, he'd been just six months away from an execution date, and his attorneys believed it could well be carried out. At the time he had no visitors, and she thought it would be a short bit of kindness. Nearly twenty years and at least two more near-death episodes later, she was still faithfully going to see Abu on death row.[9]

When I spoke to her, I was struck with the idea that, although she would continue visiting Abu, she would never have to go to Unit 2 again. That was naive.

Three weeks after the Nashville judge signed the order vacating Abu's death sentence, Tennessee Attorney General Herbert Slatery announced that his office would be appealing the order and fighting to see Abu executed on April 16, 2020, as scheduled.[10] And on the very same day, Slatery's office asked the Tennessee Supreme Court to set execution dates for nine more men, including the four remaining death row prisoners from Nashville.[11]

The attorney general's office can seek execution dates for condemned prisoners once they've exhausted their appeals—in fact, the attorney general's office argues they are required to do so. But the reason behind the timing of the requests and the men for whom they sought dates remained opaque. And to some observers—myself very much included—the move smacked of retribution.

With the state now fighting one of its own local prosecutors over Abu's death sentence, the Tennessee Supreme Court called off his execution date.[12] Abu was once again in limbo. Eventually, however, Funk proposed a new order thought to be on more solid legal ground. The judge signed off on it again, and this time, although the attorney general made it clear that he disagreed with the deal, he decided against appealing it further.

Abu would one day die in prison, but never see the inside of the death chamber.

20

I got on Terry's phone list in the fall after what turned out to be a bit of an ordeal. I first gave the prison the phone number for my desk at work, but that was rejected as it would constitute contacting the media. I then supplied my cell phone number, but it too was rejected—I still had the Florida area code of my youth and was told it would be considered a long-distance call. Finally, I got a new cell phone and replaced my old number with a local Nashville number.

One morning not long after that, I was driving my daughters to preschool, my phone rang showing a number I didn't recognize. I answered and was greeted by an automated female voice.

"Hello, this is a prepaid debit call from . . . "

She paused for a recording of Terry introducing himself—"Terry King"—before continuing.

". . . an inmate at the Tennessee Department of Correction's Riverbend Maximum Security Institution. To accept this call, press zero."

I pressed zero and, after the robot operator reminded me that our call may be monitored or recorded, there was Terry.

"Well, hello there."

We chatted, present in each other's lives in a whole new way—his voice in the car with me, mine in the prison with him. When I parked in the preschool parking lot, Terry noted that I must have stopped driving. After years away from the sounds of the outside world, he explained, his ears had become especially attuned to such things. My daughters sat in the back seat, singing to themselves, and he heard that too.

"Thank you for letting me hear that," he said.

■ ■ ■

In a letter, Terry described the day in February of 1985 when he arrived at the Walls and walked in shackles to death row:

> Trying to walk with all the chains wrapped around me was difficult to say the least. Being escorted by two police officers, I was led into the castle.
>
> "Is this King?" the big man yelled.
>
> "Yes!" responded the officers.
>
> Standing there with everyone looking on was a small group of school kids touring the prison.
>
> "All right, out of the way," the big man said to the kids. "We have one going to death row."
>
> Instantly, fear was on the faces of all those children. While being led away I thought, "I wonder what they are thinking." I never saw them again.
>
> Being led into the small flat-top building seemed like going inside a tomb. The smell of the building inside smelled like paint, cleaning materials and DEATH! "I'm never coming out of here," was my first thought inside the building. "I need to call someone." Upon entering the hallway while being led to the cell that was assigned to me, I asked the officer, "could I use the telephone?"

"When it's put on the rock, son!" replied the officer.

I called my family and after minutes of crying with them on the phone I began to assure them that things would work out . . . don't worry, I said, I have appeals.

I am told, by Terry and others, that I would not recognize the man who arrived on death row that day. One attorney who worked with him soon afterward told me that back then, Terry was young and brash and "wasn't worth the powder it would've taken to blow him away." He was a cocky young man who hadn't come close to reckoning with what he'd done.

He settled into his cell, number eleven on the first of four rows. In those early years, he would go out to the yard—an encaged concrete slab—and play handball or lift weights. He became friends with Ed Zagorski, the barrel of a man he came to know as Diamond Jim. Once, during a pickup basketball game, Ed fell sideways into Terry's knee, leaving Terry in a heap on the ground with torn ligaments. A prison doctor operated on the knee but only made things worse. With the help of Joe Ingle, Terry was brought to an outside hospital where his knee was repaired. He was hospitalized for around a week, with good food and nurses caring for him—a vacation for a man on death row.[1]

Looking back years later, Terry would feel some nostalgia for the old prison, despite its dungeon-like atmosphere. Compared to the constant surveillance made possible by myriad cameras at Riverbend, the Walls offered privacy and various quirks that made life there less mundane. An enormous population of cats, for instance, took up residence underneath the infirmary, and Terry used to love sitting outside and throwing bread to them, watching as they sped toward it like fish to a crumb in a pond.

But a heavy depression was Terry's regular companion during his four years at the Walls. He was clear-headed enough to know the depths of the trouble he was in but not mature or repentant enough to live as a new man. He existed in a valley between who he'd been and who he would become.

"What began in the summer of 1983 was the ending to several chapters of different people's life," he wrote during that time in a short essay he sent to me. "I never knew that such violence, anger, and rage could consume me during a few short weeks, but what transpired during that short period would take years to finally reach an end."[2]

■ ■ ■

It took the better part of three decades by Terry's estimation for him to become an altogether different person than the one who'd been consumed by violence and anger and rage.

It started in January 2011, when a friend of his gave him *The Shack*. The novel, in which a man named Mack faces a crisis of faith after the murder of his young daughter, then meets the Father, the Son, and the Holy Spirit in the form of a Black woman, a Middle Eastern carpenter, and an Asian woman, became a sensation, stirring praise and controversy among the faithful. In one chapter, Mack comes into contact with Sophia, a personification of God's wisdom, who confronts Mack about the way he judges others and exposes the shallow nature of his judgments. To Terry, it was a revelation.

"Here in Unit 2, there were a few men convicted of killing children," he wrote to me in a letter, "and I had always looked at them with contempt and never [allowed] myself to even get to really know who they were because I was better than them because I hadn't done *that*."

The book's allegory triggered a spiritual experience for him that years of hard time had not.

"Being trapped in that 10' × 12' cell I was forced to look at who I was," he wrote to me. "The words of my grandmother [slapped me] right in the face. 'You will be forced to cry out to the good LORD.' . . . Sadly, for the first time since my incarceration and conviction I realized that I had taken the life of one of God's children."

The experience changed his life in tangible ways. The next year he started giving money to a small country church that his grandmother used to attend. He'd never given a cent to a church before in his life, but he started giving ten dollars a month, sometimes twenty-five or fifty dollars. And he believed that not his money but his faithfulness led to what happened next.

In his letter to me, Terry referenced the Book of Malachi, specifically Malachi 3:8–10, in which God tells a prophet to test him by bringing all the tithes and offerings into the storehouse, and seeing if God will not "pour out so much blessing that there will not be room enough to store it."

To Terry's mind, it was no coincidence that in June 2013—while he happened to be studying the Book of Malachi as part of a monthly devotional provided to men on the row by the Seventh-day Adventist Church—he received a letter, many pages long, from a woman named Mary. Slowly, over the course of those many pages, she explained who she was and why she was writing.[3]

Decades earlier, Mary wrote, when she was just fourteen, she'd met a handsome older boy. He was kind and caring and they started spending more and more time together. When she was fifteen, he told her he loved her. She loved him too. But as she got older, she grew restless, and despite his protests, she left their little town and him behind. He would write her letters and even visit her mom in an effort to get her to come back. Eventually, he joined the Army in what he said was an attempt to forget her.

Their roles reversed, and soon she found she was desperate for him to return. She called the Army base where he was in basic training and told him that she was sorry she ever left and that she still loved him. He told her he'd never stopped. They rekindled their relationship and looked forward to the day they would be reunited.

Only that day never came. Mary was seventeen when she got a call from her mother telling her that the boy she loved was dead. Not only that—he'd been murdered. The details were sketchy. He'd gotten a ride from two men who apparently robbed him, killed him, and buried him in a shallow grave.

It all came crashing in on Terry. Mary had been in love with Todd, the young soldier who he and his friend had met that awful night. The young man they'd killed.

"Yes," she wrote, "The man you and Joe Sexton murdered without any thought for him, me, his brother, father, mother and all others. That 19-year-old man Todd Lee Millard was my love, my life, my future, and he was taken away from me before he could return to me."

It turned out that Mary's sister had recently gotten a text message from Mary telling her that she'd found a thirty-year-old letter from Todd that had never been opened. The unopened letter had been moved from home to home in various states. The discovery prompted Mary to Google Todd's name and to read the details of his murder. She came across Terry's name and decided to write to him, tearing up several drafts before settling on the one she finally sent.

The letter was blunt and unsparing but also, to Terry's bewilderment, gracious.

"I'm sad for you," she wrote, "and I write to tell you I forgive you and that the Todd I knew and love to this day, he would want me to tell you he forgives you."

Mary and Terry began corresponding, and eventually she even moved to Nashville from Minnesota so that she could visit him. During their first visit she held his hand, looked him in the eye, and told him again, "I forgive you." But it was something else she told him that affected him just as much. She told him it was time for him to forgive himself.

After I had gotten to know Terry and heard his story, I reached out to the family of Diana Smith, the woman he'd killed that summer in 1983. Years earlier, with Terry's permission, an investigator working for his attorneys had gone to see Leonard Smith, Diana's husband at the time of her murder, to see if he wanted to talk to the defense team or to Terry. He did not. By the time I contacted the family, Leonard Smith was long remarried, and his children had grown well into adulthood without their mother. I spoke to his wife. She told me that he was in poor health and expressed frustration at the fact that he might not live to see Terry's death sentence carried out. I told her that I wanted to give her husband or anyone else in the family the chance to talk about Diana and the case and she said that they would contact me again if they decided they wanted to speak. In the end, they did not.

■ ■ ■

The Terry I'd come to know had been shaped by all that, the sins and the forgiveness of sins. He was now one of the longest tenured men on the row, part of a community that defied its location. When new men arrived on the row, Terry and others would put together a sort of welcoming package for them, a few necessities to help ease the transition into Unit 2.

But the knowledge that such a community existed in such a place was weighted by the fact that the state was intent on killing all its members. The visitors had attached themselves to a group of people meant to meet a violent end. At this point, so had I. And that realization could be anxiety provoking.

One Monday night after a visit to the prison, David Bass and I went to dinner at a nearby Mexican restaurant. An NFL game played on the television above our table as we ate chips and salsa, and David confessed to me that he sometimes wondered if he'd made a mistake by letting himself and some of his children get so close to death row and to Terry. He was conflicted. Terry was one of his best friends, and yet, because of that, he feared that if Terry were executed, he might not recover from it.

In the end, we agreed that the beauty of these unique and radical relationships was worth the trauma that was likely to result. Or at least we agreed to keep believing so.

21

The state of Tennessee was preparing to execute a blind man.

Lee Hall would not see clearly the guards approaching his cell to take him to death watch. He would not get a good look at his last meal. And in what was either a small final blessing or an additional final curse, he would not take in the sight of the execution chamber. He would shuffle blind into the last room he would ever enter alive.

His attorneys blamed prison officials for the loss of his vision. In a 2018 court filing they wrote that Lee had been hospitalized in 2010 with glaucoma which had previously gone undiagnosed and untreated. In the years since, they wrote, prison officials had "routinely failed to comply with the directions and recommendations" of his doctors. They added that Lee's scheduled visits to the eye clinic had been regularly delayed or ignored. Now he was "blind and vulnerable," they wrote. Referencing the Supreme Court precedent that ostensibly prohibits executing "the insane," they argued that "the spectacle of his execution—guiding him to the gurney—would 'offend humanity.'" As far as they could tell, he would be just the second blind person executed in the death penalty's modern era.[1]

What could not be disputed, though, was that nearly thirty years earlier, long before he became "blind and vulnerable," he'd burned his estranged girlfriend alive. Traci Crozier, then twenty-two, had recently broken up with Lee, leaving what family members would later describe to reporters as an abusive relationship. Traci moved out of the trailer they'd shared and started living with family. But Lee would not let her go. He called the home frequently late at night. Once, court documents said, he came to the house and lit Traci's car on fire. Less than two weeks later, around midnight on April 16, 1991, Lee did it again, only this time with Traci in the car. After an argument, he stuffed a paper towel into a container full of gasoline, lit the crude fuse, and tossed it onto Traci in the front seat. A neighbor came to her aid, court documents said, pulling her from the car and helping to extinguish the flames that were engulfing her body and melting her hair and skin. Horrifically, Traci remained alert enough to worry to the neighbor about her appearance and to identify the man who'd set her on fire—Lee Hall. She survived until the next day.[2]

At his trial, Lee said he'd never meant to kill Traci, only to burn her car in anger. He also said that since she'd left him, he'd been drinking heavily and smoking crack. His attorneys would later note that Lee "broke down sobbing uncontrollably during medical testimony" about how Traci had suffered.[3]

This provided little comfort to Traci's surviving family, though. They supported Lee's death sentence and waited decades to see it carried out. If Lee's blindness meant his execution would be worse, it seemed like justice to them.

"So that when that juice is going in his arm, he won't even know when it is going to hit," Traci's sister Staci Wooten told the *Chattanooga Times Free Press* in 2014. "And he has to suffer while he sits there and wonders. The longer, the better. Traci had to suffer, and now he needs to suffer."[4]

He was about to. But his real execution would be slightly different from the just end Staci imagined, or the offensive spectacle his attorneys had described. When the time came to choose between lethal injection and the electric chair, he chose the latter.

■ ■ ■

I never met Lee, but I knew of him. He was one of Terry's best friends on the row. And because Lee had remained close with his own mother and brother, he could occasionally be seen in the visitation gallery with them. That's where Dan and Bethany Mann were on Thanksgiving Day, bringing a holiday meal to Larry and Abu-Ali, when they unexpectedly met Lee. Abu had helped him out to the gallery where he was planning to have a final visit with his family.

Dan told me later, with awe and sadness, how a stray comment about the Hall of Fame pitcher Nolan Ryan triggered an enthusiastic conversation about baseball with Lee, who had an encyclopedic knowledge of the sport.

"It was like an uncle or a nephew you'd have a conversation with over Thanksgiving dinner," Dan told me.[5] I thought of the picture of Lee his attorneys had sent me to use with stories about his upcoming execution. It showed him smiling in an Atlanta Braves hat.

Soon, Lee's family arrived—his stepfather, mother, and brother. Dan recalled to me how Lee's brother handed chocolate bars to Lee, describing them so that Lee, who could not see them, knew what he was about to eat. As visiting hours came to a close, one week before Lee would be strapped into the electric chair, he and his family stood together to take a picture, a privilege only allowed on state holidays.

Several days later, on Monday night, I went to see Terry at the prison where the atmosphere was once again weighted by an imminent execution. Terry was feeling heavy too. He told me how he'd seen Lee before coming out for our visit. They'd embraced and said they loved each other, before Terry had to walk away to keep his composure. To Terry, a good man was about to be killed for no good reason. Terry told me he'd be perfectly comfortable having Lee live next door to one of his family members, so convinced was he that Lee was not who he'd once been.

Terry had also become convinced that his friend was about to receive a stay from the courts. A week earlier, the Tennessee Court of Criminal Appeals had ordered a new trial for a former death row prisoner named Hubert Glenn Sexton, who'd been convicted in 2001 for the murders of Stanley and Terry Sue Goodman. His death sentence had been previously set aside because of errors at his trial including improper striking of jurors, improper admission of evidence, and improper comments by the prosecution. But the appellate court had now determined that he was entitled to a new trial because two jurors had not disclosed that they were victims of domestic violence, denying him a fair and impartial jury.

There turned out to be a similar issue in Lee's case. In a nearly eleventh-hour filing with the Tennessee Supreme Court, Lee's attorneys sought a stay of his execution based on the recent admission by one of his trial jurors that she had been raped and abused by her husband. The juror said that she "hated" Lee because of her experience.[6]

If there was any justice in the system, Terry believed, Lee would get some relief. But for now, the process continued as planned, moving Lee ever closer to the death chamber. After our visit, Terry went back into the unit. He and others helped Lee gather up the things in his cell, doing for their friend the final tasks he could not do for himself. Around midnight, the guards came to lead him in the dark to death watch.

I did not know how to respond to Terry's optimism about Lee's chances or how to feel about them myself. Any kind of helpful intervention from this court or this governor seemed unlikely to me. At the same time, Terry's view of the legal issue involved didn't seem wrong. His manic belief that legal relief for Lee was imminent calls to mind a passage from Viktor Frankl's *Man's Search for Meaning*, a book I later read at Terry's urging.

"In psychiatry there is a condition known as the illusion of reprieve," Frankl writes. "The condemned man immediately before his execution gets the illusion that he might be reprieved at the very last minute."[7]

There was a vicarious form of this illusion, in my experience, in which the whole community around death row became gripped with the belief—or the hope, at least—that an execution would be called off. Of course, reprieves were real. Courts and governors did sometimes intervene. But in Tennessee, five men had been executed in a little more than a year, giving little reason to believe there wouldn't be a sixth.

And so it was. The day after my visit with Terry, the Tennessee Supreme Court rejected Lee's request for a stay. A day later, Governor Bill Lee announced that he would not stop the execution.[8] Terry called me that afternoon.

"[Lee] is the most kindest, meekest, forgiving human being I believe I've ever met," he told me. "That's just a fact, a fact that they can't change. Someone who did a bad thing. A horrible thing. But I just, I don't get it. Killing people to show that killing is wrong."[9]

He insisted on preserving a fuller image of his dear friend.

"I knew who he really was. I knew him. Not what the case says or whatever. That's one moment in time. That doesn't define who he is as a human being. It doesn't. And it never will. It might to some people, because they want to define him by that. But that's not who he is by any stretch of the imagination."

Terry had known Lee for more than twenty-five years, and without Lee, Terry would not have one of the most important relationships in his life. Terry had been married once while on the row, to a woman he'd met through Lee. The marriage, perhaps not surprisingly, didn't last. But Terry's relationship with her son, Eric—who was just a toddler when they met—did. More than twenty years later, they remained close, and Terry credited Lee with that gift.

His friendship with Lee was extraordinary because of the location in which it had developed but ordinary in most every other way. They'd been there for each other and made meals together, getting creative with ingredients they bought from the commissary. Once, Terry and another friend had made a customized Georgia Bulldogs wooden frame for Lee's brother, who was a big fan. Lee knew that Terry was a lifelong Buffalo Bills fan.

With Lee on death watch, Terry told me he couldn't stop thinking about him. He was grateful, though, that he'd gotten the chance to be there for his friend one last time. Lee's mother had called Terry's attorneys to send a message to Terry. Could he help make sure that Lee's family got copies of their final photo together? Terry had made arrangements to make sure it happened.

"You know what I hope for out of all this?" Terry later told me on the phone. "I hope that the victim's family has some sort of closure. But I don't believe they will have. And the reason I say that is, their loved one is still gone. If he dies tomorrow, true, he will no longer live on this earth. And maybe there's some comfort in that with them. But their loved one is still gone. And that's what's gonna always be missing in their life, the void of their loved one not being there. And I don't see how killing him is going to change that. Because at the end of the day, even if he's dead, they're still gonna be gone. And as sad as that is, and it is sad. It is sad that young girl lost her life. It's horrible. You know, no one in their right mind could say what happened was good. Like the things that I've done—nothing about any of that is good. But for heaven's sakes, if killing somebody all of a sudden brings about closure and that sort of thing, then you gotta wonder . . . "

He paused.

"I just wonder if that's really gonna happen. I don't know that it will."

The following evening, outside Riverbend, an armed officer leaned down toward my open driver-side window.

"You been here before? You know the drill?"

I did. It was the sixth time I'd driven out to the prison for an execution and the third night on which I'd gone to join the small group that gathered in the field outside the prison. Everyone knew their role in the grim drama by now.

It was around 6:30 p.m. Inside the prison, the witnesses were making their way to the execution chamber. Reporters were there to watch, but so were family members. Lee's brother was there and so was Traci Crozier's sister, Staci.

Outside, in the field, the regular assemblage of death penalty opponents—activists and death row visitors—were holding their vigil. On the other side of the fence, five people stood in support of the execution. They had with them a large photo of Traci and one of them was dressed in priestly robes with rainbow-colored lights draped around his neck. I'd entered the field around the same time as him and watched as the officers at the security checkpoint flipped through the oversized Bible he'd brought with him.

It was cold and the evening's bite seemed to slow the terrible minutes. A generator hummed as the group worked through a liturgy under the flood lights, led by the Reverend Matthew Lewis. The young priest from Christ Church Cathedral, an Episcopalian church in downtown Nashville, had served as Lee's spiritual adviser as the execution date approached. Standing in the doorway of Lee's cell, during their final moments together, he'd read one of his favorite Biblical passages from Romans 8.

"For I am convinced that neither death nor life, neither angels nor demons, neither the present nor the future, nor any powers, neither height nor depth, nor anything else in all creation, will be able to separate us from the love of God that is in Christ Jesus our Lord."

The reverend later joined others in recording final audio messages for Lee, who was not able to read letters.

In the field, the vigil continued with readings and prayers. They declared many complicated truths, about who Lee was now but also about what he'd done many years ago. They prayed for Traci Crozier and for her family. At one point, as the group waited for news from inside the prison, John Dysinger—whose family had faithfully visited Don Johnson for years—asked everyone to join him in singing "Soon and Very Soon," the hymn that had been Don's last.

Word came at 7:27 p.m.

"The death sentence of Lee Hall was executed by means of electrocution on December 5, 2019, in accordance with the laws of the
state of Tennessee. The sentence was carried out at the Riverbend
Maximum Security Institution in Nashville. Hall was pronounced
dead at 7:26 p.m."[10]

Soon, the witnesses would emerge from the prison and give
their accounts of the execution under the white canopy tent. They
described what they said looked like smoke coming from Hall's
shrouded head. Later, the state would tell Kimberlee Kruesi of the
Associated Press only that it was "steam and not smoke as a result of
the liquid and heat."[11]

One of Lee's attorneys read a final statement from Lee in which
he apologized to the Crozier family.

"I ask for your forgiveness, and I hope and pray that someday you
can find it in your heart to forgive me."

Lee also apologized to his own family.

"I'm sorry for the pain I've caused my brother, David, and my
mother and my family. I hope this brings peace and I don't want
them to worry about me anymore."

John Spragens, an attorney who was once a *Scene* reporter himself and had witnessed the execution, then read a statement from
Lee's family.

"We are devastated by the loss of Traci and now Lee. Lee loved
Traci more than anything, and we welcomed her into our family and
love her too," they said. "We also love Lee and wish that we could've
changed the events of that tragic day. Lee did not intend to cause her
death, nor the pain she endured. He admitted the truth and accepted
his punishment. He also accepted Jesus Christ and only wishes for
the Crozier family to accept his sincere apology and hopes they find
the peace and closure they so deserve. Lee and his family want to
extend a thank you to all the prison staff and inmates in Unit 2 for
their support and assistance to Lee through the loss of his vision.

We also want to thank all the attorneys and staff who represented him. We deeply appreciate the love and kindness that our friends and church members have shown us, and for keeping us in your prayers through these difficult times. Now we have all lost, but we find peace in knowing that they are both with the Lord. Thank you."

Traci's sister, Staci, then read a statement of her own, on behalf of Traci's family.

"The day has come and gone now. The day my family has waited on for twenty-eight years. Now our family's peace can begin, but another family's hell has to begin. Today will not bring my sister or my dad's daughter back. But now, may she find her peace in heaven with our mom. She will always be greatly missed by her family and everyone who knew her. But hopefully today, ending this monster's life will bring some peace within everyone who has had to suffer throughout these twenty-eight years without my beautiful sister. We all fought this battle for you, Traci, and today we won."

Each family acknowledged the painful truth that the execution would at best represent an exchange of grief. Another family's hell has to begin. Now we have all lost.

■ ■ ■

Terry called me nearly two weeks after Lee's execution. Bitterness at the state's killing of his friend had settled into sadness that his friend was gone. He expected the sadness would linger for some time. He said he still felt Lee's presence on the row, a feeling that could both relieve and exacerbate grief.

Unexpectedly, he'd recently gotten a piece of mail from Lee. Several days earlier, a Christmas card had arrived. Lee had asked an attorney to transcribe it and arranged for it to be sent after his execution. Terry was stunned by this act of kindness, planned as it was in Lee's final days, when an existential stress must have been weighing on him.

Although he struggled even to begin, Terry said he wanted to read me the letter.[12]

Terry,

I've known you longer than anyone here, since 1994. So I just wanted to tell you how much I appreciate your friendship. You've done a lot for me. You're like a brother to me. We've both been up and down together. We did football and baseball playoffs. I cherish a lot of those memories of knowing you. I hope you get the break you're looking for in the courts sooner or later. Thanks for everything, including introducing me to Joe Ingle. I hope you have a good holiday under any circumstances. I hope the holiday goes well for you and I hope you enjoy the concert. In Christ's love, Lee.

PS—I'm going to be pulling for your Bills all the way.

22

The best night I ever spent on death row was a Monday night in January of 2020. It came in between two executions, in the valley of the shadow of state killings where peace and foreboding coexisted. The grief of Lee's execution was giving way to stressful anticipation of the next, but in between there was space to breathe a little.

I arrived at the prison before 6 p.m. as usual, making my way through security and following a guard to Unit 2 as I had several times before. But when I got to the visitation gallery, I joined what was already a lively gathering. Terry was sitting in one of two private visitation rooms, along with several visitors sitting closely together on plastic chairs. Al was there, as were David and Spencer, David's future son-in-law. Also crammed into the small room was KB, the condemned man and ordained minister I'd heard about but never met. The energy in the room was good, so good, as if it weren't connected to a place called death row.

I took a seat next to KB, who looked down at my shoes—a pair of gray high-top Converse—and reared back in his seat, exclaiming that he liked my kicks.

I looked over and noticed his bright high-top basketball shoes. When I asked about them, he identified them proudly—Kevin Durant Nikes. I didn't know you could have those on death row.

Terry reached over and offered me a Styrofoam cup, the contents of which he identified as "prison ice cream." The cup was filled with a heaping pile of reddish pink crushed ice, almost like a snow cone. I asked him what the recipe was, and he eagerly explained.

One of the items available to men on the row from the commissary or a private company charging them exorbitant rates was Crystal Light packets. Terry liked to buy them in bulk so he'd have a supply for months. And many of the men liked to use them to make prison ice cream. The process was pretty simple, really, he explained. They would mix the Crystal Light powder with water in individual cups, then put them in the freezer. Once they were frozen, the men would dump the colored ice into a thick plastic bag and smash it on the floor, breaking up the ice, before serving it back into individual cups. Prison ice cream.

I took my cup and joined everyone else in the dessert. From then on it felt as if we could've just as easily been on my back porch. The only thing missing was a few beers. When I said as much, Terry looked at me and shook his head.

"Man, I can't imagine."

We told stories and laughed as hard as any of us had in a long while. Al told us about a family tradition he had coming up, one known as the Burning of the Christmas Village. We leaned forward, insisting that he fill us in. He explained that as his sons aged out of more childish holiday traditions, he searched for something to keep them engaged with the family during the season. Given he was dealing with teenage boys, he settled on something with fire. After one Christmas had passed, early in the new year, he purchased some small wooden houses from a hobby shop, brought them home and informed his sons that the family was going to string them together in the backyard, light them on fire and watch them burn. Unwittingly it became a tradition, and not just for their family. Neighbors had begun to join in, bringing their own gingerbread and birdhouses to burn. We roared with laughter at the dark and delightful absurdity of it all. We laughed so hard and loud that later, other visitors would ask us what had been going on in there.

Still, it was impossible to completely escape from the reality of what was up ahead. That same night, Nick Sutton was visiting with friends and family. I'd met Nick, but I only really knew him from the times he'd ambled over from his seat in the visitation gallery to say hi to me and David. Nick was a Tennessee Volunteers fan and would regularly toss a deadpan comment our way about the latest Auburn loss or Tennessee victory.

But Terry had known Nick since their days at the Walls. His stepson had played with Nick's granddaughter in the visitation gallery.

Now Nick's execution date was around a month away, and he'd started the process of saying goodbye.

■ ■ ■

Some five years earlier, Frances Christian was sitting in a service at Christ Church Cathedral in downtown Nashville when Joe Ingle got to speak about visiting death row.[1] Frances had known Joe for several decades by that point, and she was familiar with his work in prisons. But for some reason, that day, his pitch piqued her interest. She went to Joe and told him she wasn't sure she'd be able to go through with it but that she wanted to attend one of his orientations for visitors at the prison.

Later at the orientation, Joe led the group back to Riverbend's Unit 2 as he'd done with many groups before. He showed them the visitation gallery where they'd sit with men from the row on weekends or Monday nights. But on this occasion, a guard allowed the group to go back into the unit, to see where the men lived. Frances went into a cell. And when they got to the unit's small library, a man was there in his standard Tennessee Department of Correction–issued garb. It was Nick Sutton. Joe asked him to tell the group about the library and life in the unit.

"Nick could be very eloquent, and he was well read," Frances told me. "He gave a beautiful description of things. And I left thinking, 'Well you know that guy was really neat. If there are more people like that back here . . . ' I expected everybody to be Hannibal Lecter. And here was this charming, well-read host. A gracious man welcoming this group in."

By chance, when Joe informed Frances sometime later of who she'd be visiting on the row, it was Nick. She wrote Nick a letter introducing herself and he wrote back, ensuring that their first meeting would be a little bit less like a dark first date. She did not research his crimes. She knew generally what it took to get to death row and that was enough for her. The details would come out one piece at a time in conversation. During their first visit, Frances told Nick that she wasn't sure how often she'd be able to come out to see him but that she wanted to come out once a week at first so they could get to know each other. That schedule lasted four-and-a-half years.

By the time they met, Nick had already exhausted his appeals. He'd even had an execution date only to see it called off because of issues with the state's lethal injection protocol. So, from the beginning, Frances knew their relationship would end with an execution, and she even meditated on this fact before each of their weekly visits—*Nick will be killed, Nick will be killed.*

I asked her later how she was able to deal with a relationship like this, one where a violent end was all but inevitable. She told me that her husband had been diagnosed with lung cancer at the age of thirty-six. He lived with it for seventeen years before he died.

"But those seventeen years we lived CAT scan to CAT scan," she said. "So, I've had a little practice with that Sword of Damocles feeling. I knew what was going to happen."

■ ■ ■

Nick Sutton's life before death row was defined by abuse, intoxication, and abandonment. In all the places that should have provided comfort and stability, he found none.

His mother left the family when he was still an infant, leaving him with his maternal grandparents. After a few years they sent him to live with his paternal grandparents and his father, Pete Sutton, a mentally ill man who was also a violent, drug-addicted alcoholic. In his request for clemency, Nick's attorneys quoted Nick's cousin, who said Pete's "idea of parenting generally consisted of yelling at, beating, and terrorizing his son."[2] Nick's grandfather, his attorneys wrote, acted as a buffer between Nick and his father. But that bit of protection would disappear when Nick's grandfather died while Nick was still in grade school. Afterwards, Nick often wore the evidence of his father's violent attacks, showing up to school with various injuries. His cousin recalled one incident in which "Pete beat Nick so badly that he broke his arm and another time where Pete flew into a rage and took Nick and Aunt Dorothy hostage at gunpoint, resulting in an armed stand-off with the police."

When Nick's father wasn't assaulting his son, he was soothing him with drugs and alcohol. By the time Nick was twelve years old, his attorneys wrote, he was regularly using drugs with his father. Not long after, when Nick was just a teenager, his father was found dead in the yard from hypothermia and exposure after an apparent alcohol binge.

The crimes that sent Nick to prison followed shortly after, when he was just eighteen. What actually happened is likely an amalgam of investigators' theories and Nick's various confessions. In any case, he killed three people in East Tennessee over the course of a few months—John Large, his old high school friend; Charles Almon, a local contractor; and Dorothy Sutton, the grandmother who'd raised him and suffered her own beatings from his father. In an article weeks before Nick's execution date, Travis Dorman of the

Knoxville News-Sentinel detailed the investigation into the killings.[3] Investigators pulled Dorothy Sutton's body from an icy river and concluded that Nick had knocked her unconscious with a piece of firewood, tied her to a cinder block, and threw her alive into the river where she drowned. Nick later struck a deal with prosecutors, agreeing to lead them to Large's body so that he could avoid the death penalty. A former detective recounted to the paper how Nick informed authorities that they would find Large with a big tobacco stick coming out of his mouth. Nick told them he'd killed Large by shoving the stick through his mouth and up into his brain.

His death sentence would come for a killing less than five years into his life sentence at an overcrowded East Tennessee prison. There, Nick and two other inmates were accused of murdering a man named Carl Estep, with whom they were said to have a dispute over drugs that had led to Estep threatening Nick's life. Estep, who was serving time for the rape of a nine-year-old girl, was found dead in his bunk with thirty-eight stab wounds.

"If you don't execute Nicky Sutton, then why have the death penalty?" former detective Martin Coffey told the *News-Sentinel*. "If you don't execute him, who do you execute?"[4]

In their application for clemency, Nick's attorneys focused on what they described as a transformation from a life-taker to a life-saver. On the inside, Nick had saved the lives of five people, they wrote, including three prison guards. One of the guards, Tony Eden, described Nick's actions during a 1985 prison riot:

"A group of five inmates, armed with knives and other weapons, surrounded me and attempted to take me hostage. Nick and another inmate confronted them, physically removed me from the situation and escorted me to the safety of the trap gate in another building. I firmly believe that the inmates who tried to take me hostage intended to seriously harm, if not kill me. Nick risked his safety and well-being in order to save me from possible death. I owe my life to Nick Sutton."

Eden also told Nick's attorneys that "if Nick Sutton was released tomorrow, I would welcome him into my home and invite him to be my neighbor."[5]

Nick was also one of the men on the row who helped care for Lee Hall, helping to guide him around the unit and making sure he wasn't taken advantage of by other inmates. Also among Nick's supporters was Paul House, a man who left Tennessee's death row after he was exonerated in 2009, and Paul's mother, Joyce. She told The Intercept ahead of Nick's execution date that when her son's multiple sclerosis stole his ability to walk, Nick had been carrying him to the shower and helping him wash.[6]

Beyond the testimony of people whose lives Nick saved, his attorneys also presented testimony from some of the family members of people whose lives he'd taken. Among those supporting his request for clemency were Carl Estep's eldest daughter. She told Nick's attorneys, "It breaks my heart that Mr. Sutton has lost so much of his life on death row for killing my father." Nick also had the support of five former members of the jury that sentenced him to death.[7]

Pulling together Nick's history of childhood abuse and drug use, his life-saving acts in prison, the support of victims' families, and Nick's own remorse, his attorneys implied an opposite question to the one posed by the former detective: If you don't grant clemency to Nick Sutton, then why have clemency?

■ ■ ■

As Nick's execution date approached, he made a schedule for his visitors, deliberately carving out time for final visits with each of them. Frances moved her regular visits around in order to accommodate Nick's family members and other visitors from East Tennessee who could not see him as often. Her own final visit with Nick was ultimately unsatisfying, she told me. She crammed into one of the private rooms in the visitation gallery with distraught family members and felt they weren't able to focus on Nick like she'd hoped.

Frances, who'd long been stoic about this likely outcome, had maintained her composure. She was the last visitor to leave the prison on the night of her final visit with Nick. She went to sign out at the desk near prison's front security checkpoint and was surprised when the sometimes thorny and unpredictable corporal leaned over and took Frances' hands.

"It's rough. I know it's rough. But we're going to get through it."

The tears came then.

■ ■ ■

On February 19, 2020, the governor washed his hands of Nick.

"After careful consideration of Nicholas Sutton's request for clemency and a thorough review of the case, I am upholding the sentence of the State of Tennessee and will not be intervening," he said in a statement.[8]

Two days earlier, around 11:15 p.m., a group of guards in camouflage—known to men on the row as the Green Team—had come to get Nick from his cell and bring him to death watch. Now he knew he would not be going back.

Frances would not be either. She'd been out to the prison for previous executions, to stand vigil in the field with the others, but found it wasn't helpful to her.

"You stand around and wait," she told me. "And then the word comes, they're dead. And then you just kind of go home. I found it very uncomforting."

Instead, she planned to stay home, drink wine, and read through the Episcopalian burial liturgy.

When the night came, there was an air of grief and exhaustion among the small crowd that gathered under the floodlights. Many of them had done this six times before. They were doing it again, out of duty or lack of anywhere else to go with this complicated mix of sadness and frustration. It was bitterly cold.

At first, no one occupied the area designated for supporters of the execution. It seemed an illustration of a broader, maddening fact. Although the death penalty persists, and executions continue, few of the people in whose names they are carried out are demanding them. When a pollster calls, many Americans say they support the death penalty, but if executions ceased, would they really even notice?

One man did show up eventually, a regular. He wore a cowboy hat and paced, occasionally stopping and clapping his hands as if to urge on the executioners. Inside, they were strapping Nick to the electric chair and offering him a chance to say his last words.

"Don't ever give up on the power of Jesus Christ to take impossible situations and correct them," Nick said, according to the media witnesses. "He can fix something that's broken. He fixed me."

Later, he added: "I'm just grateful to be a servant of God, and I'm looking forward to being in his presence—and I thank you."[9]

When word came to the field that it was finished, the crowd did not linger.

The next morning, I spoke to Kevin Sharp, a federal judge-turned-private attorney who had represented Nick for his clemency effort.

"I don't know what I want to say because I'm so mad," he told me.[10]

He felt that the governor had proven now that his supposed openness to clemency, his "careful consideration," was anything but.

"They'll say, 'Well, the criminal justice system worked, I'm not interfering with that,'" he said. "But what they don't understand is they are part of the criminal justice system. The Constitution makes them part of that. So, they want to abdicate that responsibility, but you can't. That is your responsibility."

If the governor was not willing to show mercy, he should just come out and say it.

"But don't act like you care," he said.

For Frances' part, Nick would be the last man she visited on death row. She told me later that she had no desire to visit the prison.

"I don't ever want to go in that place again."

23

By the time I met her, Rolanda Holman had spent thirty-two years believing that her brother was on death row for a crime he didn't commit. She'd lived most of her life keeping faith in the innocence he'd always maintained, all the while knowing the state intended to kill him. Now they'd put a date on it.

It was March 5, less than two weeks after the Tennessee Supreme Court set a December 3, 2020, execution date for Pervis Payne, the older brother Rolanda still called "Bubba." She smiled and welcomed me into her Murfreesboro home, urging me to take my pick of a dozen donuts she'd bought earlier that morning. She seemed to have a surplus of kindness despite an ordeal that might have justified a deficit.

I'd come to interview her for a story I was writing for the non-profit criminal justice news outlet *The Appeal*.[1] Pervis was one of four Tennessee prisoners still set to be executed in 2020, putting the state on track to kill eleven men in less than three years. But Pervis' case stood out. A Black man with a history of intellectual disability, he'd been convicted and sentenced to death for the murder of a white woman named Charisse Christopher and her two-year-old daughter Lacie Jo in an attack that also left her three-year-old son seriously wounded. At his trial, Shelby County prosecutors leaned on circumstantial evidence to tell a story that echoes throughout American history and quite loudly in the South. What's more, they told it in the Tennessee county with the most known lynchings in the state's history, a jurisdiction which as of March 2020 was responsible for nearly half of the state's death row. Pervis was portrayed as a drug-using, hyper-sexual predator who'd attacked a white woman after she refused his advances.

His story about what really happened had never changed and his family had never believed the state's. But the state was unmoved, and after more than three decades, Roland and her family found themselves shaken by the announcement of an end date. To them, a December filing from Pervis' attorneys had thoroughly made the case that he should not be executed for two inextricable reasons.

"Mr. Payne is unquestionably intellectually disabled and suffers from neurocognitive impairment," they wrote. "He is innocent. He was wrongfully convicted and sentenced because he was unable to assist his lawyers and made a poor witness who was no match for the experienced prosecutor."[2]

We sat at Rolanda's dining room table with her father, Carl Payne, on the phone from his home three hours northwest of Nashville. He was seventy-eight years old, a minister who spoke in a deep and deliberate voice.

"As Christian people, we have to think positive," he said. "Every time something like that comes, it's a knock-down thing or it's a step-back thing. But we can't park there. We can't stay in that rut. We have to start praying and try to trust the Lord to bring us up out of there. So, we know it's in God's hands and we know God gonna work it out. But it's not a good feeling. It's not a good feeling at all. But we can't live there."[3]

Pervis was a joyful, kind-hearted young boy, they told me. He struggled academically in school but didn't make trouble. His nickname, Bubba, came from when Rolanda was a toddler unable to say his real name.

The house they grew up in was strict. Their father was not just a minister, but a minister in the Pentecostal church. Rolanda was never allowed to wear lipstick and the kids were forbidden from playing secular music. As kids do, though, they had their ways. When their parents would go to church on Sunday nights, Rolanda recalled, Pervis would be left in charge.

"We would look down the road and Bubba would say, 'We can't see the lights,'" Rolanda said. "When we couldn't see the red lights anymore, it was time to turn up. So, we would put our music on, and we would dance."

They would get out their parents' fine glassware and pretend to be at the club, spinning records by Prince and Rick James.

Pervis was also involved at his father's church. He played drums at services and often took his dad's blue station wagon to pick up people who couldn't make it to church. As he got older, Pervis worked with his father outside the congregation. They had a painting business called Payne and Son.

"He and I worked together, we got along real good together," Carl said. "We had money in the bank. We were doing real well. Then all of a sudden he's snatched from me and gets caught up in this kind of stuff. I never did believe that it was true."

The story Pervis had been telling for more than three decades goes like this. On the Saturday afternoon of June 27, 1987, a twenty-year-old Pervis was in Millington, a small town outside of Memphis, waiting for his girlfriend to return home from a trip. They had plans to spend the weekend together. This was years before cell phones, so he'd been checking in at her apartment throughout the day. But when he came by to look for her around 3 p.m. that afternoon, he later told authorities, a man came running down the stairs past him, dropping change and papers from his pockets. Pervis picked up some of the items and went upstairs to the second floor where his girlfriend

lived. There, he noticed the door across the hall was ajar and disturbing sounds were coming from inside. After calling out, he entered the
apartment and encountered a horrific scene. Charisse Christopher
lay in a bloody mess, a knife stuck in her throat. A medical examiner later determined she'd been stabbed forty-one times. Her two
children, two-year-old Lacie Jo and three-year-old Nicholas, had also
been stabbed.

"I saw the worst thing I ever saw in my life and like my breath
just had—had tooken—just took out of me . . . she was looking at
me," he would later testify in court. "She had the knife in her throat
with her hand on the knife like she had been trying to get it out and
her mouth was just moving but words had faded away. And I didn't
know what to do."[4]

Pervis fumbled around the scene, checking on the children and
pulling the knife from Charisse's throat before running off to get help.
As he ran from the scene, he saw police arriving.

"As soon as I left out the door I saw a police car, and some other
feeling just went all over me and just panicked, just like, oh, look at
this," Payne testified. "I'm coming out of here with blood on me and
everything. It going to look like I done this crime."[5]

Later that day, as he was arrested, he told the officers taking him
into custody, "Man, I ain't killed no woman." He would tell his family later that the officers who interrogated him after his arrest told
him, "You think you're Black now, wait until we fry you."

Authorities accused Pervis of having used drugs all day leading
up to the alleged murder. But they refused his mother's pleas to test
him at the time of his arrest. They also pointed to supposed scratches
on his chest as a sign that he'd struggled with the victim; they turned
out to be stretchmarks from his weightlifting. He had no prior criminal history, much less one of violence. But nearly eight months later, a
Shelby County jury convicted him and sentenced him to death.

More than thirty years later, with Pervis facing execution, his
attorneys were arguing that he was not only innocent, but also that

his execution would violate a 2002 U.S. Supreme Court decision prohibiting the execution of people who were then known as the "mentally retarded." They'd long argued that Pervis met every legal definition of intellectual disability and said his functional IQ was 68.4. His case, they argued, provided the perfect ingredients for a wrongful conviction.[6]

The stress of this belief had taken a toll on the Payne family. Pervis' mother, Bernice, died in 2005, and his father believed that the immense weight of her son's case and death sentence played a role.

"She died believing that he was gonna come out of there," he told me through the phone. "She knew he wasn't guilty of the crimes. She knew he was coming out. She told Rolanda when she was on her deathbed that God made her a promise. She wasn't giving up."

Ten years later, Pervis' sister died, and Rolanda told me that the loss sapped him of his will to go on.

"He stopped fighting," she told me. "He felt like he had no hope. Like, 'who am I going to come to when I get home?'"

"I said, 'Bubba, I'm gonna be here.'"

Rolanda had an insistent hope that her brother would be vindicated, that he would come home. But she remained deeply aware that another family was involved.

"It's not to discredit what has happened to the victim's family because we are very empathetic and sympathetic to that," she said. "We're gonna fight for justice for them too. Not just for us, because they deserve justice. Because y'all got the wrong guy. It is not Pervis Tyrone Payne who did this to your family."

I left Rolanda's home believing in Pervis' innocence and yet unconvinced that his case would move the state and its seemingly indifferent leaders.

Then came the virus.

■ ■ ■

Terry called me on March 20, a week after then President Donald Trump declared the COVID-19 pandemic a national emergency and the same day that the first Tennessean died of the illness. He said he was calling around to check on everyone he knew.

Our family was fine for the most part. Our two daughters were, for now, blissfully unaware of the unfolding global crisis which was bewildering their increasingly anxious parents. We were, like most people we knew, staying inside and obsessing over the rapid spread of a virus about which we still knew very little. We also watched Steven Soderbergh's 2011 pandemic thriller *Contagion*, which turned out to be a mistake.

I asked Terry if death row was as consumed by it as the free world. The dynamic in the unit sounded pretty similar to the one outside.

"Some people more than others," he said. "Some people just love drama. They go on and on and on and on and on. I try to stay busy doing arts and crafts."[7]

He did say that he usually kept headphones in while he worked, listening to the radio and sharing the latest coronavirus updates with others around him.

Watching on TV as young revelers partied without a care in the world as the pandemic worsened around them made Terry think of how he'd been as a young man.

"Seeing those crazy-ass kids down on the beach down there in Florida and out there in California—drinking Corona beer no less— I thought to myself, you know, I would be doing that. You know, if I was that age again, I would be that stupid."

Just like people in the free world, many of the men on Tennessee's death row had good reason to be concerned. Most of them were older and many had chronic health issues that made them more vulnerable if they became infected. Beyond that, they had little ability to socially distance, as those of us on the outside were learning to do everywhere we went. They also had little confidence that they'd receive anything like true care if they got sick.

"Knowing that we all got a death sentence and they're not going to go out of the way to seriously try to treat you," Terry said.

But Terry had also called to make sure I'd received something he sent me in the mail. Around a month earlier, on President's Day—before the pandemic shut down visitation at the prison—I'd remembered that the men on death row were allowed to take pictures with visitors on state holidays and that visitation hours were extended. I'd been wanting to get a picture with Terry, and George Washington's birthday would do just as well as any other occasion. I rushed over to the prison in the middle of the day, and we got our picture. Now he'd mailed a printed copy to me.

He was working on something else that would be coming in the mail too. Earlier in the year, he'd called and asked me if it'd be OK if he made a gift for my wife, something he hoped would make her happy and show his gratitude for her support of our friendship. He'd decided on a jewelry box which he'd carve out of red and white cedar. He was planning to put her name across the front and a pair of praying hands on the top. For some time, he'd been fretting over whether to paint the nails on the hands a certain color, peppering me with questions about what my wife would like. Ultimately, we opted for something natural-looking, and he was happy with how it was turning out.

It felt like the pandemic was putting more and more of the outside world on pause, but at the time, there were still execution dates on the calendar, and our conversation soon turned to those. Two days earlier, the assistant federal public defender Kelley Henry had filed a motion asking the Tennessee Supreme Court to stay the upcoming execution of Oscar Smith because of the pandemic.[8] Oscar, who'd been sentenced to death in Nashville for the 1989 murders of his estranged wife Judy Smith and her two sons, Chad and Jason Burnett, had always maintained his innocence, but he was set to be executed in just over two months.

The request already had a precedent. The state of Texas—far from hesitant to use its execution chamber—had just stayed an execution because of the ongoing public health crisis, with attorneys arguing that the rapidly spreading virus made it unsafe to crowd family members, prison officials, and media witnesses into the prison for an execution. In other words, carrying out a state killing would come with the risk of someone getting sick.

Kelley's motion argued that the pandemic was affecting the ability of Oscar's legal team to do their jobs and prepare his case for clemency as the execution date approached. She asked the court to "stay the execution for six months to permit the virus outbreak to run its course and allow for Mr. Smith's legal team to conduct its crucial work in representing him."[9]

In those naive early days, we did not know how optimistic the six-month timeframe was. But less than a month later, the court granted the request, rescheduling Oscar's execution for February 4, 2021.[10]

I talked to Terry on the phone the day the court released that order. When Oscar got word that he needed to call his lawyers, Terry had told him it was good news. After all, Terry reasoned, there was no more bad news to deliver—Oscar already had an execution date. I thought out loud that Oscar must've been pretty relieved.

"Oh, he was on cloud nine, man," Terry said. "He really was."[11]

Terry was happy too, and not just for Oscar. His appeals were still working their way through the courts, and if the pandemic slowed that process down then that would be just fine.

■ ■ ■

Early in the first pandemic year, as the crisis caused many plans to be canceled and kept me stuck in my house like I'd never been before, I struggled with how to talk about it to Terry. It felt somewhat strange to tell a man who'd been on death row for longer than I'd been alive that I felt cooped up. In the same way, I sometimes hesitated to tell him when I was able to go out and do simple enjoyable things that for him were unfathomable. What I eventually understood, though, was that we were two people trying to have an honest relationship. He was on death row, and I was not. He understood this. Pretending as if our lives weren't dramatically different was no way to have a true friendship.

In that spirit, when Terry called me in late May, I told him I'd recently taken up a new hobby—watching birds. I would sit on my front porch or go on a walk and just intentionally notice the birds, watching their movements and keeping track of the various kinds I saw. For me, it was a sort of mindfulness practice. I found that when I focused on the birds, I was able to stay in the present moment and not be swept away by anxieties. I asked Terry, did he ever get to see birds?

"Oh sure," he said. The other afternoon he'd been sitting in a plastic chair in "the yard"—the enclosed concrete slab outside the unit—and "there was a couple of birds sitting on top of the cage and just chatting away, just singing away."[12]

He went on: "Not only that, but there's a big-ass skunk that's made this prison his home . . . I watch it just about every afternoon."

The skunk, he said, would regularly walk down the sidewalk leading to the unit like a guard coming in for a shift.

Perhaps there was something comforting in observing beings who were oblivious to the killing around them, be it by the virus or the state. In the free world, COVID was raging, and it seemed to have no trouble breaching prison walls. Earlier that month, two Tennessee prisons had been among the worst COVID hot spots in the country.[13] But there were still three executions on the 2020 calendar—Harold Nichols on August 4, Byron Black on October 8, and Pervis Payne on December 3. It seemed reasonable to hope for delays, especially given the Tennessee Supreme Court's decision to reschedule Oscar's date. But as ever, uncertainty and some fear about the state's determination to put men to death remained.

Then the court acted again. On June 12, it rescheduled Byron's

October date to the following April.[14] Byron was convicted in Nashville in 1988 for the murders of Angela Clay and her daughters Latoya and Lakeisha. But his attorney, Kelley Henry, was making the case that he was incompetent to be executed. In an April court filing she'd written that Byron had an IQ of 67 and had been diagnosed with schizophrenia. She'd asked the Supreme Court to call off his execution because the pandemic was preventing his legal team from doing what it needed to do to prove his mental status.[15]

In response to the court's decision, she released a statement elaborating on his state of being.

"He is physically infirm, can barely walk, is in need of two hip replacements, and suffers from congestive heart failure," she wrote. "He gets around the prison by being pushed in an office chair with wheels."[16]

■ ■ ■

One day during the pandemic summer, my oldest daughter—then not yet five—asked me what jail was. I didn't know where she'd even heard about jail—probably some damned television show that's supposedly for kids. Somehow she'd heard of this place called jail where people got locked up, and now she wanted to know more about it. And she was persistent.

My wife and I always tried to be honest with her when these sorts of things came up. We tried to tell her the truth without overwhelming or scaring her. I also wanted her to know that people in jail weren't necessarily bad people, just people who had once—allegedly, at least—done a bad thing, maybe hurt someone or taken something that wasn't theirs. A lot of them didn't have families like ours, I told her. And as I tried to explain this to her, I realized one of the many ways that my relationship with Terry was a gift. You know that friend that daddy talks to on the phone sometimes, I asked her? She did. She'd crashed our conversations more than once.

Well, he's in jail, I said. A long time ago, he did a very bad thing but he's different now. He's nice now and he's daddy's friend.

That was enough for her, for then at least.

▩ ▩ ▩

The Tennessee Supreme Court had ultimately agreed that the public health crisis was blocking Byron's ability to prove his incompetency claim. But Harold Nichols had no such claim and because of that, the court denied a motion to reschedule his date. His name remained on the execution calendar.

By late June he'd started giving away his belongings. Paint brushes, paint, other supplies. He'd been spreading it out among his friends on the row, and Terry was among them. Terry told me he protested at first but eventually relented at Harold's insistence. Accepting anything felt to Terry like accepting the execution's inevitability, and he still believed Harold's would get called off.

"I don't know how strongly I believe that," he told me over the phone. "I think I'm trying to believe it stronger than maybe the reality is."[17]

By early July, Harold had chosen his execution method—the electric chair. One Monday morning, a little more than three weeks before he was scheduled to be killed, I talked to him on the phone. The days hadn't really changed all that much for him yet. He worked maintenance on the row, doing plumbing and electrical repairs, and that's what he'd keep on doing.

"Nothing's gonna change until they come to get me and take me over to death watch," he told me.[18]

Harold was born and raised in East Tennessee, near Chattanooga, and had been on death row for nearly thirty-two years. I could hear those roots, and all those years, in his voice. The crime that sent him to death row was brutal. He admitted he did it. And it wasn't the only one.

He was convicted and sentenced to death in 1990, for the rape and murder of twenty-one-year-old Karen Pulley. He was eighteen when he broke into her Chattanooga home and, according to court documents, found her alone in an upstairs bedroom. He raped her and beat her over the head with a board. One of her roommates found her alive, but she died the next day. After police determined that Nichols was a primary suspect in several other area rapes, they arrested him, and he confessed.[19]

"I've never said that I was innocent," he told me. "I did do the crimes that they've got me in here for and I fully regret that."

Now the only thing that would keep him out of the death chamber was the governor's mercy, or concern that an execution would end up being a superspreader event. Evidence of the former was in short supply—Bill Lee had heard four pleas for mercy so far as governor, and he'd rejected them all.

"I feel good," Harold told me when I asked how he was feeling as the execution date approached. "I'm not scared of dying, OK? I'm a Christian and I know what waits on the other side. Death doesn't scare me. I would rather go on living. But death itself does not scare me. I'm not that troubled about it. The way I see it, I've been locked up now for almost thirty-two years and death is a way out. It's like a release, you know?"

He did seem troubled by the prospect of being taken to death watch only to receive a last-minute reprieve. He envisioned having final conversations with his daughter and his sister, only to have his execution called off to then have to do it all over again.

"To me, it would be almost a mental torture," he said. "You know, if they're gonna take me over there, don't bring me back for just three or four days and take me back, you know. Get it done, be done with it."

He was born in 1960 in Cleveland, Tennessee. His mother, Nanny Lou, died when he was ten years old, leaving him and his thirteen-year-old sister, Deborah, with their abusive father. A 2013 opinion from the Sixth Circuit Court of Appeals described Mac Nichols as "a mean, abusive, and outright vile man."[20]

His abuse—which was both physical and sexual, according to court documents—was so bad that the children were eventually placed in an orphanage by leaders of a church where the Nichols family were members. Harold recalled a time shortly after his mother's death when he took part in a fundraising campaign for the orphanage, even winning a bicycle for his outstanding efforts. He did not know that only months later, he and his sister would be living there.

"At the time we were told, 'if anybody asks why you're in the orphanage just say that your dad couldn't take care of you,'" he said. "But he was abusive. So that's why we ended up in the orphanage. I always wondered what it was that I had done wrong, because I've seen a lot of families where the parents might pass away or something and the aunts and uncles take the kids and raise them, you know. And I always wondered what I had done wrong that my family didn't take me and my sister."

He said that weighed on him for years, well into his time on death row, until one of his uncles came to visit him in 1997. The uncle admitted that he hadn't believed the abuse allegations until years later, when he saw Mac Nichols behave the same way with other children.

"Growing up, I lived with a lot of guilt," Harold said. "But that conversation with him, that was a big help to me to become who I am now."

Sobriety too had been a part of making him a different person than the young man who attacked women.

"I've had problems with drugs and alcohol over my life," he told me. "You know, I'm not using that as a reason, that's no excuse. But I've gotten away from that."

Now he was a professing Christian who worked his maintenance job and spent a lot of his free time making art and writing poetry. He had contributed to exhibits of work from Tennessee's death row, including one at Vanderbilt University that was on display as we spoke.

"I want to be a person that is known for peace and known for kindness rather than hating everything," he said. "When I first got to prison, I blamed everybody for my problems. I blamed the courts, the DAs, the jury, I blamed pretty much everybody. Until it dawned on me one day—and this wasn't anything that happened overnight—there's only one person that's responsible for me, OK, and that's me. I put myself here. Nobody else did, OK? When I came to that realization, I said that's not who I wanted to be, so I set about to make change."

When he expressed his regret for the way he harmed people decades ago, he also noted the policy that prevents him from expressing that remorse directly. Death row prisoners are not allowed to contact their victims.

"I mean, I understand why," he said. "But they prevent our attorneys from doing it and everything. So, there's never an opportunity to say I'm sorry, you know? I would've liked to have said that a long time ago. But I've never had that opportunity."

I asked him what he would say to his victims if he had the chance.

"The main thing is not just that I'm sorry that I hurt them, but that they were not responsible for any of that," he said. "That it was not their fault, any of it at all. All the blame and all the responsibility of that is on me. Just like growing up, like I said, I carried a lot of guilt wondering what I had done wrong. So, I know what it's like to be on both sides of that fence. That's why I wish I could've said this years ago. It would've been, I think, more helpful for them back twenty years ago, thirty years ago, but I just would've liked the opportunity to let them know that the blame is mine solely."

He paused throughout our conversation, and through the phone it was hard to tell whether he was holding back emotions or trying to find the right words. He said he knew the damage he did extended beyond the physical victims of his crimes.

"Not just the people that I've hurt, but the community," he said. "That's one of the things that I've learned in prison is that the things we do, whether it's crime or otherwise, our actions go beyond the moment. They have a rippling effect. The things I did hurt more than just the individuals, it hurt the community, and I regret that. I regret everything I did."

I asked him why he'd chosen the electric chair.

"The way I see it, there's going to be some pain either way you go," he said. "And I figure electrocution will be the quickest. That's the sole reason why I've chosen electrocution. To lay there on the gurney and you're basically having your veins shot with bleach, you know, burning from the inside out even though they tranquilize you so that you can't move so that you can't exhibit that pain—everybody thinks, well, it's real peaceful. But it's not. You just can't move."

I also asked him about giving away his things and about his relationship with the other men on the row.

"I've spent more time with most of these guys around here than I did with my own family," he said. "So, these guys, a lot of 'em, we're like brothers. Over the years if somebody had something that was bothering them, they could come talk to me. If I had something that was bothering me, I could come talk to them. If we were having some kind of problem or something we could work it out amongst ourselves. It created a bond between us."

We talked a bit longer and finally I asked him what he'd say to the governor if he had the chance.

"Governor Lee says that he's a Christian," he said. "And if he is, you know, I hope he is. But as Christians, the Bible teaches us that we can't serve two masters. We can't serve God and man. And if God is directing us, saying, 'Thou shalt not kill,' and man is directing us to kill, and we kill because man says we should, then he's not serving God he's serving man. I just hope that he understands that.

"But I also want it known that I have no animosity, I have no hatred for anybody that's involved in this. The warden, the executioner.

They've chosen this to do and, you know, I'm not accountable for them. If me and my executioner are standing before God on judgment day, I'm not gonna be held accountable for what he did. I'm only gonna be held accountable for the way I treated him. So, I have no hatred for any of 'em.'"

We hung up the phone and I felt sure I'd just talked to a man who would soon be strapped into the electric chair. But four days later, the governor granted Harold a reprieve "due to the challenges and disruptions caused by the COVID-19 pandemic."[21]

Later, Terry told me that after hearing the news Harold had joked that he was gonna need some new boots. He'd already given his away.

The stress of preparing for his execution only to have it called off just weeks before was not Harold's alone, of course. After the governor announced the reprieve, Lisette Monroe—Karen Pulley's sister—told the Associated Press that it was yet another excruciating and re-traumatizing development in the decades-long slog. She even called on family friends to write to the governor and express their disappointment in his decision.

"The pain and the hurt won't stop when he's gone," she said. "It won't bring Karen back. It won't bring my girls the opportunity to know their aunt. But it'll be over."[22]

■ ■ ■

One day in late July of 2020, I met David around lunch time to sit outside—around six feet apart—and catch up. It had been a while and in-person interaction felt like an indulgence.

Although executions were being called off instead of carried out, David still felt a soul-deep stress about the possibility of Terry's being scheduled. That's the thing about being on death row or caring about someone who is. The passage of time is an enemy, always dragging you closer to the moment when your name appears next to a date.

David's wife had expressed concern about what would happen to David when that day came. So had mine.

He thought out loud through the scenario in which Terry was sent to death watch.

"I'm not, at this point, a religious volunteer," he said. "So that would prevent me, we think, from being with Terry on the last few days. But my goal would be to be with him . . . As I understand it, he would be sitting in a cell, I'd be sitting in a chair outside the cell, and we'd have hours every day to sit for about three days. What would we talk about? Would I vomit? Would I do like the hard-ass people and go, 'Don't show your emotions,' or would I continue to bring my true self and weep with my friend and in front of my friend? Would I be there when the last meal comes? What would we say? What would we feel?"[23]

He tried to believe that Terry would not be executed, but he'd also seen the state's determination to carry out the executions it scheduled. Only a global pandemic had stopped the state's historic spree of killing.

Terry had contemplated this too, and we talked about it on the phone a couple months after my chat with David. Terry was intent on fighting his case and doing whatever he could to stay out of the execution chamber. But he'd also made a decision to fight that fight now rather than holding out hope that a flurry of last-minute filings would save him. In part, it was strategic—he felt that the courts had made it clear they didn't look kindly on eleventh-hour claims. But he also wanted to avoid the stress and trauma they could produce, even if successful. He'd seen men on the row go to death watch only to be sent back to the row. They weren't the same. He didn't want that for himself or his loved ones.

"Now, I might change my mind if I was sitting over there," he said with a laugh. "But I don't think so."[24]

■ ■ ■

Only one man was left on the 2020 execution calendar, and it was the man with a convincing innocence claim.

As Pervis Payne's December 3 date approached, his attorneys were rallying support for his cause on two fronts. The first was his claim of actual innocence, the one he had maintained since the day he was arrested in 1987. The second was his intellectual disability. Proving the former was difficult, although they were making some progress. In September, a Shelby County judge had approved DNA testing—over the objections of Shelby County District Attorney Amy Weirich—on previously untested evidence including the knife used in the murders.[25] The latter was actually impossible for Pervis to prove in court due to a quirk of the Tennessee legal system. Despite the U.S. Supreme Court ruling against the execution of people with intellectual disabilities, there was no legal procedure in Tennessee through which a court could hear a condemned person's claim on the matter. The Tennessee Supreme Court had acknowledged this problem and called on the state legislature to create such a procedure. In November, the Tennessee Black Caucus of State Legislators announced they were filing a bill to do just that.[26] But Pervis' execution was by then less than a month away.

On the phone Terry told me about the warden coming to the unit to talk to Pervis and ask him to choose his execution method. Then, several days later, the governor announced that he was granting Pervis a reprieve. When he did so, though, his stated reason was not to wait for the results of court-ordered DNA testing or to allow the legislature to create a way for a court to hear Pervis' intellectual disability claim. Instead, it was, again, "due to the challenges and disruptions caused by the COVID-19 pandemic."[27]

24

A few days before the pandemic Christmas of 2020, I was sitting at my desk at home when I got a call from Riverbend. I answered the phone and heard the familiar automated voice of a woman on the other end.

"Hello, this is a prepaid debit call from . . ."—then came Terry's recorded introduction—"an inmate at the Tennessee Department of Correction's Riverbend Maximum Security Institution. To accept this call, press zero."

I accepted the call, and Terry greeted me as he often did.

"Well, hello there."[1]

He'd called to tell me a story. Recently, he'd been sitting with Oscar Smith, the man who'd seen his 2020 execution date rescheduled because of the pandemic but was now a little more than a month away from his February 4, 2021, date. Terry believed Oscar had resigned to the fact that this date was not going to move. "I know they're gonna execute me," Terry had heard him say, "I know they're gonna execute me." As it happens, a couple weeks later, the Tennessee Supreme Court would issue a stay in his case, calling off his execution again because, among other reasons, his attorneys had become infected with COVID-19. But as 2020 neared its end, Oscar believed he was weeks away from going to the death chamber.

The story Terry wanted to tell me, though, was about Oscar and our mutual friend David. Oscar and David didn't know each other well, but they'd been speaking on the phone one day recently because Oscar had made something for a friend on the outside and David was relaying the proper mailing address. Terry was nearby as they spoke, hearing only one side of the conversation, when he saw a strange expression take over Oscar's face. Later, he overheard Oscar telling some of the other men in the unit about the call.

"I was talking to David earlier, he told me he loved me," Oscar said.

Terry had known Oscar since Oscar arrived on death row in 1989, and he also knew that there was abuse in Oscar's past. He gathered that his old friend had not often heard the words "I love you," certainly not from a relative stranger who would seem to have every reason not to care much about Oscar's situation. Terry later told David that by saying those words to Oscar, he opened up for Oscar the radical possibility that someone could still see good in him, could see him for more than the crimes that defined him in the eyes of the law.

Moving on, Terry asked me about my family's Christmas plans, and I told him we were headed down to see my in-laws in Alabama, where we'd celebrate Christmas morning outside to try to keep from spreading the virus amongst ourselves. Then, with some urgency, Terry told me that the following night, on December 21, we needed to go outside to see what he called "the Bethlehem star."

Apparently, he explained, Jupiter and Saturn were going to be very close together—closer than they'd been in 800 years, I later learned—and their proximity would produce a sight that wouldn't occur again until 2080.

"But you know what's really cool about that?" he said. "No one living on the planet Earth has ever seen that before. Think about that for a moment. Last time that happened was 800 years ago. And it won't happen again, Steven, for another 60 years. So, tell all your friends, man, that's gonna be so cool. I got to live to see that. That's pretty cool."

That thought stirred up another, more upsetting one for Terry. He thought of his friends Nick Sutton and Lee Hall, he said, and how they didn't live to see it. Emotion caught his voice, tripping him up.

"It just tells me how precious life is," he said.

It turned out that Terry wouldn't really be able to see it, either. Although he did have a window to the outside, the prison floodlights were so bright that they washed out any view of the stars above. But it made him think of a time when he did see the stars.

Years earlier he'd had knee surgery, and afterwards he was taken to the nearby special needs facility for therapy.

"A lot of times they used to leave your ass over there all day, just to kind of punish you for going," he said. "You know, locked in a cell with nothing. But anyway, that's my theory and I'm gonna stick to it."

In any case, Terry was there late waiting on transportation to bring him back to the main prison. When he finally did get back it was dark and—in what he spoke of as an absolute privilege—he got to walk down an access road, around most of the prison, to get back to Unit 2.

"Of course, I was in shackles and chains but who cares?" he said.

I could hear him begin to cry on the other end of the line.

"I got to see the stars. Man, it had been forever."

He would shuffle for a bit, then stop to look up. Then shuffle on farther, then stop again.

"Man, I got to look at that, it was just the most beautiful thing."

Silence for a beat and then he went on.

"I'd just look you know, and go, 'Man oh man. That's sad. To give all that up for this.' You know what I'm saying? Give all that up. The freedom and the pleasure and the joy of walking out at night in the dark and seeing the beautiful stars that are in the sky. I thought, 'Man, how crazy was I?'"

I promised him I'd go outside to look at the stars that night. And I hoped, or at least hoped for hope that he could one day walk un-shackled beneath the stars again. More than thirty-seven years—more than thirteen thousand nights—had passed since the summer when he participated in the killing of Todd Millard and took the life of Diana Smith. The Terry King who stole a lifetime of nights from them was unrecognizable to the man I was speaking to on the phone. And I thought that maybe some of the stars that looked down on him then had since faded away, and a new light would shine on him now.

■ ■ ■

A few weeks later, early in the new year, Terry called me again and caught me in line to get my car's emissions test. When I told him where I was an almost childish enthusiasm came through in his voice.

"Hey that's pretty cool, I've never been to the vehicle emissions place."

Our conversation quickly moved to the pandemic which would soon be entering its second year and to the vaccines that were beginning to roll out. I'd been a bit anxious about Terry on this front. As COVID-19 had raged throughout the country, including its jails in prisons, many of us had been looking with hope to the eventual arrival of vaccines. But Terry had been expressing serious reservations about getting the shot. Not wanting to overstep my bounds, I'd simply told him that I trusted the vaccines and planned on getting one as soon as I could. His concerns remained, and he seemed increasingly dead set against getting vaccinated when it became available to him.

That's why I was surprised when he told me that he'd changed his mind. Although he continued to have his doubts about getting such a new vaccine, he said he'd decided to go ahead with it because he didn't want the prison to have any reason to block him from having visitors once visitation resumed.

He did confess, though, that he was feeling torn about the arrival of the vaccines. In one sense it was an obvious relief. But there was another twisted reality. The virus, the thing that had been killing so many people in the free world, was the only thing keeping the men on Tennessee's death row alive. After a historic run of executions, the state had gone nearly a year without putting anyone to death. But the prospect of the pandemic receding also meant the prospect of that reprieve coming to an end. Terry felt certain that once the vaccines were widely available, the state would get back to scheduling executions. Men on the row would start getting dates and the line would start moving again.

Acknowledgments

The first people I must acknowledge are the men on Tennessee's death row and the victims of the crimes described in this book. It is no small thing to put a person's story in print and I did not take it lightly. I hope I have done so in a way that honors the humanity and dignity of all. I am grateful to those who spoke to me for this book or who told their stories to other reporters whose work is cited here. I am also deeply indebted to the visitors of death row who invited me into their community and shared a difficult and beautiful part of their lives with me; the attorneys who shared their insights, experiences, and files with me; and the investigators whose interviews with far-flung friends and family allowed me to color in the details of these men's lives. In particular, Demetria Kalodimos, David Bass, Al Andrews, Joe Ingle, and Kelley Henry made much of this book possible. As for Terry King, I told him some time ago that I wished in a strange way that we had never met; that his life had not led to death row where our paths could cross. But given that it has, I consider it an honor to now call him a friend.

I never would have been in a position to write these stories, or much at all, if a couple of editors in Nashville weren't willing to give a chance to a twenty-two-year-old who walked in off the street with little experience and fewer sources. Stephen George and the late Jim Ridley were inexplicably kind and patient with me, and I won't forget it. Soon I got to be a staff writer at *The City Paper* (RIP) and later the *Nashville Scene*, working under Jim and Steve Cavendish, who also became a mentor and a friend in addition to serving as the editor who would calmly tell me not to delete my stories and start over from scratch as I panicked about them on the phone. Much of the reporting that expanded into this book was done at the *Scene* under the editorship of Patrick Rodgers. He gave me the space and (extra) time to pursue stories I cared about, helped hammer them into shape and was my first call as I left the prison after the executions recounted in this book. He is as smart, passionate, fun, and loyal as an editor or friend could be. He only fired me three times, but he didn't mean it. No matter what else happens in my life, I will always be proud to have worked at the *Scene* and I hope (almost all) of the wonderful freaks I worked there with over the years know how much they mean to me. A special thanks goes to Nancy Floyd, who allowed me to walk into her office without warning, raid her mini-fridge, and vent my neuroses about this book when few other people knew I was working on it at all. My pal and fellow Steve, Stephen Elliott, also knew about this work-in-progress in the early stages and was kind enough not to ask me about it too often.

The first person I pitched this book to was my wife, Mallory. She encouraged me to pursue it without hesitation and, even though the nearly five years that followed were more difficult and painful than she could have imagined, she was a constant source of love, encouragement, and real talk. With our two young daughters at home, she regularly gave me nights or weekends alone with my writing and once put me up in a hotel to help get this manuscript across the finish line. Her name is among the many that should be with mine on the cover. The next person I pitched was the aforementioned Steve Cavendish. His sign-off—"I like this plan, I'm proud to be a part of this plan"—has always given me the confidence to move ahead. Next,

I got on the social media site formerly known as Twitter and DM'd Lauren MacLeod, who would thankfully become my indefatigable agent. We'd met only once before but she agreed to hear me out over a cup of coffee, and I have given her only brief stints of peace and quiet ever since. Thank you, Lauren, for your belief, your patience and for usually answering the phone.

There are many other people who have encouraged me along the way and helped me even though I was not in a position to return the favor. Radley Balko and Liliana Segura were writing and reporting heroes of mine who became friends and supporters who treated me as a peer. Their work and their friendship mean a great deal to me. Margaret Renkl has also been a champion of me and my work in ways that have truly kept me going when the work was at its most difficult. As I was drafting my book proposal, Kathryn Miles, Christopher White, and Kyle Swenson allowed me to see their successful proposals. These were a lifeline to me.

Of course, the Microsoft Word file I eventually produced would not be a book you can hold if it weren't for the skilled work of my editor Carl Bromley and the team at Melville House. I have not made this easy on them and they have all been more patient than I deserve. They have all made a dream of mine come true. Carl's thoughtful editing made this book deeper and better and I could not have found my way there on my own. He is also truly delightful to have on the other end of the phone and has given me many excellent crime fiction recommendations. Julie Ford gave the book a thorough legal review for which I am very grateful. And I must thank Ryan Harrington, who acquired the book for Melville before handing it off to Carl. He believed in this story and gave me this opportunity, and I hope to one day buy him a beer.

Of course, I have to thank my family and friends who have been a safe and loving constant in my life. My parents, Jim and Sue Hale, have loved me, made sure I knew it, and supported me in everything I do. The stories in this book have only deepened my gratitude to them and my sense of how lucky I was to be born to them. My sister has been a playmate, a role model, and a supporter throughout our lives. I love you, Kayla. Our original Nashville crew: Brian and Anna Alpizar, Jason and Amanda Hermansdorfer, Ryan and Ashlynn Campagna, and Will and Erica Anderson. And The Thread: Alex, Brian, Dan, Jason, Ken, Matt, Nick, Raleigh, Ryan, Scott, LB, Troy, and Wilson. You're My Guys forever. I also have to thank Brian, Ryan, Jason, Wilson, and Will for meeting me on my back porch when I found myself breaking down and putting me back together. And Wilson, for so many nights on the phone talking about writing and life.

Lastly, I must come back to Mallory and our girls, Leighton and Holland. You are what I always wanted to have in my life and I will take every chance I get to tell you that I love you. Thank you for loving me.

Endnotes

Chapter 1

1   Tenn. Code Ann. § 40-23-116.

2   "Rules of Department of Correction Adult Services Division: Chapter 0420-3-4 Selection of News Media Agency Representatives to Attend an Execution of a Death Sentence." Tennessee Department of Correction. www.tn.gov.

3   "Tennessee Executions." Tennessee Department of Correction. www.tn.gov.

4   "The Death Penalty in 2022: Year End Report." Death Penalty Information Center, December 16, 2022. www.deathpenaltyinfo.org.

5   "The Death Penalty in 2017: Year End Report." Death Penalty Information Center, December 14, 2017.

6   Hale, Steven. "Is Tennessee Going to Torture Billy Ray Irick?" *Nashville Scene*, July 25, 2018.

7   *Glossip v. Gross*, 576 U.S. (2015). Justia. www.supreme.justia.com.

8   Hale, Steven. "Judge Upholds Tennessee's Lethal Injection Protocol." *Nashville Scene*, July 26, 2018.

9   *Billy Ray Irick v. Tennessee,* 585 U.S. (2018). Supreme Court decisions are archived at www.supremecourt.gov.

10   Billy Ray Irick, Tennessee State Courts.

11   The information on Irick's childhood and youth is from the Supreme Court of Tennessee, "In Re: Billy Ray Irick: Response Opposing Motion to Set Execution Date, Request for Certificate of Commutation, and Claim of Incompetency to Be Executed," May 27, 2010. The Supreme Court of Tennessee documents are archived at www.tncourts.gov.

12 Brown, Peter I. "Psychiatric Evaluation of Billy Ray Irick." www.tncourts. gov.

13 Matheny, Jim. "Remembering Why: Rape and Murder of 7-Year-Old Paula Dyer." WBIR, July 22, 2018.

14 Matheny. "Remembering Why."

15 Brown. "Psychiatric Evaluation."

16 *Billy Ray Irick v. Ricky Bell*, Warden, No:3:98-CV-666 (United States District Court Eastern District of Tennessee Chattanooga Division November 3, 1999). "Affidavit of Ramsey Jeffers."

17 *Billy Ray Irick v. Ricky Bell*, Warden, No:3:98-CV-666 (United States District Court for the Eastern District of Tennessee November 3, 1999). "Affidavit of Cathy Jeffers."

18 "Affidavit of Ramsey Jeffers."

19 C. Eugene Shiles Jr. to Dwight E. Tarwater, Special Counsel to Governor Bill Haslam, April 14, 2017.

20 Transcript of Det. Don Wiser Interview with Kathy Jeffers, April 16, 1985.

21 Transcript of Det. Don Wiser Interview with Kathy Jeffers.

22 *Billy R. Irick v. Ricky Bell*, Warden, No. 01-5638 (United States Court of Appeals for the Sixth Circuit May 12, 2009). www.govinfo.gov.

23 Lakin, Matt. "Looking Back on Paula Dyer's Last Day on Earth."

24 Billy R. Irick v. Ricky Bell, No. 01-5638.

25 Matheny. "Remembering Why."

26 *Billy Ray Irick v. Ricky Bell*, Warden, No. 3:98-cr-666 (United States District Court for the Eastern District of Tennessee September 14, 1999). "Affidavit of William D. Dipillo."

27 Affidavit of Clifton R. Tennison Jr., MD, Re: Billy Ray Irick, February 25, 2010.

28 Brown. "Psychiatric Evaluation."

29 Brown. "Psychiatric Evaluation."

30 Shiles to Tarwater, April 14, 2017.

31 Brown. "Psychiatric Evaluation."

32 Seidner, Bruce G. "Competency Evaluation." *State of Tennessee v. Billy Ray Irick*, Criminal Court for Knox County, Tennessee, Division I. August 17, 2010. www.tncourts.gov.

33 *Lethal Injection Execution Manual: Execution Procedures for Lethal Injection.* Tennessee Department of Correction, July 5, 2018. www.dpic-cdn.org.

34 Matheny. "Remembering Why."

Chapter 2

1 Hale, Steven. "Demetria Kalodimos Out at WSMV." *Nashville Scene*, January 1, 2018.

2 Lind, J. R. "Demetria Kalodimos Settles With WSMV." *Nashville Scene*, January 2, 2020.

3 Kalodimos, Demetria. Interview by Steven Hale, January 30, 2019.

4 Bass, David. Interview by Steven Hale, December 8, 2018.

5 "Facts About the Death Penalty." Death Penalty Information Center, May 23, 2023. www.dpic-cdn.org.

6 Kazek, Kelly. "10 Things to Know About Alabama's Electric Chair, Yellow Mama." AL.com, January 21, 2016. www.al.com.

7 "On Capital Punishment." Southern Baptist Convention, 2000 Annual Meeting, June 1, 2000. www.sbc.net.

8 "Capital Punishment: An Overview of Christian Perspectives." The Ethics and Religious Liberty Commission of the Southern Baptist Convention, May 29, 2014. www.erlc.com.

9 Burger, Frederick. "Graddick—The Tough-Talking AG." *The Anniston Star*, February 23, 1986.

10 Haas, Brian. "Tenn. Makes Unprecedented Push to Execute 10 Killers." *USA Today*, December 5, 2013.

11 Hale, Steven. "Tennessee Puts Remaining Executions On Hold." *Nashville Scene*, April 13, 2015.

12 "Capital Punishment, 2018—Statistical Tables." U.S. Department of Justice, Tracy L. Snell, BJS Statistician, September 2020. www.bjs.ojp.gov.

13 "Death Penalty Talk Revives Criticism of Human Rights Court." *Andean Air Mail & Peruvian Times*, February 5, 2018.

14 Barrenechea, Alvaro. Interview by Steven Hale, August 30, 2019.

15 Billy Ray Irick to Alvaro Barrenechea.

16 Billy Ray Irick to Alvaro Barrenechea.

17 Andrews, Al, and David Bass. Interview by Steven Hale, April 22, 2019.

18 Andrews and Bass. Interview.

Chapter 3

1 Tamburin, Adam. "Court Blocks Autopsy for Executed Inmate Billy Ray Irick, Citing His Religious Beliefs." *The Tennessean*, August 15, 2018.

Chapter 4

1 Ingle, Joe. Interview by Steven Hale, June 27, 2019.

2 Ingle, Joseph B. *Last Rights: Thirteen Fatal Encounters With the State's Justice* (Sterling Publishing Co., Inc., 2008), 1.

3 Ingle. *Last Rights*, 9.

4 *Attica: The Official Report of the New York State Special Commission on Attica* (Bantam Books, 1972). The Marshall Project. www.themarshall-project.org.

5 Ingle. *Last Rights*, 14.

6 Ingle, Joe. Interview by Steven Hale, January 21, 2021.

7 McFadden, Robert D. "Reverend Will D. Campbell, Maverick Minister in Civil Rights Era, Dies at 88." *The New York Times*, June 4, 2013.

8 Cooper, Peter. "Will Campbell: A Bootleg Preacher Who Tried to Love them All." *The Tennessean*, June 28, 2013.

9 Ingle. *Last Rights*, 25.

10 "A Prisoner Is Slain and 10 Wounded in Tennessee Riot." Associated Press, September 13, 1975.

11 *Furman v. Georgia*, 408 U.S. 238 (1972). Justia. www.supreme.justia.com.

12 *Gregg v. Georgia*, 428 U.S. 153 (1976). Justia. www.supreme.justia.com.

13 "Capital Punishment Chronology." Tennessee Department of Correction. www.tn.gov.

14 Ingle. *Last Rights*, 25.

15 Aldrich, Marta W. "Restorative Justice Advocate Harmon Wray Dies." United Methodist News Service, July 30, 2007.

16 Lozier, John. Interview by Steven Hale. March 30, 2021.

17 Welch, Patricia. "Christmas Visit Brightens Day On Death Row." *The Tennessean*, December 19, 1976.

18 Welch, Patricia. "End to Death Penalty His Hope." *The Tennessean*, September 11, 1976.

19 Wicker, Tom. "Old Sparky's Ready." *The New York Times*, October 10, 1976.

20 Ingle. *Last Rights,* 51.

21 Ingle, Joe. "Last Rights," C-SPAN, 55:03, June 3, 2008.

22 Rawls Jr., Wendell. "Judge Orders Tennessee to Correct Prison Conditions Found to Be Inhumane." *The New York Times*, August 13, 1982.

Chapter 5

1 Bass, David. Interview by Steven Hale, December 8, 2018.

2 Curriden, Mark. "Lawyer's Attempt to Keep His Head Above Water Landed a Client on Death Row." *ABA Journal*, March 1, 2011. www.abajournal.com.

3 "Visitation Handbook, Riverbend Maximum Security Institution." Tennessee Department of Correction, January 2021. www.tn.gov.

4 Hale, Steven. "As His Execution Nears, Edmund Zagorski Speaks." *Nashville Scene,* October 8, 2018

5 Topping, Elizabeth. "They Rehearse Death Until It Seems Easy!" *Tennessean Magazine*, March 28, 1937.

6 Hale, Steven. "The Chair: 100 Years After Its First Use, Tennessee's Electric Chair Remains the State's Most Prolific Killer." *Nashville Scene*, July 7, 2016.

Chapter 6

1 Laska, Lewis L. *Legal Executions in Tennessee: A Comprehensive Registry, 1782–2009* (McFarland, 2011), 7.

2 Laska. *Legal Executions in Tennessee*, 9.

3 Hale, Steven. "It's Time to Put the 'Boy Hero of the Confederacy' to Bed," *Nashville Scene*, l.

4 Laska. *Legal Executions in Tennessee*, 12.

5 "Presswood." *Republican Banner,* May 26, 1872.

6 Laska. *Legal Executions in Tennessee*, 152.

7 "Lynching in America: Racial Terror Lynchings." Equal Justice Initiative, 2017. www.lynchinginamerica.eji.org.

8 "DPIC Analysis: Racial Disparities Persisted in U.S. Death Sentences and Executions in 2019." Death Penalty Information Center, January 21, 2020. www.deathpenaltyinfo.org.

9 Brandon, Craig. *The Electric Chair: An Unnatural American History* (McFarland, 1999), 4.

10 Moran, Richard. *Executioner's Current: Thomas Edison, George Westinghouse, and the Invention of the Electric Chair* (Knopf, 2002).

11 Brandon. *The Electric Chair*, 58, 9.

12 Moran. *Executioner's Current*, xix.

13 "Far Worse Than Hanging: Kemmler's Death Proves an Awful Spectacle." *The New York Times*, August 7, 1890.

14 "Far Worse Than Hanging." *The New York Times*.

15 Hale, Steven. "The Chair: 100 Years After Its First Use, Tennessee's Electric Chair Remains the State's Most Prolific Killer." *Nashville Scene*, July 7, 2016.

16 "Assembly Finally Quits." *The Tennessean*, September 28, 1913.

17 Hale. "The Chair."

18 "Electrocution." *Lawrence Democrat*, October 8, 1913.

19 Vandiver, Margaret. *Lethal Punishment: Lynching and Legal Executions in the South* (Rutgers University Press, 2006), 1.

20 Laska. *Legal Executions in Tennessee*, 268–269.

21 "Tennessee Executions." Tennessee Department of Correction. www.tn.gov.

22 Laska. *Legal Executions in Tennessee*, 388-389.

23 Greene, Lee Seifert. *Lead Me On: Frank Goad Clement and Tennessee Politics* (University of Tennessee Press, 1982), 171.

24 Topp, Ed. "Clement Makes Plea: Legislators Buzzing Over Death Penalty." *Knoxville News-Sentinel*, January 9, 1959.

25 Greene. *Lead Me On*, 328.

26 Hollabaugh, Julie. "Witness to 84 Raps Executions." *The Tennessean*, March 18, 1965.

27 Lehman, Susan. "A Matter of Engineering: Capital Punishment as a Technical Problem." *The Atlantic*, February 1990.

28 *Mr. Death: The Rise and Fall of Fred A. Leuchter, Jr.*, directed by Errol Morris (Lionsgate Films, 1999).

29 Hale. "The Chair."

30 "Leuchter Report." Auschwitz-Birkenau State Museum, www.auschwitz.org.

31 "The History of the Death Penalty: A Timeline." Death Penalty Information Center." www.deathpenaltyinfo.org.

32 "Capital Punishment Chronology." Tennessee Department of Correction. www.tn.gov.

33 Barry, Dan. "Death in the Chair, Step by Remorseless Step." *The New York Times*, September 16, 2007.

Chapter 7

1 Hale, Steven. "Edmund Zagorski's Plea for Mercy." *Nashville Scene*, September 25, 2018.

2 Hale, Steven. "Haslam Denies Clemency for Edmund Zagorski." *Nashville Scene*, October 5, 2018.

3 "Death Watch." Tennessee Department of Correction. www.tn.gov.

4 Ingle, Joe. Interview by Steven Hale, June 27, 2019.

5 *Edmund Zagorski v. Bill Haslam, Tony Parker, and Tony Mays* (United States District Court for the Middle District of Tennessee). "Plaintiff Motion for Temporary Restraining Order for Denying Choice to Use Electric Chair," October 10, 2018. www.tncourts.gov.

6 *Edmund Zagorski v. Bill Haslam*, et al. No. 3:18-cv-01035 (United States District Court for the Middle District of Tennessee). "Temporary Restraining Order Granted by US Federal Court," October 11, 2018. www.tncourts.gov.

7 *Edmund Zagorski v. Tony Mays*, Warden, No. 18-6052 (United States Court of Appeals for the Sixth Circuit). "United States Sixth Circuit Court of Appeals Stay," October 10, 2018.

8 In Re: Edmund Zagorski, Movant, Application for Stay of Execution (Supreme Court of the United States). "Motion to Stay Execution, Pending Cert," October 9, 2018. www.tncourts.gov.

9 Hale, Steven. "You're Not Going to Die Tonight." *Nashville Scene*, October 12, 2018.

10 Robert L. Hutton to Dwight Tarwater, Legal Counsel to the Governor, Re: Supplemental Information, Request for Commutation of Sentence to Life Without Parole, September 14, 2018.

11 *Edmund George Zagorski v. State of Tennessee*, No. 01SO1-9711-CC-00240 (Tenn. December 7, 1998). www.tncourts.gov.

12 Declaration of Kenneth Feldman, November 15, 2000.

13 Declaration of Dewayne Knight, March 11, 2018.

14 Declaration of Doug Giessler, June 24, 2018.

15 Declaration of Lorraine Kochanski, April 10, 2018.

16 Declaration of Darrell Knight, May 1, 2018.

17 Kochanski, April 10, 2018, and Declaration of Dallas Knight, March 13, 2018.

18 Declaration of Lyle Hughes, May 21, 2018.

19 Kochanski, April 10, 2018.

20 Giessler, June 24, 2018.

21 Darrell Knight, May 1, 2018.

22 Declaration of Darryl Olterman, May 18, 2018.

23 Declaration of Theresa Olterman, March 18, 2018.

24 Declaration of Doug Knight, March 10, 2018.

25 Declaration of Dennis Miller, November 14, 2000.

26 Theresa Olterman, March 18, 2018.

27 Kochanski, April 10, 2018.

28 Darrell Knight, May 1, 2018.

29 Declaration of [name redacted for confidentiality], June 23, 2018.

30 Giessler, June 24, 2018.

31 Hughes, May 21, 2018.

32 Kochanski, April 10, 2018

33 *State of Tennessee v. Edmund George Zagorski,* 701 S.W.2d 808 (1985) law.justia.com.

34 Young, Nicole. "Three Weeks Later, Families of Edmund Zagorski's Victims Hope for Closure." *The Tennessean,* October 9, 2018.

35 Dearmore, Donna. "Zagorski Convicted, Gets Chair." *The Tennessean,* March 3, 1984.

36 *State of Tennessee v. Edmund Zagorski,* No. M1996-00110-SC-DPE-DD, (Supreme Court of Tennessee). "Edmund Zagorski's Response to State's Motion for Expedited Execution Dates and Reasons Why No Execution Date Should Be Set," March 1, 2018. www.tncourts.gov.

37 MacLean, Bradley A. and H.E. Miller Jr., "Tennessee's Death Penalty Lottery," *Tennessee Journal of Law and Policy,* Volume 13, Issue 1 (Summer 2018). www.dpic-cdn.org.

38 "Why No Execution Date Should Be Set," March 1, 2018.

39 Hale, Steven. "Zagorski Jurors Want Mercy for the Man They Sentenced to Death." *Nashville Scene,* October 8, 2018.

40 Hale. "Plea for Mercy."

41 Hale, Steven. "Edmund Zagorski Set to Die November 1 in the Electric Chair." *Nashville Scene,* October 22, 2018.

42 Bass, David. Interview by Steven Hale, December 8, 2018.

43   "Two Men Die in Explosion on Oil Rig." Associated Press, March 25, 1980; "Third Body Recovered from Gas Rig." *The Galveston Daily News*, March 29, 1980.

44   Hale. "Plea for Mercy."

45   Freedberg, Sydney P. "The Story of Old Sparky." *Tampa Bay Times*, September 25, 1999.

46   Tennessee Department of Correction, "Zagorski Media Advisory." November 1, 2018. www.tn.gov.

47   *The Tennessean*, "Witnesses Discuss the Details of Edmund Zagorski's Execution," November 1, 2018. www.youtube.com.

48   Hale, Steven. "For Some Death Row Inmates, Kelley Henry Is the Last Line of Defense." *Nashville Scene*, November 21, 2019.

Chapter 9

1   Tennessee Department of Correction, "Statement from Governor Haslam on David Earl Miller," December 6, 2018. www.tn.gov.

2   Hale, Steven. "The Two Women Closest to This Week's Execution." *Nashville Scene*, December 5, 2018. www.nashvillescene.com.

3   Stephen M. Kissinger, Assistant Federal Community Defender, to Governor Bill Haslam, November 29, 2018.

4   Declaration of Pablo Stewart, MD, February 28, 2003.

5   Declaration of Dr. David Lisak, March 7, 2003.

6   Stewart, February 28, 2003.

7   Declaration of Dr. David Lisak.

8   Declaration of Dr. David Lisak; Stewart, February 28, 2003.

9   Declaration of Dr. David Lisak.

10 Lakin, Matt. "'A Simmering Rage': David Earl Miller's Path to Tennessee's Electric Chair." *Knoxville News-Sentinel*, December 3, 2018. www.knoxnews.com.

11 Declaration of Dr. David Lisak.

12 Declaration of Dr. David Lisak; Stewart, February 28, 2003.

13 Declaration of Dr. David Lisak; Stewart, February 28, 2003.

14 *State of Tennessee v. David Earl Miller*, 674 S.W.2d 279 (1984). law.justia.com.

15 Stewart, February 28, 2003.

16 *State v. Miller* (1984).

17 Stewart, February 28, 2003.

18 Harris, Roger. "Sex Evidence Now OK in Miller Trial." *Knoxville News-Sentinel*, March 14, 1982. www.newspapers.com.

19 *State v. Miller* (1984).

20 *State v. Miller* (1984).

21 Kissinger to Haslam, November 29, 2018

22 *David Earl Miller v. Ricky Bell*, Warden, No. 301-cv-487 (United States District Court for the Eastern District of Tennessee Sep. 18, 2013). "Affidavit of Mark Evan Olive."
23 Hale. "Two Women."
24 Hale. "Two Women."
25 Declaration of Dr. David Lisak.

Chapter 10

1 Bass, David. Interview by Steven Hale. December 8, 2018.
2 King, Terry. Interview by Steven Hale. June 25, 2020.
3 King, Terry. Interview by Steven Hale. August 4, 2020.
4 *Terry Lynn King v. Ricky Bell*, Warden, Case No. 399-cv-454 (United States District Court for the Eastern District of Tennessee). "Petition for Writ of Habeas Corpus and Request for Leave to Amend," March 13, 2000.
5 "Petition for Writ of Habeas Corpus."
6 "Petition for Writ of Habeas Corpus."
7 King, Terry. Interview by Steven Hale. September 22, 2020.
8 "Petition for Writ of Habeas Corpus."

Chapter 11

1 Kalodimos, Demetria. Interview by Steven Hale. January 30, 2019.
2 Cavendish, Steve. "Anchor Down: How WSMV Walked Away from Demetria." *Nashville Scene*, February 1, 2018.
3 *State of Tennessee v. Ronald Richard Harries*, 657 S.W.2d 414 (1983). law.justia.com.
4 "Harries 'Took the News in Stride.'" *Kingsport Times-News*, May 30, 1984. www.newspapers.com.
5 Mulgrew, Tom. "Drug Issue Wins Stay for Harries." *The Tennessean*, June 9, 1984. www.newspapers.com.
6 Osborne, J.H. "Family Learns Rhonda Greene's Killer Died in Prison Four Years Ago." *Kingsport Times-News*, December 17, 2016.
7 Declaration of R. J. W., June 2, 2018.
8 R. J. W., June 2, 2018.
9 Declaration of D. W., June 2, 2018.
10 D. W., June 2, 2018.
11 Declaration of Marilyn Maples, May 23, 2018.
12 Declaration of B. W., May 23, 2018.
13 D. W., June 2, 2018.
14 Declaration of T. M. W., June 2, 2018.
15 B. W., May 23, 2018.
16 R. J. W., June 2, 2018.
17 Declaration of J. M., May 23, 2018.

18 R. J. W., June 2, 2018.
19 Declaration of Vernon Haynes, May 13, 2018.
20 B. W., May 23, 2018.
21 Loggins, Kirk. "Rutherford Man Convicted of Murder." *The Tennessean*, April 5, 1985.
22 Loggins, Kirk. "Wright Sentenced to Death; Slaying of Witness Cited." *The Tennessean*, April 6, 1985.
23 Loggins. "Wright Sentenced to Death."
24 *State of Tennessee v. Charles Walton Wright*, No. M1985-00008-SC-DDT-DD (Supreme Court of Tennessee). "Charles Wright's Response in Opposition to State's Motion for Expedited Execution Dates and Reasons Why No Execution Dates Should Be Set." March 1, 2018.
25 Hale, Steven. "Charles Wright, Death Row Prisoner from Nashville, Dies at 64." *Nashville Scene,* May 17, 2019.
26 Crabtree, Tommy. "Death Penalty Will Be Sought in Gallatin Rape, Murder Case." *The Tennessean,* December 7, 1982.
27 Sullivan, Barbara. Interview by Steven Hale. March 16, 2019.
28 Bass, David. Interview by Steven Hale, December 8, 2018.
29 Cross, Josh. "Two Murders Led to Sumner's First Death Penalty Conviction." *Gallatin News*, September 5, 2019.
30 Duncan, David. Interview by Steven Hale, June 30, 2021.
31 Hale, Steven. "Attorneys and Supporters Seek Clemency for Nashville Man Dying on Death Row." *Nashville Scene*, January 16, 2019.
32 Bob Clement to Governor Bill Haslam, September 21, 2018.

Chapter 12

1 Andrews, Al, and David Bass. Interview by Steven Hale, April 22, 2019.
2 Mills, Russell "Hank." Interview by Steven Hale, June 2018.
3 "Chief Henry Standing Bear." Crazy Horse Memorial. www.crazyhorse-memorial.org.
4 Russell "Hank" Mills to Monique Ziolkowski, September 12, 2018.

Chapter 13

1 Burgess, Katherine. "Their Father Killed Their Mother. Now, the Siblings Disagree on Whether He Should Be Executed." *The Commercial Appeal*, May 8, 2019.
2 Hale, Steven. "Ahead of May 16 Execution, Don Johnson Says 'I Am at Peace'." *Nashville Scene*, May 1, 2019.
3 "Application for Executive Clemency on Behalf of Don Johnson," April 3, 2019, 1.
4 "Application for Executive Clemency," 15.

5 Nolan, Hamilton. "Letters From Death Row: Donnie Johnson, Tennessee Inmate 109031." *Gawker*, January 22, 2015. www.gawker.com.

6 Smith, Bob. "Do 'Reformatories' Reform?" *Kingsport Times-News,* February 9, 1969. www.newspapers.com.

7 "Humans Treated Worse Than Animals, Report Says." *Daily News-Journal* (Murfreesboro), September 22, 1969. www.newspapers.com.

8 "Application for Executive Clemency," 19.

9 Nolan. "Letters From Death Row."

10 Haggard, Amanda. "Finding Forgiveness on Death Row." *Nashville Scene,* February 8, 2017.

11 *State of Tennessee v. Donnie Edward Johnson,* 743 S.W.2d 154 (1987). law.justia.com.

12 *State v. Johnson* (1987).

13 Garrett, Celeste. "Johnson Draws Electric Chair in Wife's Death." *The Commercial Appeal*, October 5, 1985. www.newspapers.com.

14 *State v. Johnson* (1987).

15 Nolan. "Letters From Death Row."

16 Haggard. "Finding Forgiveness."

17 Haggard. "Finding Forgiveness."

18 Andrews, Al, and David Bass. Interview by Steven Hale, May 13, 2019.

19 Hale, Steven. "Governor Denies Clemency for Don Johnson." *Nashville Scene,* May 14, 2019.

20 Loller, Travis. "Man Executed for Killing Wife Decades Ago in Memphis." Associated Press, May 16, 2019.

21 Hale, Steven. "The Execution of Don Johnson." *Nashville Scene*, May 17, 2019.

Chapter 14

1 Hale, Steven. "Charles Wright, Death Row Prisoner from Nashville, Dies at 64." *Nashville Scene*, May 17, 2019.

2 Hale. "Charles Wright Dies at 64."

3 Hale. "Charles Wright Dies at 64."

Chapter 15

1 King, Terry. Interview by Steven Hale, June 25, 2020.

2 *Terry Lynn King v. Ricky Bell,* Warden, No. 399-cv-454 (United States District Court for the Eastern District of Tennessee). "Petition for Writ of Habeas Corpus and Request for Leave to Amend," March 13, 2000.

3 King, Terry. Interview by Steven Hale, July 2, 2020.

4 Mulhern, Barbara. "Pair Held in Slaying of Missing Edgerton Soldier." *The Capital Times*, August 13, 1983.

5 King, Terry. Interview by Steven Hale, July 30, 2020.
6 "Bodies of Women Found in Quarries; Suspects in Custody." *Johnson City Press*, August 9, 1983.
7 *King v. State,* C.C.A. No. 03C01-9601-CR-00024 (Tenn. Crim. App. July 14, 1997). www.casetext.com.
8 *King v. State* (1997).
9 *King v. State* (1997).
10 King, Terry. Interview by Steven Hale, August 4, 2020.
11 *Terry Lynn King v. Ricky Bell,* Warden, No. 3:99-cv-454 (United States District Court for the Eastern District of Tennessee), August 12, 2011.
12 "Petition for Writ of Habeas Corpus."
13 *State v. Terry Lynn King,* 718 S.W.2d 241 (1986). law.justia.com.
14 *State v. Terry Lynn King* (1986).

Chapter 16

1 Ingle, Joe. Interview by Steven Hale, June 27, 2019.
2 Terry King to Katie, June 25, 2019.

Chapter 17

1 Hale, Steven. "Death Row Prisoners to Governor: Come Pray with Us." *Nashville Scene*, August 8, 2019. www.nashvillescene.com.
2 Mann, Dan, and Bethany Mann. Interview by Steven Hale, December 15, 2020.
3 *State of Tennessee v. Larry McKay and Michael Eugene Sample,* 680 S.W.2d 447 (1984). law.justia.com.
4 Segura, Liliana. "'One by One, They're Dying': Activists Protest Tennessee's Fifth Execution in a Year." The Intercept, August 17, 2019.

Chapter 18

1 *State of Tennessee v. Stephen Michael West,* No. M1987-00130-SC-DPE-DD (Supreme Court of Tennessee). "Response in Opposition to the Attorney General's Motion to Set an Execution Date and Stephen Michael West's Request for a Certificate of Communication." March 1, 2018. www.tncourts.gov.
2 Affidavit of Vestor West, December 1998.
3 Dudley, Richard G. Jr. "Psychiatric Evaluation." February 21, 2002. www.tncourts.gov.
4 "Response in Opposition to the Attorney General's Motion to Set an Execution Date." March 1, 2018.
5 Affidavit of Pablo Stewart, MD. December 13, 2002. www.tncourts.gov.

6   "Clemency Petition." July 17, 2019.

7   "Clemency Petition." July 17, 2019.

8   *State of Tennessee v. Stephen Michael West*, 767 S.W.2d 387 (1989). law.justia.com.

9   "Response in Opposition to the Attorney General's Motion to Set an Execution Date." March 1, 2018.

10 *State v. West* (1989).

11 "Response in Opposition to the Attorney General's Motion to Set an Execution Date." March 1, 2018.

12 Mattise, Jonathan. "No Clemency for Tennessee Man Set to Be Executed Thursday." Associated Press, August 13, 2019. www.apnews.com.

13 Terry King to Steven Hale, August 24, 2019.

14 Affidavit of William D. Kenner, MD. February 21, 2018. www.tncourts.gov.

15 Hale, Steven. "Rudy Kalis Finds Friendship with the Condemned Stephen West." *Nashville Scene*, August 13, 2019.

16 Hale. "Friendship with the Condemned Stephen West."

17 Hale. "Friendship with the Condemned Stephen West."

18 "Statement from Governor Bill Lee on Stephen West." August 13, 2019. www.tn.gov.

19 Matheny, Jim. "'There Was a Time When I Thought It Would Never Happen' | Steve West Set to Be Executed by Electrocution Thursday." WBIR, August 10, 2018. www.wbir.com.

20 "Statement to Be Read to the Press on the Day of Execution of Stephen West in Remembrance of Wanda and Sheila Romines and Also Jack Romines."

21 Kruesi, Kimberlee. "Tennessee Governor 'Not Compelled' to Witness Execution." Associated Press, August 26, 2019.

Chapter 19

1   *Abdur'Rahman v. Bell*, 999 F. Supp. 1073 (M.D. Tenn. 1998).

2   "The Full Story." Justice for Abu. www.justiceforabu.org.

3   Pulle, Matt. "Reasonable Doubt." *Nashville Scene*, December 6, 2001. www.nashvillescene.com.

4   Hale, Steven. "Nashville Death Row Prisoner Abu-Ali Abdur'Rahman Gets a New Hearing." *Nashville Scene*, August 13, 2019. www.nashvillescene.com.

5   Curriden, Mark. "Lawyer's Attempt to Keep His Head Above Water Landed a Client on Death Row." *ABA Journal*, March 1, 2011. www.abajournal.com.

6   *State of Tennessee v. Abu Ali Abdur'rahman*, No. M1988-00026-SC-DDTDD (Supreme Court of Tennessee). "Response to State's Motion for Expe-

dited Execution Dates and Reasons Why No Execution Date Should Be
Set." March 1, 2018. www.tncourts.gov.

7   Hale, Steven. "DA Glenn Funk Seeks to Drop Death Penalty in Abu-Ali
Abdur'Rahman Case." *Nashville Scene*, August 28, 2019.

8   Hale. "Funk Seeks to Drop Death Penalty."

9   Hale, Steven. "Abdur'Rahman's Death Sentence Vacated Months Before
Scheduled Execution." *Nashville Scene*, September 3, 2019. www.nash-
villescene.com.

10 Hale, Steven. "Tennessee AG Challenges Decision to Drop Abdur'Rahman
Death Sentence." *Nashville Scene*, September 20, 2019.

11 Hale, Steven. "State Attorney General Seeks Execution Dates for Nine
Death Row Prisoners." *Nashville Scene*, September 24, 2019.

12 Hale, Steven. "Tennessee Supreme Court Halts Abu-Ali Abdur'Rahman
Execution." *Nashville Scene*, December 11, 2019.

Chapter 20

1   Loggins, Kirk. "Death Row Athlete Has Knee Surgery." *The Tennessean*,
February 7, 1989. www.newspapers.com.

2   King, Terry. "Out of Darkness Into the Light." Personal essay, undated.

3   Mary McPherson to Terry King, June 24, 2013.

Chapter 21

1   *State of Tennessee v. Lee Hall, Jr.*, E1997-00344-SC-DDT-DD (Supreme
Court of Tennessee). "Lee Hall's Response in Opposition to State's Mo-
tion for Expedited Execution Dates and Reasons Why No Execution Date
Should Be Set." March 1, 2018. www.tncourts.gov.

2   *State of Tennessee v. Leroy Hall, Jr.*, 958 S.W.2d 679 (1997). www.case-law.
vlex.com.

3   "Response in Opposition to State's Motion for Expedited Execution Dates."

4   Bradbury, Shelly. "'He Needs to Suffer' - 23 Years Later, Burning Death
of her Sister Still Pains Woman." *Chattanooga Times Free Press*, August 20,
2014.

5   Hale, Steven. "The Execution of Lee Hall." *Nashville Scene*, December 6,
2019. www.nashvillescene.com.

6   Hale, Steven. "As Lee Hall's Execution Nears, Juror Bias Triggers a New
Trial in a Similar Case." *Nashville Scene*, December 3, 2019.

7   Frankl, Viktor E. *Man's Search for Meaning*. Beacon Press, 2006), 7.

8   Hale, Steven. "Governor Lee Won't Delay Lee Hall's Execution." *Nashville
Scene*, December 4, 2019.

9   King, Terry. Interview by Steven Hale, December 4, 2019.

10 Tennessee Department of Correction, "Media Advisory." December 5,
2019. www.tn.gov.

11 Kruesi, Kimberlee. "Blind Inmate Executed in Tennessee for Woman's 1991 Killing." Associated Press, December 5, 2019. www.apnews.com.

12 King, Terry. Interview by Steven Hale, December 18, 2019.

Chapter 22

1   Christian, Frances. Interview by Steven Hale, February 26, 2021.

2   "Request for Commutation of Death Sentence of Nicholas ("Nick") Todd Sutton." January 14, 2020.

3   Dorman, Travis. "Nicky Sutton's Twisted Tale May End Soon in Tennessee's Electric Chair." *Knoxville News-Sentinel*, January 30, 2020.

4   Dorman. "Sutton's Twisted Tale."

5   "Request for Commutation."

6   Segura, Liliana. "Will Tennessee Kill a Man Who Saved Lives on Death Row?" The Intercept, February 16, 2020. www.theintercept.com.

7   "Request for Commutation." January 14, 2020.

8   "Statement from Governor Bill Lee on Nicholas Sutton." February 19, 2020. www.tn.gov.

9   Allison, Natalie. "'He Fixed Me': As He Was Put to Death, Nicholas Sutton Had Nothing but His Faith." *The Tennessean*, February 20, 2020.

10 Hale, Steven. "The Execution of Nick Sutton." *Nashville Scene*, February 21, 2020.

Chapter 23

1   Hale, Steven. "Tennessee Set to Execute Intellectually Disabled Black Man in Killing of White Woman Even Though Innocence Questions Persist." *The Appeal*, April 29, 2020. www.theappeal.org.

2   *State of Tennessee v. Pervis Tyrone Payne,* No. M1988-00096-SC-DPE-DD (Supreme Court of Tennessee). "Response in Opposition to Motion to Set Execution Date; Notice That Defendant Is Incompetent to Be Executed and Request for a Hearing; and Request for Certificate of Commutation." December 30, 2019. www.tncourts.gov.

3   Holman, Rolanda, and Carl Payne. Interview by Steven Hale, March 5, 2020.

4   *State of Tennessee v. Pervis Tyrone Payne,* 791 S.W.2d 10 (1990). law.justia.com.

5   *State v. Payne* (1990).

6   *State v. Payne* (1990).

7   King, Terry. Interview by Steven Hale, March 20, 2020.

8   *State of Tennessee v. Oscar Smith,* No. M2016-01869-SC-R11-PD (Supreme Court of Tennessee). "Motion for Stay of Execution Due to Covid-19 Pandemic." March 18, 2020. www.tncourts.gov.

9 "Motion for Stay of Execution."

10 *State of Tennessee v. Oscar Smith*, No. M2016-01869-SC-R11-PD. "Order for Execution Reset to February 4, 2021." April 17, 2020. www.tncourts. gov.

11 King, Terry. Interview by Steven Hale, April 17, 2020.

12 King, Terry. Interview by Steven Hale, May 28, 2020.

13 Hale, Steven. "Two of the Country's Worst COVID-19 Hot Spots Are in Tennessee—Both Are Prisons." *Nashville Scene,* May 4, 2020. www.nashvillescene.com.

14 *State of Tennessee v. Byron Lewis Black,* No. M2000-00641-SC-DPE-CD (Supreme Court of Tennessee). "Order Resetting Execution Date for April 8, 2021." June 12, 2020. www.tncourts.gov.

15 *State of Tennessee v. Byron Lewis Black,* No. M2000-00641-SC-DPE-CD (Supreme Court of Tennessee). "Motion to Reset Execution Date Due to COVID-19 Pandemic." April 29, 2020. www.tncourts.gov.

16 Hale, Steven. "Tennessee Supreme Court Reschedules Byron Black Execution Due to COVID-19." *Nashville Scene,* June 12, 2020.

17 King, Terry. Interview by Steven Hale, June 23, 2020.

18 Nichols, Harold. Interview by Steven Hale, July 13, 2020.

19 *State of Tennessee v. Harold Wayne Nichols,* 877 S.W.2d 722 (1994). law.justia.com.

20 *Harold Wayne Nichols v. Stanton Heidle,* No. 06-6495 (6th Cir. 2013). law.justia.com.

21 Hale, Steven. "Governor Grants Reprieve for Harold Nichols." *Nashville Scene*, July 17, 2020.

22 Kruesi, Kimberlee. "Woman Seeks Justice for Sister as Killer's Execution Delayed." Associated Press, August 20, 2020. www.apnews.com.

23 Bass, David. Interview by Steven Hale, July 28, 2020.

24 King, Terry. Interview by Steven Hale, October 7, 2020.

25 Hale, Steven. "Judge Grants DNA Testing in Pervis Payne Case." *Nashville Scene*, September 16, 2020.

26 Hale, Steven. "Black Caucus Files Bill Aimed at Preventing the Execution of the Intellectually Disabled." *Nashville Scene*, November 5, 2020.

27 Hale, Steven. "Governor Grants Reprieve for Pervis Payne Due to COVID-19." *Nashville Scene*, November 6, 2020.

Chapter 24

1 King, Terry. Interview by Steven Hale, December 20, 2020.